Glory and Dishonour

Glory and Dishonour

Victoria Cross Heroes Whose Lives Ended in Tragedy or Disgrace

BRIAN IZZARD

AMBERLEY

First published 2018

Amberley Publishing
The Hill, Stroud
Gloucestershire, GL5 4EP

www.amberley-books.com

British Library Cataloguing in Publication Data.
A catalogue record for this book is available from the British Library.

ISBN 978 1 4456 7648 7 (hardback)
ISBN 978 1 4456 7649 4 (ebook)

Typesetting and Origination by Amberley Publishing.
Printed in the UK.

Contents

For those men who found it easier
to win the medal than to wear it

Introduction

For some of the men who were awarded the Victoria Cross it did prove harder to wear the medal than to win it.

As Ian Fraser put it, 'A man is trained for the task that might win him the VC. He is not trained to cope with what follows. He is not told how to avoid going under in a flood of public adulation.' Fraser and James Magennis both won the Victoria Cross for a bold X-Craft attack on a Japanese cruiser in 1945. Fraser coped; Magennis didn't.

There have been many books on holders of Britain's highest gallantry award. *Glory and Dishonour* takes an unusual path, exploring – sympathetically – the lives of twenty-seven men who received the Victoria Cross but fell from grace. 'Public adulation' was one factor, but there were others. Today there is treatment for what is commonly known as post-traumatic stress disorder. In Victorian times there was no such help. Clearly, John Byrne, a hero of the Crimean War, was in need of psychiatric treatment when he shot and wounded a labourer who had insulted him. Shortly afterwards Byrne killed himself, and it was revealed that he had spent time in what was then called a lunatic asylum. Robert Jones, who took part in the remarkable defence of Rorke's Drift in 1879, died in tragic circumstances many years afterwards, still suffering from his wounds. An inquest heard that he had been 'acting in a rather peculiar manner'. A verdict of suicide while temporarily insane was recorded, and his local church refused a full burial service on the grounds that he had committed a sin.

During the First World War there was controversy over what was termed shellshock. Hospital admissions were high, and army commanders were concerned about their depleted forces. The war saw the birth of military psychiatry, but there were critics. Viscount Gort, who won the Victoria Cross as a Grenadier Guards officer in 1918, declared that shellshock was 'practically non-existent' in 'first-class divisions' and should be thought of as 'a form of disgrace to the soldier'. During the Second World War the Royal Air Force took a dim view of men who were seen as 'lacking moral fibre'. With its staggering losses, it was not surprising that Bomber Command had significant numbers unwilling to fly on operations. Even the Victoria Cross winner Leonard Cheshire, who would later show himself to be so compassionate, took a hard line with 'LMF' cases: 'You couldn't have a bloke saying he would not fly.'

A number of Victoria Cross holders had brushes with the law. George Ravenhill is perhaps the saddest case. After leaving the army, the hero of Colenso was so short of money to feed his family that he was forced to give up three of his children to foster care, never to see them again. He was jailed for stealing some metal worth 6 shillings.

A few men were rogues before their displays of outstanding bravery. William Mariner, who created havoc in German trenches with a one-man bombing raid in 1915, was a convicted burglar. But he won the respect of the police. His name was on a Metropolitan Police roll of honour of criminals who lost their lives fighting during the First World War.

John Kenneally of the Irish Guards fooled everybody, including King George VI and Winston Churchill. He was actually Leslie Jackson from Birmingham, who pretended to be Irish after deserting from the artillery. In Tunisia in 1943, he twice single-handedly charged large groups of German troops, firing his Bren gun from the hip and 'bowling them over like ninepins'.

At a London reunion of Victoria Cross holders, New Zealander Clive Hulme expressed 'shock and horror' that so many holders were on the dole. Hulme, a hero of the Battle of Crete in 1941, was branded a war criminal after his death.

Nothing, however, can detract from the courage of these men.

1

The Mystery Sailor
William Johnstone

One of the earliest awards of the Victoria Cross may have gone to the wrong man. Was the hero William Johnstone, John Johnstone or James Johnson? Or even someone called Johanssen? The mystery probably will never be solved.

The medal was engraved 'Stoker William Johnstone 12 Aug 1854', and it had been awarded for an act of heroism during the Royal Navy's Baltic campaign. This sailor was supposed to have served in the frigate HMS *Arrogant* – but no one of that name appears on the ship's muster list. There were, however, a John Johnstone and a James Johnson on board. John Johnstone is usually credited as the hero, but serious doubts remain. He met a tragic end in 1857 after attacking another sailor.

The Baltic campaign stemmed from the war in the Crimea, which saw Britain and France go to the aid of Turkey to oppose Russian advances in the region. The task of dealing with Russia's fleet in the Baltic and hitting the country's trade was given to Vice Admiral Sir Charles Napier. Known as Black Charlie because of his swarthy appearance, Napier was a popular figure whose service stretched from the Napoleonic Wars. He was known for his boldness, but before his ships sailed from Portsmouth on 4 March 1854 he sounded a note of caution: 'I will do the best I can. We are going to meet no common enemy. We are going to meet an enemy well prepared. I am sure every officer and man in the fleet will do his duty gloriously, but at the same time, I warn you again that you must not expect too much.' Black Charlie would be proved right.

Arrogant, under the command of Captain Hastings Yelverton, was involved in one of the earliest exploits. On 19 May the forty-six-gun frigate, accompanied by HMS *Hecla*, a paddle sloop, was fired on by Russian troops as she examined a channel on the south-west coast of Finland, then part of Russia. The two vessels opened up with broadsides and the enemy withdrew. Yelverton learned from a local pilot that there were three merchant ships at Ekness [Ekenas], 8 miles to the north, and the next day *Arrogant* and *Hecla* went in search of them, sailing up narrow and difficult passages inland. Artillery engaged the warships, killing two of *Arrogant*'s crew before being silenced. *Hecla* towed away one of the merchant ships.

In a letter to the Admiralty, which was published in *The London Gazette* of 2 June, Napier paid tribute to Yelverton's 'smart operation' at Ekness. The admiral wrote: 'Great credit is due to him for his perseverance in threading up so narrow and intricate a navigation; and it will show the enemy they are not safe even in their country towns. Captain Yelverton very properly abstained from damaging the town [Ekness].' He added: 'All the officers and men behaved as British seamen and marines were wont to.'

On 7 August Yelverton paid a visit to Napier, who was on board his flagship, HMS *Duke of Wellington*, with the fleet stationed off Wardo [Vardo], one of the Aland Islands at the southern end of the Gulf of Bothnia between Finland and Sweden. The admiral complained that despatches from Tsar Nicholas I for the commander of the strategic fortress of Bomarsund on the nearby island of Sund were being landed on Wardo. Returning to *Arrogant*, Yelverton told one of his lieutenants, John Bythesea, of the admiral's annoyance. The ambitious Bythesea suggested a plan to intercept the despatches. Sweden had ceded the islands to Russia in 1809, but many of the inhabitants were still Swedish. The lieutenant found a foreign national who spoke Swedish among the crew – the mysterious William Johnstone. He pushed for the pair to carry out the raid, but Yelverton thought a larger group would be necessary. Bythesea pointed out that too many men might compromise the operation and he won the argument.

On 9 August, only two days after the admiral's complaint, Bythesea and Johnstone rowed across to Wardo. After hiding their boat, they went to a farmhouse. They were in luck. The owner, presumably

Swedish or perhaps Finnish, understood them and offered to help, revealing that he was no friend of the Russians because they had taken all his horses. The men were fed and told they could stay at the farmhouse, which was near the road used by the tsar's messengers. But the Russians learned that British sailors were on the island and sent out search parties. Bythesea and Johnstone evaded capture after the farmer's daughters dressed them as peasants.

On 12 August the farmer informed Bythesea that the boat carrying despatches for the Bomarsund fortress would be arriving that night. There would be a military escort, but only for part of the way. The lieutenant was even told where the escort would leave. That night he and Johnstone hid in bushes near the road, armed only with a pistol. They ambushed five couriers, two of whom fled. But the three other men were seized, along with the despatches. The prisoners were taken to the boat and forced to row to *Arrogant*, with Bythesea covering them with his pistol and Johnstone steering.

Yelverton was impressed. So too were Napier and General Louis-Achille Baraguey d'Hilliers, commander of French forces, the latter having joined the Baltic campaign in a second fleet. The general's troops helped to capture Bomarsund fortress on 16 August after a naval bombardment.

Bythesea and Johnstone were both awarded the Victoria Cross. The medal was first instituted on 29 January 1856, but awards were backdated to cover the campaigns in the Baltic and in the Crimea. The first award went to Lieutenant Charles Lucas of *Hecla*, who threw a live shell overboard during an unsuccessful attack on Bomarsund fortress on 21 June 1854. Bythesea and Johnstone were the second and third recipients. The first investiture was held in Hyde Park on 26 June 1857, and Bythesea was one of the sixty-two men who were presented with the Victoria Cross by Queen Victoria. Thirty-one recipients, including Johnstone, were serving overseas at the time, and their medals were sent out for individual presentations, although the sailor may have received his medal in a registered packet.

There was, of course, no William Johnstone serving aboard *Arrogant*, and details of leading stoker John Johnstone are sketchy. According to a muster book entry for 26 September 1852, this Johnstone had been born in Hanover and was aged thirty-two. He was 5 feet 5½ inches tall, with a fair complexion, blue eyes and light brown hair. There was an anchor tattoo on his left wrist. Married, his home was in Liverpool. His character varied from 'good' to 'very good'. Before joining the navy he had served in merchant ships.

By 1856 Johnstone was serving in the third rate HMS *Brunswick*. His appearance had apparently changed. He was listed as 5 feet 6 inches tall, with a ruddy complexion and grey eyes. No longer a leading stoker, he was working as a cook. There appears to be no explanation for this change of role; perhaps he had been injured.

On 20 August 1857 *Brunswick* was off St Lucia in the Caribbean. That morning Johnstone committed suicide. The ship's log records that 'in a fit of insanity' he slashed leading stoker Charles Wood 'on various parts of his body' with a very sharp razor and then cut his own throat. Johnstone died from 'the effects of the cut to his throat'. He was 'committed to the deep' in the afternoon.

Curiously, there was no mention that he had won the Victoria Cross. No explanation for the attack was given, but it might be significant that the target of his anger was a leading stoker. Had Johnstone been taunted about his lower status as a cook? Or were doubts expressed about his Victoria Cross? The key to Johnstone's recruitment for the Wardo operation had been his ability to speak Swedish, but it is doubtful whether the man born in Hanover and with a home in Liverpool possessed that language skill. Napier's ships were seriously undermanned during the Baltic campaign and Swedes were taken on to ease the problem. Indeed, the admiral had a Swedish lieutenant serving in his flagship. Was the real hero someone called Johanssen, who had not appeared on *Arrogant*'s muster list because of his short time on board? Recommendations for Baltic and Crimea honours were made long after the heroic acts, and by the time of Johnstone's citation in *The London Gazette* of 24 February 1857 he was serving in a different ship. If Bythesea had come across John Johnstone at the London investiture, it might have been a revealing moment.

In his many official letters sent in 1857, *Brunswick*'s captain, Henry Broadhead, made only one reference to Johnstone and that was in a list of crew members who had decided to allot pay to wives or parents. Broadhead's successor, Captain Erasmus Ommanney, showed more interest. In January 1858 Ommanney wrote to Vice Admiral Sir Houston Stewart, Commander-in-Chief, North America and West Indies Station, to make sure that Johnstone's widow received the annual Victoria Cross payment of £10 and the pension that the sailor had accrued – £28 17s 2d.

In the 1930s the Victoria Cross named to William Johnstone was acquired by the London dealer Spink and sold to a wealthy and eccentric American collector, Robert B Honeyman Jr, who amassed large quantities of medals, stamps and scientific books. David Spink recalled: 'He usually came to our premises at short notice – just enough to allow us to assemble some choice items to show him – and he never stayed long. He would quickly look over the pieces we had ready for him with his experienced eye and his flair for quality and historical interest, pick out what he wanted, pay for them, and walk out with his acquisitions. The whole operation probably only took a quarter of an hour – thirty minutes at most.'

Honeyman never bothered to research any of his orders, decorations or medals, and in 1954 he donated his collection – without any documentation – to the Natural History Museum of Los Angeles County, an odd choice. The collection holds more than 5,000 pieces, including William Johnstone's Victoria Cross. In 2016 the award was not on display. Honeyman died in 1987, aged ninety.

John Johnstone was not the only man to find shame – Napier and Bythesea would experience it also. Napier had gone to sea at the age of twelve and been given his first command, a sloop, at nineteen. His reputation grew in major campaigns, and his enthusiasm for conflict even saw him being appointed an admiral in the Portuguese navy in 1833, a move that led to him being struck from the Navy List. Napier did not endear himself to their lordships at the Admiralty with his frequent criticism of poor conditions and inadequate ships. King William IV, who served in the navy during his youth and took exception to Napier's reprimands, described him as an 'unprincipled firebrand and adventurer of the most dangerous description'. Napier eventually bounced back and played a key role in the war in Syria in 1840.

One of his criticisms concerned the age of senior officers. He had long campaigned for younger men to be given key positions, so it was with some surprise that at the age of sixty-eight he agreed to take command of the hastily convened Baltic fleet. The ships might have looked good on paper, but they were not fully manned and many of the men on board lacked experience. Even coastguards had been called up. Of HMS *Monarch*, Napier noted that there was 'hardly a man in her who knows a rope – she could barely sail, let alone fight'. Stores in the fleet were short and there was not enough ammunition. Sailors did not have adequate clothing for the icy Baltic. Napier lacked gunboats for the shallow waters ahead, as well as pilots and charts. To add to his problems, the Russians mined areas around the strategic forts of Sveaborg and Kronstadt, and the Swedish government declined to join the campaign. Britain had been counting on Sweden's 300-plus gunboats. Fog and gales were other enemies. Furthermore, the Russian fleet refused to come out and fight.

Political pressure for a decisive outcome mounted at home, and the First Lord of the Admiralty, Sir James Graham, complained that the Russians were 'skulking within the harbour'. Graham told Napier that he was 'well aware of the impossibility of triumphing over an enemy that will not fight you on fair terms', but he warned that 'it would be madness to play her game and rush headlong on her granite walls, risking our naval supremacy'.

Yet more problems arrived for Napier – cholera and smallpox. By early July 1854 more than 100 men had died of cholera. In Britain disquiet was growing. John Delane, editor of *The Times*, told Napier after the storming of Bomarsund: 'We want some exploits. The public, though very patient, look to you and your fleet for greater results.' The admiral hit back: 'I'm sorry I have not been able to give the public a good butcher's bill, but had I attacked either Kronstadt or Sveaborg with my fleet, they would have had a bill with the loss of the fleet, or had we succeeded in withdrawing disabled, we should have fallen an easy prey to the Russian fleet, which would have been worse.'

Delane would prove to be a greater enemy than the Russians. He told Graham that the lack of action in the Baltic had caused 'extreme dissatisfaction to the government and to the public'. Apparent successes in the Crimea added to the pressure on Napier, who by September was facing worsening weather. The French soon withdrew their fleet. The British ships left a few weeks later. When *Duke of Wellington* arrived back in Portsmouth in December, Napier was expecting to resume the campaign the following year when conditions improved. But he lost his command. There was no official recognition of his efforts, and the admiral concluded that 'my character has been attacked by the First Lord of the Admiralty, and by the Board, and, coupling that with my dismissal from the command, I have nothing left but to demand that my conduct be investigated before a court martial'. The request was refused, and their lordships complained that the admiral had repeatedly 'thought fit to adopt a tone in correspondence which is not respectful to their authority'.

In April 1855 Britain sent a fleet, better equipped, to the Baltic under the command of Rear Admiral Richard Dundas, who went on to bombard Sveaborg, whose defences were hardly dented. When Dundas returned, the Admiralty thanked him warmly. The Crimean War ended in 1856.

Napier never put to sea again. He died at his Hampshire home on 6 November 1860, aged seventy-four. Many sailors attended his funeral but there was no official representation.

John Bythesea was born at Freshford, Somerset, on 15 June 1827, the son of a rector. He joined the navy as a volunteer first class in 1841. Bythesea flourished after his exploit on Wardo. The lieutenant was promoted commander in May 1856 and two years later found himself in command of the sloop HMS *Cruiser*, formerly *Cruizer*. He took part in operations against China in 1859–60, including the Taku forts action, and was promoted captain in 1861. Various appointments followed until he was given command of the battleship HMS *Lord Clyde*. It would be his last ship. In March 1872 *Lord Clyde* went to the aid of a paddle steamer that had run aground on the island of Pantelleria, west of Malta. But the warship also became trapped, needing a tow from her sister ship, HMS *Lord Warden*. Bythesea and his navigating officer were court-martialled. They were severely reprimanded and dismissed their ship, never to be given any further appointments at sea.

For the dedicated Bythesea it must have been a bitter blow. There would be one consolation: after leaving the navy in 1877 he was promoted rear admiral on the retirement list. He died at his home in South Kensington on 18 May 1906.

Some seventy years after selling William Johnstone's award, Spink offered Bythesea's Victoria Cross at auction. It was bought in April 2007 by the noted Victoria Cross collector Lord Ashcroft through his trust for a hammer price of £135,000, and later went on display at the Imperial War Museum, London.

2

A Police Siege and Suicide
John Byrne

John Byrne was an excellent soldier on the battlefield – and a poor one off it. His troubled life would end in a police siege and suicide.

Byrne was born in the village of Castlecomer, County Kilkenny, on 27 September 1832. A print exists of Castlecomer in 1832, showing a tree-lined main street with neat rows of houses on each side and a church in the background – an apparently idyllic place to be. The reality was different, however. Little is known of Byrne's early life but, as with many families living in the area, his parents were probably poor and desperately trying to make a living.

One family, the Wandesfordes, owned the village and the surrounding lands. It was mainly an agricultural area, with limited employment opportunities. To get a job as a tenant farmer, a tradesman or a labourer was good fortune. The Wandesforde family originally came Kirklington, near Richmond, Yorkshire, and their roots can be traced to the thirteenth century. Christopher Wandesforde was the first member of the family to settle in Ireland. He arrived in 1636 and later became Lord Deputy of Ireland. The family lived in a castellated mansion, Castlecomer House.

Those who struggled to survive often ended up at the workhouse in Kilkenny town, which served the county. In early 1847, when Byrne was fourteen, there were around 2,000 people in the overcrowded workhouse, and within twelve months there would be 1,000 deaths from fever. At that time Ireland was in the grip of its great potato famine. Potatoes were the main food, but crops failed because of disease, and between 1845 and 1852 some 1 million people died, mostly of starvation, despite the fact that the country was exporting huge quantities of grain. There were few options to escape the misery. Those who could afford a ticket boarded a ship and headed to the United States. The British Army provided another route for many Irishmen, among them the probably illiterate Byrne, who enlisted on 27 July 1850, aged seventeen. He had made his way to Coventry to join the 68th (Durham) Regiment of Foot (Light Infantry), later the Durham Light Infantry.

It was soon clear that Byrne had problems with authority. There were several run-ins, and in November 1853 the private was court-martialled and given a six-month prison sentence, though the offence remains a mystery. In July 1854 he was jailed again but released the following month because his regiment was setting sail to take part in the Crimean War.

He showed the other side of his character on 5 November, distinguishing himself at the fiercely contested Battle of Inkerman. The Russians launched a major attack on the British Second Division, which had 2,700 men and twelve guns holding positions on and around a hill known as Home Ridge, east of Sebastopol. The enemy had a total force of 42,000 soldiers and 134 guns, although not all of the men took part in the action. They advanced in two columns in a flanking movement. An early morning fog helped to shield their approach, but there were too many men for a comparatively small area and only 6,300 Russians made the initial attack, supported by artillery on Shell Hill to the north of Home Ridge. British pickets played a key role in slowing the advance, and the aggressive acting divisional commander, Major General John Pennefather, sent units forward to engage the Russians rather than keep them in defensive positions. A bayonet charge saw the enemy being driven down a slope and across a valley to Shell Hill.

The second column, with greater numbers, was also forced to retreat. But Russian attacks continued as reinforcements, including French troops, arrived to help beat them off. The fighting was often savage, and led to Inkerman being described as The Soldier's Battle. After the 68th was ordered to retire Byrne went back to the battlefield and rescued a wounded soldier under fire. This would earn him the first of two recommendations for the Victoria Cross. Despite their greater numbers, the battle ended in defeat for the Russians. Casualty figures vary but the Russians may have had more than 15,000 men killed and wounded, against about 2,500 for the British and around 900 for the French.

The Russians were not the only enemy. A harsh winter and disease took their toll on the British troops, who were poorly equipped for the conditions. However, Byrne did not lose his fighting spirit, and on 13 January 1855 he was wounded in the foot during a skirmish.

On the stormy night of 11 May, Byrne was involved in a savage fight. A large Russian force left besieged Sebastopol and attacked trenches near the Woronzoff Road. Only two companies of the 68th held the position, and the action saw fierce hand-to-hand fighting. At one point in the darkness and driving rain Byrne struggled with a Russian on the parapet of a trench, eventually killing him with a bayonet. The attack was repulsed. Byrne's bravery on that night was acknowledged in the citation to his Victoria Cross, published in *The London Gazette* of 24 February 1857. It was the regiment's first VC. He did not receive the medal until 22 July because the regiment was on the island of Corfu. Major General Sir George Buller made the presentation.

A history of the Durham Light Infantry described Byrne as 'a fine fighter who in peace spent most of his time in the cells'. His name appeared in the regimental defaulters' book on sixteen occasions. Despite his poor disciplinary record, he was, surprisingly, promoted corporal in 1861.

The ten years after Inkerman must have been a difficult time for Byrne because the 68th was engaged in peacetime service, mostly in Burma. But in late 1863 the regiment sailed from Rangoon to Auckland to take part in the Maori war that had broken out in New Zealand some three years earlier. The conflict had intensified and reinforcements were necessary. The country had seen a similar conflict in 1845–47. Maoris were once again objecting to their lands being sold to settlers at low prices with the complicity of the authorities. Maoris lacked sophisticated weapons – shotguns and tomahawks were their usual choice – but they proved to be ferocious and wily opponents, relying on a special fortification known as a pa. These wooden stockades, surrounded by deep ditches, were cleverly constructed, with rifle pits, trenches and underground shelters. They were usually in isolated areas and could be reached only after hacking through forest and scrub or wading across swamps.

On 28 April 1864, the 68th was part of a mixed force of 1,700 soldiers and sailors that assembled to attack the strategic Gate Pa on the east coast of North Island. The Maori were heavily outnumbered. The pa consisted of two redoubts, one large and one small, and artillery opened up during the afternoon on the main target. Under cover of darkness men of the 68th were sent to the rear of the large redoubt to cut off escape routes. The bombardment continued for most of 29 April until a breach was made. Little firing had been returned and, in the belief that resistance would be minimal, 300 men were ordered to storm the fortress. After some fierce fighting it was reported that the pa had been captured. But suddenly firing came from concealed positions and the British began taking heavy casualties. A reserve of 300 men entered, adding to the confusion in confined spaces. With many officers among the casualties, panic set in and soldiers and sailors fled, leaving behind dead and wounded. *The New Zealander* newspaper claimed that men 'ran away howling'. That night the defenders escaped through the lines of the 68th. It was the worst defeat suffered by British forces in the Maori wars. Thirty-five were killed and seventy-five wounded, roughly twice the number of Maori casualties.

In June the British learned that Maoris were building another, more formidable pa at Te Ranga, a few miles inland from Gate Pa. There were 600 warriors, and it was decided to attack before they had time to finish the fortress. On 21 June, with only rifle pits dug, the Maori saw a force of about 700 men, mostly from the 68th, advancing towards them, led by Lieutenant Colonel Henry Greer, a hot-tempered Irishman. The British soldiers were determined to avenge the deaths of their comrades at Gate Pa and soon overwhelmed the unfinished defences. There was fierce hand-to-hand fighting, similar in intensity to some of the Crimean clashes.

Byrne jumped into one of the rifle pits and was involved in a life-or-death struggle with a Maori. He managed to thrust his bayonet into the man, who kept fighting, grabbing the soldier's rifle with the steel still inside him. Byrne was saved by the actions

of Sergeant John Murray, who dashed to his aid as the Maori lashed out with a tomahawk. Murray had already killed at least eight warriors 'without any assistance'. The Maoris were routed and took heavy casualties as the British fired at them from their own rifle pits. The next day the pits became a mass grave for more than 100 warriors. British casualties were nine dead. It was a decisive battle, although the war continued until July 1866. Most of the British troops were withdrawn from New Zealand soon afterwards.

Murray, an Irishman, was awarded the Victoria Cross for his bravery at Te Ranga, and Byrne received the Distinguished Conduct Medal. Another Irishman, Captain Frederick Smith, of the 43rd (Monmouthshire) Regiment of Foot (Light Infantry), also received the VC. Despite being wounded, Smith, a Crimea veteran, had jumped into the rifle pits 'where he commenced a hand-to-hand encounter with the enemy, thereby giving his men great encouragement and setting them a fine example'. The awards were announced in *The London Gazette* of 4 November 1864.

Byrne was promoted sergeant in 1866. Returning to Ireland, he was discharged at Cork in May 1869 after nearly nineteen years' service. A civilian life did not appeal to him, and within days he was back in uniform as a sergeant with the Queen's County Militia. But by the October he had transferred back to the 68th. He also did service with the North Durham Militia. Once again he had problems with a peacetime role, and in May 1872 the newly promoted colour sergeant was finally discharged after being court-martialled for 'insubordination and highly improper conduct'. Drink was probably the cause of his downfall, and he was lucky not to forfeit his Victoria Cross.

Byrne returned to Ireland and his activities over the next six years remain a mystery. In 1878 he surfaced in Bristol, apparently destitute and claiming that he had lost all his possessions in a fire. After being spotted by an old comrade he managed to get a job as a labourer with the Ordnance Survey, despite being considered too old at forty-five. Soldiers were supervising survey work, and his decorations impressed a colonel who was in overall charge. Byrne was sent to join a group of workers in Newport, and he took lodgings at a small terraced house, 7 Crown Street, Maindee.

According to his landlady, Eliza Morgan, an elderly widow, he was 'most civil and respectable' and did not drink much – 'a pint of beer now and then'. He had been living there for about six months when he returned from work one lunchtime 'excited'.

He told Mrs Morgan: 'I'll never go again to be insulted.' An eighteen-year-old workmate called John Watts had apparently made disparaging remarks about him and the Victoria Cross. It appears that Byrne wore his medal. 'He threw his Cross on the table,' Mrs Morgan recalled.

Byrne asked if he could borrow a dagger hanging on a wall but she refused. He also asked if she had any guns in the house. Instead of returning to work he went to Cardiff, arriving back in the evening. The next morning, 10 July 1879, he was still excited. 'I'll never be insulted,' he said. 'I have served my queen and country for twenty-one years, and I'll never be insulted by a cur puppy. He isn't fit to black my boots.'

Byrne went to work as usual. The labourers would meet at the Maindee home of a Royal Engineers corporal who was in charge of them. When Byrne arrived, he went straight to Watts and pulled out a revolver, shooting him in the shoulder. The ex-soldier did not say anything. Then he smiled and walked away as Watts ran off with a flesh wound.

Byrne went straight to his lodgings, and Mrs Morgan sensed that something was wrong. 'Do tell me what's the matter,' she said, 'You frighten me.' He replied: 'I shall be arrested.'

Mrs Morgan's concern was immediate: 'Oh my God, what have you done? I hope no police will come as they have never been in my house.'

News of the shooting soon spread in the small community. The police were alerted and a neighbour turned up at the back door to tell Mrs Morgan that her lodger was a wanted man. The landlord of the nearby Crown Inn, William Davey, who knew Byrne as a customer, also arrived to persuade him to give himself up. The ex-soldier might have suggested that the shooting was an accident.

From a window Byrne saw that police and a crowd were outside. He warned that he would fire at any officers who tried to force their way in to arrest him. Later he told Davey: 'I'm not going out through that crowd and I'm not going to be dragged out. If you bring your cab here at three o'clock I'll come with you and not before that.' The landlord agreed. Byrne asked for some brandy but Davey said he would only fetch lemonade.

Shortly before 3 p.m. Davey returned with his cab. 'Well, Mr Byrne, the time's nearly up.' Byrne, who was in the ground-floor front room, replied: 'Yes, I'll go with you now.' He buttoned up his coat and stood with his hands in his pockets. At that moment a police sergeant opened the front door in an attempt to arrest him. Byrne ordered 'Stand back!' and pointed the revolver at him. Then he put the gun in his own mouth and pulled the trigger. He died instantly.

One newspaper reported: 'The multitude who gathered are wont to censure the police for not adopting measures to apprehend the man, and thus, in all probability, have saved his life.'

On 12 July Colour Sergeant John Byrne VC DCM was buried in an unmarked grave at Newport's St Woolos Cemetery.

An inquest was held at his local, the Crown Inn. One of the witnesses was Watts, who denied that he had insulted Byrne or the Victoria Cross. The teenager said that on the morning of 9 July the corporal in charge of the labourers had asked them not to smoke their pipes when on parade before setting off for work. Byrne turned up shortly afterwards lighting his pipe, and Watts said he passed on the corporal's request. He told the inquest that Byrne laughed but later mumbled something that he did not understand. Watts thought he had been drinking.

The inquest also heard from a Lieutenant Barklie, who said that the War Office had written about Byrne. It emerged that he was held in a lunatic asylum before being employed by the Ordnance Survey. The jury quickly returned a verdict that Byrne had committed suicide 'whilst in an unsound state of mind'.

After the inquest, the authorities, including the War Office, were criticised for their lack of welfare. In the *Cardiff Weekly Mail And South Wales Advertiser*, a columnist using the Greek mythical name Aeolus commented:

Everyone who has read the tragic story of his death must feel deep regret that such a life should have ended in that ignominious manner. How he came to be set at liberty, and how he was not looked after by someone who knew his antecedents, seems strange. The War Office, according to Lieutenant Barklie, had an inkling that possibly all was not quite right; yet there was no suspicion of mental illness. This is attributable, Aeolus believes, to ignorance on the part of those around him. Naturally there is a shrinking from suspicious watchfulness of a man who has suffered mental aberration. And it may be that the few who knew the man hoped the worst was passed. Now, however, that the whole truth is out, we see how unwise it may be to act reticently where the subtleties of madness are concerned.

On 4 November 1985 Major General [later General Sir] Peter de la Billière took part in a ceremony at St Woolos Cemetery, laying a wreath at Byrne's grave, where representatives of the Durham Light Infantry had erected a new headstone.

General de la Billière, who had served with the regiment, wrote in 2004:

He was typical of many outstanding soldiers who are at their best in the close-knit society of the army and under the tight code of discipline that governs service existence. Without these props, he lacked the self-discipline and control to run his life effectively. He was certainly a wild Irishman, but he was also an extremely brave soldier who risked his life on many occasions for Queen and Country, and stood out among his contemporaries on the battlefield. In his day the Victoria Cross was not held in the regard and respect that it is accorded today, but his story emphasises the ease with which sacrifices made in battle are forgotten once the priorities of conflict are overtaken by those of the ensuing peace.

There is no known photograph of John Byrne.

3

Vanishing Act
Edward St John Daniel

By the age of eighteen Edward St John Daniel had performed three acts of bravery worthy of the Victoria Cross, and he seemed set for a promising career in the Royal Navy. But within six years he would have the unhappy distinction of being the first man to forfeit the medal and he remains the only officer.

Daniel, born in Clifton, Bristol, on 17 January 1837, joined the navy as a cadet shortly before his fourteenth birthday. The son of a Bristol lawyer, his mother had died less than a year earlier. After training in Nelson's flagship HMS *Victory* and the frigate HMS *Dauntless* he served briefly in HMS *Blenheim*, a third rate. In March 1852 he joined the frigate HMS *Winchester* under Captain Granville Loch – and went to war, aged fifteen.

Winchester formed part of a punitive expedition to Burma. British merchants had complained that the King of Ava was refusing to abide by a treaty of 1826, which ended the First Burma War and gave territory to the Honourable East India Company. New hostilities were declared and the Irrawaddy delta around Rangoon saw most of the fighting. Loch was shot leading an attack on an enemy position at Donabew on 4 February 1853. Loch's force withdrew and he died two days later. The captain was buried in Rangoon. It is not clear if Daniel took part in the raid, but the swamps and jungles left him with insect bites and cuts that were not treated, and leg ulcers would trouble him for the rest of his life. The war officially ended on 30 June 1853, although no formal treaty was signed.

In the September Daniel joined the sixth rate HMS *Diamond* and was promoted midshipman. *Diamond*'s captain was William Peel, third son of Sir Robert Peel, the former prime minister. In 1854 Daniel sailed to another conflict, the Crimean War.

After arriving in the Black Sea, officers and men formed part of the naval brigade supporting British and French troops against the Russians. Daniel and another midshipman, Evelyn Wood, a future field marshal, were appointed Peel's aides-de-camp.

Daniel and Wood found Peel an inspirational leader. The navy set up its own batteries overlooking the Balaclava Plain, and Wood would recall in his memoirs:

Before the first bombardment, Captain Peel asked Lieutenant Ridge and Midshipman Daniels [*sic*] of HMS *Diamond*, and Lieutenant Douglas and Midshipman Wood of the *Queen*, to disregard fire in the battery, by always walking with head up and shoulders back and without due haste. He himself was a splendid example. I know he felt acutely every shot which passed over him, but the only visible effect was to make him throw up his head and square his shoulders.

In a letter home dated 16 October 1854, Daniel wrote: 'We are encamped with a thousand of our blue jackets and we have twenty of our guns ashore. We have had a good many shots fired at us, but none of our men have been wounded. I am the Captain's aide-de-camp. I have been obliged to provide myself with a horse as we are six miles from Admiral Sir E. Lyons [Rear Admiral Sir Edmund Lyons, commander of the Black Sea fleet] and very often I have to go to him twice a day, and after that to go to the trenches all night with the Captain.' He added: 'I am very much obliged to you for the pistols.'

Two days later Daniel carried out his first recognised act of bravery. He volunteered to get boxes of ammunition under heavy Russian fire from a wagon whose horses had been 'disabled' as it made its way to *Diamond*'s battery. From 17 October naval guns took part in a major bombardment of enemy positions in and around Sebastopol. The next day Captain Peel displayed his own heroism in an act that would help him to win the Victoria Cross.

A Russian shell landed in the battery close to cases of powder but did not explode. With the fuse still burning, sailors dived for cover in a futile attempt to save themselves. Peel heard shouts and picked up the 42lb shell, clutched it to his chest and went to the edge of the parapet, throwing it over the side. It exploded seconds later, but there were no casualties.

During the Battle of Inkerman on 5 November, when the allies were heavily outnumbered, Daniel again showed his bravery. He stayed at Peel's side throughout the day. At one point they hurried to warn some 100 officers and men of the Grenadier Guards who were in danger of being cut off and helped to save the regiment's colours.

Daniel was slightly wounded in the trenches at Sebastopol on 6 June 1855 but soon carried out the third of his acts of bravery, which would see him awarded the Victoria Cross. On 18 June an unsuccessful assault was made on the Redan fortifications. Peel was shot in his left arm as he led a ladder party and fell back. Under heavy fire Daniel tied a tourniquet on his arm and took him to safety, probably saving the captain's life. Daniel escaped injury even though bullets tore through his clothing and pistol case.

Daniel's Victoria Cross was announced in *The London Gazette* of 24 February 1857. It was on the recommendation of Rear Admiral Sir Stephen Lushington, commander of the naval brigade, who had noted the three acts of bravery in a despatch. Evelyn Wood, Peel's other aide-de-camp, was also recommended for the Victoria Cross but it was not approved, most likely because he had signalled that he wished to leave the navy and join the army, apparently believing that he would see more action as a soldier.

Diamond paid off in February 1857, and Daniel and Peel missed Queen Victoria's first Victoria Cross investiture in London in June. Peel had been given command of HMS *Shannon*, an experimental steam frigate, which had sailed for the China Station in March. The captain's trusted midshipman, Daniel, was on board. When the ship reached Singapore, Peel received new orders because of the Indian Mutiny. *Shannon* went to Hong Kong, embarked detachments of marines and soldiers of the 90th Foot, and headed to Calcutta with two other ships, HMS *Sanspareil* and HMS *Pearl*, arriving in August.

Peel, with his experience gained from the Crimea campaign, formed a naval brigade of some 400 sailors and marines from *Shannon*, with six 68-pounders and other heavy weapons. This force, with Daniel acting as an artillery officer, would distinguish itself. It was soon making its way to Allahabad. Other forces joined the *Shannon* brigade and on 1 November mutineers at Kudjna were defeated. In later fighting at the heavily defended Shah Najaf [Nujeff] mosque in Lucknow four naval Victoria Crosses were won, and the brigade also took part in the relief of Cawnpore. Peel, knighted in January 1858, was shot in the thigh at Lucknow in March. Later he contracted smallpox and died in Cawnpore on 27 April. He was buried the same day. In total, the *Shannon* brigade lost four officers and ninety-nine men to combat, wounds or disease.

The Times correspondent William Russell paid tribute to Peel: 'The greatness of our loss we shall in all probability never know.' Daniel must have felt Peel's death keenly, although Mate Edmund Verney suggested that the captain might have been getting exasperated with the midshipman's behaviour. Peel had sent Daniel alone on a special mission to Cawnpore and there were whispers that 'the Captain was very glad of an opportunity of sending him away, because twice already he has come under his notice, when he had drunk too freely'. In another letter to his father, Sir Harry Verney, in June 1858, he complained that Daniel was 'such a drunkard that none of us would mess with him'.

At a special parade in Gyah, Bengal, on 13 July 1858, attended by the *Shannon* brigade, Daniel was presented with his Victoria Cross by Peel's successor, Captain Frances Marten. In September 1859 the midshipman was promoted lieutenant and posted to a new ship, the second rate HMS *Mars*. He was invited to a gathering at St James's Palace in April the following year and shook hands with Queen Victoria, who was 'much impressed by him' – but not for long.

On 24 May 1860, while serving in the sloop HMS *Wasp*, he was severely reprimanded for twice being absent without leave. On 9 June he was found drunk in the wardroom after failing to turn out for the middle watch. At a court martial on board HMS *Impregnable* at Devonport a week later he admitted the offence but pointed to his service in three campaigns – Burma, the Crimea and India – and his impressive array of medals. As well as campaign medals, he had received the Legion d'Honneur from France, the Sardinian Medal for Valour and the Turkish Order of the Medjidie (5th Class). The court decided that it would not be harsh on the twenty-three-year-old lieutenant, who had no doubt seen more active service than many senior officers, and he was sentenced only to be dismissed his ship and to be placed at the bottom of the list of lieutenants for two years.

In January 1861 he was appointed to the second rate HMS *Victor Emmanuel* in the Mediterranean. But Daniel was still unable to control his drinking. and on 21 June he was placed under arrest. It is not entirely clear what he did. One claim suggests that in a drunken rage he attempted to drown another member of the crew who had insulted him. In a letter to Rear Admiral Sydney Dacres, a senior officer in the Mediterranean fleet, the ship's captain, William Clifford, disclosed that Daniel had taken 'indecent liberties' with four subordinate officers. According to the Victoria Cross collector Lord Ashcroft, this would have been a euphemism for sodomy.

The *Victor Emmanuel* went to Corfu and Daniel was set to face another court martial, this time with more serious consequences. However, on the night of 27 June he disappeared from the ship. Two marines were sent ashore to try to find him, but the navy never saw him again and he was soon listed as a deserter. The search does not appear to have been extensive. Perhaps the navy did not want the embarrassment of finding its disgraced Victoria Cross hero.

Under the royal warrant instituting the Victoria Cross on 5 February 1856, a holder of the decoration could forfeit it if he was 'convicted of treason, cowardice, felony, or of any infamous crime, or if he be accused of any such offence and doth not after a reasonable time surrender himself to be tried for the same'. It was the responsibility of the War Office to make such recommendations to the queen.

On 29 July 1861 the Admiralty informed the War Office of the Daniel case. Officials moved quickly, suggesting on 7 August that the relevant warrant could be prepared. A minute to Under-Secretary General Sir Edward Lugard noted: 'I privately heard of this bad case, but we now have it on record from the Admiralty that it was disgraceful, tho' not specified fully.' It is not clear who wrote the minute but the Secretary of State for War, Sir George Lewis, was also involved.

There seem to have been double standards at the time. Lugard was told of a soldier of the Coldstream Guards who had been awarded the Victoria Cross and was later 'accused of felony'. The commanding officer, however, refused to pursue the matter. As the man had not been convicted he kept the award, although he was not allowed to receive his medal 'from Her Majesty's hands'. Clearly the commanding officer in this case had not wanted to bring shame on his famous regiment so soon after the institution of such a prestigious decoration. By that time three men had been awarded the Victoria Cross while serving with the Coldstream Guards – Private William Stanlake, Captain Gerald Goodlake and Private George Strong, all for the Crimea. Captain Goodlake and Private Strong both attended the first investiture. Private Stanlake, who also won the Distinguished Conduct Medal, was not present.

On 23 August 1861 the War Office wrote to the queen pointing out that Daniel was accused of a 'disgraceful' offence and had 'evaded enquiry by desertion'. His name had been removed from the Navy List. The queen was asked to sign a warrant to 'erase' Daniel's name from the registry of Victoria Cross holders. This she did on 4 September.

He returned to England in secret and on 16 September boarded an American clipper in Liverpool that was bound for Australia. Daniel may have spent the next two years digging in the gold fields around Melbourne. In January 1864 New Zealand was recruiting men to fight in the Maori wars, and Daniel enlisted in Victoria, one day after his twenty-seventh birthday, giving his occupation as 'baker'. The following month No. 428 Private E. St J. Daniel of the Taranaki Military Settlers arrived at New Plymouth on North Island. He had not changed his ways. His drinking led to 'intensive labour' punishments in August and September.

He saw some action but the conflict ended in July 1866, though skirmishes continued for many more years. His unit was disbanded in May 1867, and he received land rights for his service, which he soon sold because farming did not appeal to him. He was also entitled to yet another campaign medal. Daniel joined up again, this time as constable No. 154 in the New Zealand Armed Constabulary Field Force at Patea, South Taranaki. Some sixty members of the force, including Daniel, who had been promoted lance corporal, were sent to Hokitika, South Island, in March 1868 to deal with rioting among the Irish community in the West Canterbury goldfields. The disturbances, stirred by Fenians, were soon quelled.

On 16 May Daniel, who had been 'ailing for some time', was admitted to Hokitika Hospital and died four days later, aged thirty-one. The death certificate gave the cause as 'delirium tremens', more commonly known as the DTs, which are normally associated with alcohol withdrawal. A full military funeral was held on 21 May, and a local newspaper reported: 'The deceased during his connection with the Armed Constabulary Force was much respected by his comrades, and certainly, on this mournful occasion, everything was done that lay in their power to testify their regard for their now lost friend and comrade.' He was buried in the local cemetery.

Or was he?

There is a theory that Daniel secretly returned to England after switching his identity with another man in New Zealand, Robert Daniels, originally from Birmingham. Daniel (No. 428) and Daniels (No. 427) enlisted in the Taranaki Military Settlers on the same day and sailed to New Zealand in the same ship. Daniels would have enjoyed the status of a Victoria Cross winner and may have turned to drink – like Daniel – because of the burden of keeping up the pretence.

Victoria Cross researcher Victor Tambling came up with the theory after buying a sepia photograph said to be of Daniel. A London photographer had taken the portrait around 1875, seven years after Daniel's 'death'. The image bore an uncanny likeness to a photograph of Daniel in uniform. The theory was explored in a 1992 BBC radio documentary, *Switched Identity*, and in 2001 a New Zealand television programme returned to the subject, using a leading forensic pathologist, Dr Tim Koelmeyer, who compared the bone structures in the pictures and said he was 'quite convinced that the portrait and the photograph are one and the same person'.

There was another twist. In 1902 the American author and social campaigner Jack London decided to spend several weeks among the poor in the East End of London. The result was a bleak book, *The People of the Abyss*. In one chapter he recalled an afternoon when he joined a queue for the Whitechapel workhouse and met a man who was 'strong-featured, with the tough and leathery skin produced by long years of sunbeat and weatherbeat ...'

The man claimed to have served in the Royal Navy and to have won the Victoria Cross. There were some remarkable similarities to Daniel's service – enlistment as a boy, war in Burma, the Crimea campaign, the Indian Mutiny. And he said he was court-martialled and discharged from the navy, forfeiting his Victoria Cross. His downfall came after he attacked a lieutenant who had insulted him.

But there were also discrepancies. The man said he served in the first war in China. After the attack he had been reduced to the rank of ordinary seaman and received a two-year prison sentence. He pointed out he was 'seven an' eighty years', but Daniel would have been sixty-five in 1902.

Eight men have forfeited the Victoria Cross, but Edward St John Daniel was the only one from the Royal Navy to have done so. It is possible that the man had known of Daniel's case and found it easy to spin a yarn to impress the American visitor. However, London appears to have believed him.

4

Jailed over a Cow
James McGuire

James McGuire was awarded the Victoria Cross for an act of bravery during the Indian Mutiny in 1857. He became the first army recipient to forfeit the medal. Bizarrely, a cow had led to his downfall.

Like another Irish Victoria Cross winner, John Byrne, little is known of McGuire's early life. But the two men probably had similar backgrounds – poverty and the misery of Ireland's great potato famine. For many young men there were limited prospects, the army offering one of the few avenues of escape.

Even McGuire's surname has been disputed, with references to M'Guire and Maguire. His place of birth is usually given as Enniskillen, County Fermanagh, but he probably came from Largy, a village to the north of the town. He was born in 1827, though the date is another mystery. At Enniskillen in 1849 the East India Company was recruiting for its regiments, and on 29 March McGuire, then a labourer aged twenty-one or twenty-two, signed on for ten years. He sailed for India in the troopship *Ellenborough*, arriving on 10 October to join the 1st Bengal European Fusiliers.

The regiment was involved in the Second Burma War of 1852–53, which broke out after British complaints that local rulers were failing to comply with the treaty that had ended the country's first war in 1826. The fusiliers were sent as reinforcements, sailing from Calcutta in several frigates and arriving in Rangoon in November 1852. They were soon in action. On 19 November it was decided to send an expedition to recapture the town and fortress of Pegu, which had been taken in the June but abandoned soon afterwards because there were not enough troops to form a garrison. The Burmese simply sneaked back. McGuire was among 300 men of the regiment who joined the force under Major General Henry Godwin, which also included the 1st European Madras Fusiliers, the 5th Madras Native Infantry and detachments of artillery and sappers.

The soldiers travelled part of the way by steamer, but after landing they had to hack their way through jungle in oppressive heat, with the enemy firing at them from concealed positions. When they arrived near the gateway of the town, Godwin found that his men were too exhausted to attack and needed to rest. On 21 November the general addressed the fusilier regiments: '*You* are Bengalies and *you* are Madrassies. Let's see who are the best men.' The response was 'a hearty cheer', and the two regiments led the assault. The town and fortress were soon recaptured. Three officers were wounded and up to forty other ranks were killed, wounded or reported missing. The next day the Bengal Fusiliers headed back to Rangoon, leaving a garrison of around 400 men.

On the evening of 27 November the Burmese mounted a daring attack on Pegu, which was repulsed. The following month saw further raids, and Major General Godwin was forced to send a relief expedition that included nearly 600 men of the Bengal Fusiliers. Pegu was eventually saved but the soldiers faced a new enemy – cholera, which took the lives of twenty fusiliers.

A new expedition was formed to drive the Burmese from numerous stockades they had erected in the southern part of the country. Again, the Bengal Fusiliers were involved. It was a challenging operation in unknown country, with seemingly endless miles of jungle and swamp. On 19 January 1853 the force entered an abandoned stockade identified as Gongho to find that the enemy had thrown many of their dead into wells to poison the water. The force carried on – unopposed – with fatiguing marches, arriving at the important city of Shoe Gyne, where 'the natives seemed well-disposed to the British'. There were further operations, and in April the 1st Madras Fusiliers relieved the Bengal Fusiliers. Most of the men returned to Rangoon, although detachments were left at Pegu and Shoe Gyne. Hostilities ceased at the end of 1853, with a vast increase in territories controlled by the British. The Bengal Fusiliers returned to India in February 1855 after an absence of nearly two-and-a-half years.

Unrest among sepoys, mainly Hindu, had been simmering for some time when in March 1857 the Bengal Native Infantry mutinied at Barrackpore. On 10 May there was another mutiny at Meerut. The mutineers fled to Delhi and were joined by other native regiments. Europeans – many of them women and children – soon became the target for mass slaughter in what would become known as the Indian Mutiny.

On 13 May the 1st Bengal Fusiliers, based at Dugshai in the foothills of the Himalayas, were alerted and later joined other regiments for an advance on Delhi, marching at night because of the excessive heat. In June, at Budlee-ka-Scrai, on the road between Alipore and Delhi, the force met fierce resistance, artillery fire causing a high number of casualties. But the mutineers were poorly led and allowed their flanks to be exposed. They retreated in disorder to Delhi. The Bengal Fusiliers had been marching and fighting for fifteen consecutive hours.

Skirmishes would continue for weeks. The regiment's Private John McGovern, frequently in trouble for unruly behaviour, was awarded the Victoria Cross for carrying a wounded soldier back to camp under heavy fire on 23 June. The 2nd Bengal Fusiliers were also involved in much of the fighting. Casualties mounted and cholera and sunstroke claimed some of the lives. On the morning of 5 July the British commander, Major General Sir Henry Barnard, was struck down by cholera; by the evening he was dead.

Conditions in camp were appalling:

The heat at this time was terrific, and it appears marvellous that disease was not more prevalent. The men were exposed during the day to a tropical sun, and all night to malarious dews. The air was tainted with every kind of nauseous smell. There was a total absence of any attempt at sanitary arrangements. Camels and other animals that had died or been killed lay in all directions in close proximity to the camp, and dense clouds of flies rendered it unsafe to eat or drink without muslin having been placed over the face, the drinking pot and plate. There thus appeared to be every enticement for disease but, with the exception of occasional cases of sunstroke and cholera, and the casualties of war, our troops were far more healthy than we had any reason to expect.

Delhi was under siege for weeks, but that was not the only challenge. The rebels also had strangleholds on Lucknow and Cawnpore as well as other places in Bengal.

It was not until the evening of 13 September that siege guns made significant breaches in Delhi's north walls, including the Kabul and Kashmir gates. A major assault was planned for the following morning using some 5,000 troops in five columns. The 1st Bengal Fusiliers left Dugshai 800 strong but they had been reduced to about half that number. James McGuire, promoted sergeant, was one of the survivors. The regiment formed part of the first column under Brigadier John Nicholson, with the Kashmir breach their target using scaling ladders.

One account gave a vivid description of the fighting:

On emerging into the open, a terrific fire was poured on the escaladers who, with a cheer, ran forward at the double, followed closely by the rest of the regiment. On nearing the Kashmir bastion, it was seen that the ditch was so filled with masonry that our men were enabled to glide down the incline and plant the escalading ladders with such rapidity that the top of the ramparts was quickly reached amidst a storm of bullets, and missiles, hurled down from the walls above. Notwithstanding this opposition, the ramparts were gained before the mutineers had collected their forces in sufficient numbers to make a very determined resistance, and thus a firm footing was obtained on the breach before any attempt had been made to blow open the Kashmir Gate.

Our men, though vastly outnumbered, fought with uncontrolled vehemence, striking down the mutineers with their clubbed muskets where they could not succeed in thrusting home their bayonets. The dense masses of the Sepahis now crowding to the front could not withstand the eager onslaught of our men, who for nearly three months had been thirsting for this day of retribution. This was not the usual excitement of battle, it was the individual burning lust of revenge for the atrocities committed by the mutineers, and it is hardly possible to realise the intensity of passion that animated every British heart that day. There were volunteers in our ranks, conductors and non-commissioned staff who had lost all that had made life most dear. And these men dealt death around at every stroke, crying aloud, above the din of war, 'Where is my wife?' 'Where are my poor children?' It was just almighty retribution, beyond the influence or control of men.

It was on 14 September that Sergeant McGuire won the Victoria Cross. The fusiliers and soldiers from other regiments had fought their way to the Kabul gate and were waiting for orders and fresh ammunition. Suddenly three boxes of ammunition exploded, setting fire to two others. At great risk to themselves McGuire and Drummer Miles Ryan rushed into the 'burning mass' and grabbed the boxes, throwing them one after the other over the side of the parapet. In the confusion soldiers had been rushing towards 'certain destruction' and the actions of McGuire and Ryan, who was also awarded the Victoria Cross, saved many lives.

The 1856 warrant creating the Victoria Cross allowed soldiers or sailors to elect someone who had shown outstanding bravery to receive the medal, and this appears to have happened in McGuire's case. According to Lieutenant General Sir George MacMunn, the sergeant was unanimously chosen because of his honesty. He had been picked as the canteen sergeant for that month, a job that involved distributing the rum ration.

Lieutenant General MacMunn explained: 'In the field, when rum was a daily ration, the men would file past the canteen sergeant, each with his mess tin, and into this the sergeant would pour the tot of rum from the little copper measure which had no handle and which was held usually between finger and thumb, the tip of the latter inside. Thus the sergeant saved for himself each day close on a thousand times the thickness of his thumb tip. It was a fair perquisite and so recognised, but this particular sergeant helped the measure in with finger and thumb both outside, and such self-denial deserved formal recognition from the regiment, so they chose him unanimously for the Cross.'

Delhi was finally captured on 20 September. Among the dead was Brigadier John Nicholson, who had taken command the previous month.

The mutineers had declared the old Mughal emperor Bahadur Shah their ruler. After the fall of Delhi, Major William Hodson, an intelligence officer who also commanded a cavalry unit known as Hodson's Horse, learned that the emperor and his two sons were hiding in a tomb on the outskirts of the city. The 'indefatigable' Hodson was highly respected by his Sikh cavalry, 'a commander after their own hearts'. He obtained permission to capture Bahadur Shah, but was told the emperor must not be harmed or insulted. He galloped off with a small number of troopers. Reaching the tomb, he found a mass of people, soldiers and followers. As guards approached he calmly drew a cigar box from a pocket and ordered one of them to fetch a light. The bluff worked. Bahadur Shah surrendered without a fight.

The next day Hodson, with only five men, returned to the area of the tomb, where there were still thousands of the emperor's followers, to search for the two sons, both princes. The officer had kept his word and delivered the emperor safely, but he had given no assurances about the princes, who were soon found. On the way back to Delhi Hodson shouted that they were 'the butchers who had murdered our wives and children', grabbed a carbine from one of his troopers and shot them dead. The major was quoted as saying: 'I cannot help being pleased at the warm congratulations I receive on all sides for my success in destroying the enemies of our race.'

The capture of Delhi was a significant turning point in the Indian Mutiny, but many months of fighting lay ahead because tens of thousands of rebels had scattered across the country. The 1st Bengal Fusiliers were fully engaged in the action, especially at Lucknow and Cawnpore. The fall of Gwalior on 20 June 1858 signalled the virtual end of the mutiny, although clashes continued into the following year.

The British government decided to take over the administration of India, and the East India Company, which could trace its origins to 1600, was dissolved. In 1861 the company's European troops were transferred to the British Army. The 1st Bengal European Fusiliers became the 101st Regiment of Foot (Royal Bengal Fusiliers) and later the Royal Munster Fusiliers.

After completing ten years' service Sergeant James McGuire was discharged in May 1859 with a pension of 1 shilling a day. As the holder of the Victoria Cross he was also entitled to an annual payment of £10. On 4 January 1860 Queen Victoria presented him with the medal at Windsor Castle.

McGuire, placed in the army reserve, returned to Ireland and at some stage went to live with an uncle, also called James McGuire, who had a small farm near Enniskillen. The ex-soldier was persuaded to loan the family £6 – from his Victoria Cross payment – but the debt was never fully repaid. On 13 June 1862 McGuire senior reported that the door to his cow shed had been broken open and one of his three cows was missing. The animal was recovered several days later and police arrested McGuire VC. He had been on his way to a fair, presumably to sell the animal.

The following month he appeared at the local assizes facing two charges – stealing a cow and having the animal in his possession knowing it to be stolen. The court heard that McGuire thought he was entitled to take the cow because the debt had not been cleared. It will be remembered that the Bengal Fusiliers had noted his honesty over tots of rum. The lawyer representing McGuire showed his medals to the jury and spoke of his valiant service, which included fighting in 'the burning fields of Hindustan'. It was really a family dispute, the lawyer insisted, and not a case of theft. But the court was not sympathetic and sentenced McGuire to nine months' hard labour.

The War Office soon learned of McGuire's felony conviction, and the matter was referred to the Under-Secretary of State for War, General Sir Edward Lugard, who was told there were mitigating circumstances. McGuire was a 'simple, quiet man and not up with the ways of the world'. The India Office was consulted, and there was a sharp reply on behalf of Sir Charles Wood, the Secretary of State for India: 'Sir Charles Wood believes that as the Secretary of State for War takes Her Majesty's pleasure as to the granting of the Victoria Cross, so he should in like manner receive Her Majesty's commands as to the withdrawal of that distinction. In the case of James McGuire, who belonged to HM's Indian Military forces, Sir Charles Wood considers that the Victoria Cross should be taken away and the pension cease.'

It appears that McGuire's ten years' service in India and his brave conduct counted for nothing as far as Wood was concerned. The Liberal MP, who became Viscount Halifax, was not always noted for his generosity of spirit. He had opposed help for Ireland during the great famine.

General Lugard, who had served during the Indian Mutiny, may have felt some sympathy for his fellow veteran, but he was advised that under the warrant for the Victoria Cross the medal and pension would have to be forfeited. On 12 December 1862 Queen Victoria signed the relevant document.

From that date on the story of James McGuire takes a bizarre course. He reportedly died on 22 December. It is not clear where his death took place. It has been stated at Londonderry prison, where he was still serving his sentence, or at 'Lisnaskea Hospital', near Enniskillen. Curiously, there was a workhouse with an infirmary at Lisnaskea but not a hospital, and it is unlikely that McGuire would have been transferred from prison to a workhouse. Even stranger, he was recorded as having been buried at Donagh cemetery, about 3 miles from Lisnaskea, in an unmarked grave under the name Patrick Donnelly, raising the possibility that it might have been a double grave.

But War Office papers show that McGuire petitioned for the restoration of his Victoria Cross and pension in 1863. In an apparent change of heart, he was even supported by the stipendiary magistrate involved in his case. At Enniskillen on 18 May, the magistrate wrote: 'From what I have learnt of the man's character I believe it quite possible he may have thought he was justified in taking the cow. He has undergone a severe punishment and I respectfully recommend that the pension to which his gallantry has entitled him be restored.' Other local dignitaries supported the petition, one of whom wrote: 'The petitioner lives in my neighbourhood ...' Clearly, they were supporting a man who appeared to be very much alive.

General Lugard was asked to consider the petition in the June. In another twist he was told that the Victoria Cross had been forfeited on 22 December 1862, the date of McGuire's supposed death. It was pointed out that under the original warrant of 1856 the decoration could be restored. A minute paper noted: 'It is stated that there is reason to suppose that the man may have considered himself justified in taking the property of the person indebted to him as the only means in his power of recovering the value of what was due to him. He has undergone the term of his sentence, and it is submitted that, in pursuance of the reservation in the warrant, Her Majesty may now be advised to restore the Cross and pension.' The general wrote on the paper: 'Approve of the restoration under the circumstances.'

However, at this point McGuire seems to have disappeared from the records. The army did not return his Victoria Cross, which he had been forced to hand over after his conviction. Had he died? Or had he taken on a new identity, perhaps joining the army again, an easy thing to do in those days?

The answer may never be known. It seems that no picture of McGuire exists.

5

Oats, Hay and Prison
Michael Murphy

Michael Murphy was another Irish hero who suddenly fell from grace, but his regiment held him in such regard that he was accepted back after serving a prison sentence.

Murphy was born in the fortress town of Cahir, County Tipperary, on 5 September 1831, the son of John and Honora Murphy, although his date of birth has been disputed. His father was a local blacksmith, a trade that Murphy took up in his teenage years. It is doubtful that he received much formal education. In 1854, aged twenty-two, he married one Mary Walsh, and months later decided to join the army, prospects and money no doubt being the factors. As he had some experience with horses, he enlisted in a cavalry regiment, the 17th Lancers, at Cork, receiving a bounty of £9. Most of the regiment was serving in the Crimea, where 'the death or glory boys' took part in the Charge of the Light Brigade, and Murphy trained briefly with the 16th Lancers before returning to the 17th Lancers, which was conveniently based at Cahir.

In October 1856 he volunteered for the 2nd Battalion Military Train, a supply and transport unit, which was being formed at the Curragh. The forerunner of the Army Service Corps was selective and many volunteers were rejected. Murphy, 5 feet 3 inches tall, was one of the lucky ones, joining as a farrier and picking up another bounty, 21 shillings.

Major J. P. Robertson, who was involved in the recruiting process, noted: 'I was sent off to the different cavalry regiments stationed in England or Ireland to select volunteers for the new corps and my orders were to take none but those of really good character. I caused a tremendous disturbance by rejecting about half of the offered volunteers ...' But his actions were supported by senior officers 'and I got together 500 as fine young men as could be seen anywhere'.

After a short spell at Woolwich the 2nd battalion sailed in the *Blervic Castle* for Hong Kong on 28 April 1857. When the ship reached Indonesia, the battalion was diverted to Calcutta because of the Indian Mutiny. Murphy and his comrades arrived on 27 August and on 25 November they joined several thousand soldiers at Alum Bagh [also Alumbagh or Alambagh], a camp near besieged Lucknow. The battalion, led by Major Roberstson, took on the role of a light cavalry unit and was involved in the relief of Lucknow, drawing praise from Major General [later Lieutenant General] Sir James Outram, one of the key figures during operations to suppress the mutiny.

In one attack, men of the Military Train routed enemy cavalry and captured several guns that had ended up in a ravine. But they soon faced around 2,000 infantry and although heavily outnumbered held them off until reinforcements arrived. Outram 'was particularly pleased with the very cool and soldierlike behaviour of the Military Train'.

By the end of 1857 Delhi, Lucknow and Cawnpore were back in British hands, but thousands of rebels were still at large in strategic areas of the country. Orders were given to hunt them down, and the 2nd battalion became part of the Azimghur field force.

It was on 15 April 1858 that Michael Murphy won the Victoria Cross. A large number of rebels led by Koer Singh had left Azimghur [Azamgarh], a town south-east of Lucknow, and were being pursued by a squadron of the Military Train and a half troop of horse artillery. The 3rd Sikh Cavalry, led by the adjutant, a Lieutenant Hamilton, joined the pursuit. During a charge at Nathupur Hamilton fell wounded from his horse and was surrounded by sepoys who 'commenced cutting and hacking him whilst on the ground'. Murphy, whose horse had been shot from under him, rushed to the officer's aid. He fought off several of the rebels and was badly wounded. Another soldier of the Military Train, Private Samuel Morley, also went to help Hamilton.

Murphy and Morley stayed with the lieutenant, fighting back to back. Eventually loyal Indian troops came to support them. By that time Murphy had killed five rebels – and received five wounds. He was sent to Calcutta for hospital treatment. Hamilton did not survive.

In April 1859 it was announced that the Military Train would return to England, and the *Calcutta Gazette Extraordinary* paid tribute to its 'short but brilliant' service in India, adding: 'Throughout the glorious and most trying summer campaign, of which the first relief of Lucknow was the fruit, the Military Train bore a part which would have reflected credit upon the oldest and most experienced cavalry soldiers. It has since served with distinction in various affairs under Lieutenant General Sir James Outram – at the capture of Lucknow, in the operations about Azimghur, and lastly in the harassing campaign of Shahabar.'

On returning to England, *The Times* of 10 October 1859 also saluted 'this gallant body of men'. The 2nd battalion went to its depot at Aldershot. Murphy's Victoria Cross had been announced in *The London Gazette* of 27 May, and he received the medal from Queen Victoria during a parade at Windsor on 4 January 1860. He qualified for the decoration's annual payment of £10, and shortly afterwards he was promoted farrier sergeant, boosting his daily pay from 1s 6d to 2s 6d. Murphy's award did not go down well with Morley, whose bravery had been ignored officially. Morley thought he deserved the Victoria Cross too. Remarkably, the private pointed this out when Brigadier Lord George Paget went to Aldershot to inspect the battalion in May 1860. And remarkably, the general was sympathetic, saying he would take the matter up at the highest level. He was true to his word, and an inquiry was carried out by a board of three generals, who sent a letter to the Under-Secretary of State for War on 12 July saying that Morley had 'a fair claim to the decoration'. Queen Victoria approved the recommendation, and she presented the medal to him at Windsor on 9 November 1860.

Murphy remained with the Military Train for the next ten years, with spells in Canada and at the Royal Military Academy Sandhurst. In 1870 the Military Train was disbanded and he joined the newly created Army Service Corps, but the following year he transferred to the 7th Hussars, stationed at Aldershot.

On 26 January 1872, forty-one-year-old Murphy's life changed. The Indian Mutiny hero was arrested and accused of theft. That afternoon a labourer, James Green, had taken his horse and cart into the hussars' barracks. Farrier Major James Watt noticed that the cart was empty, but twenty minutes later, as Green headed back to the main gate, it was found to contain a sack of oats and some hay. Asked for an explanation, the labourer said Murphy had given him the oats and hay. The feed, kept in a boiler room, was for sick horses. Murphy was questioned and reportedly said: 'For God's sake, look over it or I shall be a ruined man for life.' After his arrest the farrier sergeant was taken to a civil prison.

On 2 March Murphy, wearing his Victoria Cross and Indian Mutiny campaign medal, appeared at Hampshire Lent Assizes in Winchester, along with Green, accused of stealing oats and hay worth £1 7s, 'the property of the Queen'. Murphy's defence argued that the soldier may have been guilty of neglect or ignorance but there had never been any intention to steal. A Victoria Cross winner 'of the highest character' would not be foolish enough to send a horse and cart with stolen feed across a barrack square in full view of sentries in broad daylight.

Murphy told the court that he had asked for the oats and hay to be moved because they were surplus and he wanted to give them to underfed horses in his own troop. But the judge, Mr Baron Bramwell, dismissed this as 'a lame excuse'. He also appeared irritated that the defence had emphasised Murphy's bravery and his Victoria Cross in an attempt to win over the court. Murphy may have wished that another judge had been involved. Mr Baron Bramwell, a well-known figure in legal circles, was once described as 'domineering, entertaining and consciously concerned to mould the law to ends which he favoured'.

Green, in his defence, told the court that he had simply been asked to move the feed from one place to another. If the judge showed little sympathy for the soldier, he appears to have taken the opposite view with Green. Although Farrier Major Watt told the court that the labourer had been only two yards from the main gate when he was stopped, the judge remarked that Green's conduct 'certainly looked like that of an innocent man'.

The jury found Murphy guilty and forty-year-old Green not guilty. The *Hampshire Telegraph* reported: 'He [the judge] was sorry a man with so excellent a character, and who had seen so much service, should commit such a crime, but it could not be tolerated that sergeants should take corn in this way.' Mr Baron Bramwell said he would take into account the jury's request that Murphy be shown mercy – and then jailed him for nine months with hard labour. The soldier was taken to the county's House of Correction. That day he was reduced to the rank of private.

The conviction led to a royal warrant depriving Murphy of his Victoria Cross and pension. He was supposed to return the medal to the War Office, but in May the prison governor said he was unable to locate it. The decoration – worn by Murphy at his trial – had apparently disappeared.

On 30 November the soldier was released from prison and he returned to the 7th Hussars, which had moved from Aldershot to Hounslow. Although he had been with regiment only for a short time, it is significant that he was allowed back and not discharged following his conviction. There may well have been some sympathy over the way his court case was handled and the punishment meted out.

During the next two years Murphy's health deteriorated and he had spells in hospital. It is unclear if the serious wounds he received in India and the hard labour at the House of Correction were factors. In December 1874 he was attached to the 9th Lancers, which was set to go to India, but he remained in England, transferring to the 5th Lancers. However, his army life was coming to an end. Broken health left him unable to carry out his duties. Michael Murphy was discharged in February 1875 after twenty years' service. He was given a discharge allowance of 20s.

Murphy's life after leaving the army remains sketchy. He went to live at Bellingham, Northumberland, but over the next few years he moved several times, working for some time as a blacksmith, the trade he took up as a teenager. His wife Mary died at the age of thirty-seven. At one stage Murphy was living alone in a cottage at Blackwell, near Darlington, which had been provided by Lieutenant General Sir Henry Havelock-Allan, a Victoria Cross winner and a veteran of the Indian Mutiny who seemed happy to help an old soldier facing hard times. Later Murphy married a woman called Julia and went to live in Darlington, getting a job as a labourer in an ironworks. Julia died in 1888.

On 4 April 1893 Michael Murphy VC – as he styled himself – died of pneumonia in Darlington. He was given a pauper's funeral and buried in a local cemetery. General Havelock-Allan intervened once again and arranged for a gravestone to be erected.

The gravestone reads:

Sacred to the memory of Michael Murphy formerly Sergeant the 2nd Battalion Military Train and the 7th Hussars, who for conspicuous gallantry during the Indian Mutiny where he received five wounds in saving the life of a wounded officer obtained the Victoria Cross. Born in Tipperary – 1832 [1831], died at Darlington 4th April 1893. RIP. Three of his sons died or were killed in Her Majesty's Service. This stone is erected to his memory by his old comrade Sir Henry Havelock-Allan.

It was a remarkable tribute because the general had not been a cavalry officer and Murphy never served under him. During the mutiny Havelock-Allan was with the 10th Regiment of Foot, later the Lincolnshire Regiment. He also chose to ignore the fact that Murphy had forfeited his Victoria Cross in disgrace after the conviction for theft.

A question mark hangs over the gravestone's reference to three sons. One may have died in the Zulu massacre of British troops at the Battle of Isandlwana on 22 January 1879 and the two others during the Egyptian campaign of 1882–89. But it is not clear how many children Murphy had from his two marriages, and their identities have not been established. If Murphy did indeed lose three sons in military service, it would have been a heavy burden on top of his poor health.

Private Samuel Morley transferred to the 16th Lancers from the Military Train two years after receiving his Victoria Cross. In January 1864 he purchased his discharge. Civilian life, however, appears to have had little appeal and six months later Morley, from Radcliffe-on-Trent, Nottinghamshire, re-enlisted, this time in the 1st

Battalion Military Train. His second spell in the army was marred by indiscipline. Morley's name appeared often in the defaulters' book, and he was twice court-martialled and jailed for being absent without leave. When the Military Train was disbanded in 1870, he was discharged. Morley went to live in Nottingham where he worked in a gasworks, later marrying. He died on 16 June 1888, aged fifty-nine. The authorities in Nottingham paid for a memorial stone, part of which reads: 'He won the coveted distinction of the Victoria Cross during the trying days of the Indian Mutiny, in those terrible battles which led to the capture of Lucknow, when the Empire of India seemed almost to have escaped our grasp ... In every action in which he was engaged during the rebellion, his conduct was that of a brave, cool and gallant soldier.'

Michael Murphy's missing Victoria Cross appeared at auction in 1898, when it was bought for £44 on behalf of the sergeants' mess of the Army Service Corps at Aldershot. The sergeants clearly had the same attitude as General Havelock-Allan – Murphy was a hero who deserved to be recognised. The decoration is now held by the Royal Logistic Corps at Deepcut, Surrey, along with the Victoria Cross awarded to Samuel Morley.

6

Despair in Pentonville
Valentine Bambrick

Valentine Bambrick became aware of army life at an early age. His father John was a troop sergeant major in the 11th Light Dragoons and had fought at Waterloo. Napoleon's armies were a familiar enemy. The regiment had taken part in the Egyptian and Peninsular campaigns. It helped to defeat Marshal Marmont's troops at the Battle of Salamanca on 22 July 1812, one of Wellington's greatest victories. During the Peninsular War it acquired the nickname The Cherry Pickers after being surprised by the French in a cherry orchard. At Waterloo on 18 June 1815, the 11th broke an infantry square and took part in the pursuit of Napoleon's fleeing soldiers, capturing the last French guns still firing. When Wellington entered Paris in triumph on 7 July, the dragoons were among his escort and bivouacked on the Champs Elysees.

John Bambrick had joined the 11th Light Dragoons in August 1814 as a twenty-three-year-old labourer. By the time of Waterloo, less than a year later, he had already been promoted sergeant. In 1819 the regiment was sent to India in a posting that would last nearly twenty years. For a time it was stationed at Cawnpore, where Valentine Bambrick was born on 13 April 1837. He was named Valentine after an uncle who also served as a troop sergeant major in the 11th Light Dragoons, which had added another battle honour, Bhurtpore. The uncle joined the regiment at the age of thirteen – a mere 4 feet 9 inches tall and described as a labourer – on the same day as John Bambrick in August 1814. Both men were born in Windsor, Berkshire. A year after young Valentine's birth the 11th left India and returned to England, where his father was discharged as medically unfit.

When Prince Albert arrived at Dover in 1840 for his wedding to Queen Victoria, the 11th Light Dragoons provided part of his escort. The prince was impressed and soon afterwards he became colonel of the regiment, which changed its title to the 11th (Prince Albert's Own) Regiment of (Light) Dragoons (Hussars) and then the 11th (or Prince Albert's Own) Hussars. The new hussars also found themselves with a change of uniform, which included crimson trousers, a Saxe-Coburg livery. And there was another nickname, The Cherry Bums, which in polite company changed to The Cherubims.

Young Valentine Bambrick had a brother, John (named after their father), who joined the 11th Hussars and took part in the Charge of the Light Brigade at Balaclava on 25 October 1854. The 11th were second in the formation, with the 17th Lancers leading the attack on the Russian guns because their dropped lances were known to terrify the enemy.

The fire from the Russian guns was merciless, as Troop Sergeant Major George Smith of the 11th Hussars would recall:

> The first man of my troop that was struck was Private Young, a cannon ball taking off his right arm. I, being close on his right rear, fancied I felt the wind from it as it passed me. I afterwards found I was bespattered with his flesh. Private Turner's left arm was also struck off close to the shoulder and Private Ward was struck full in the chest. A shell too burst over us, a piece of which struck Cornet Houghton in the forehead and mortally wounded him.
>
> When Private Young lost his arm, he coolly fell back and asked me what he was to do. I replied: 'Turn your horse about and get to the rear as fast as you can.' I had scarcely done speaking to him when Private Turner fell back, calling out for help. I told him too to go to the rear.

In the smoke and confusion many of the hussars veered to the left of the guns, coming under withering fire from infantry. Private John Richardson was one of the men who reached the guns: 'There was a lot of smoke about, and I couldn't see much. I remember after we got among the artillery and came to hand-to-hand work, my horse was killed and fell with me under him.' Russian cavalry joined the fighting and the Light Brigade, with so many casualties, was heavily outnumbered. Private William Pennington of the 11th recalled: 'Of course with our handful, it was life or death, so we rushed at them to break through them. With five or six fellows at my rear, I galloped on, passing with the determination of one who would not lose his life, breaking the lances of the cowards who attacked us in the proportion of three or four to one, occasionally catching one a slap with the sword across his teeth, and giving another the point on his arm or breast.'

When officers realised 'to our horror' that the Heavy Brigade would not be charging in support, the order to withdraw was given. Of the 673 who took part, only 195 mounted officers and men returned to the British lines. Nearly 250 were killed and wounded, and the Russians took dozens prisoner. More than 400 horses were lost.

Alexander Dunn, a twenty-one-year-old lieutenant in the 11th Hussars, won the Victoria Cross for two acts of bravery in rescuing a sergeant and a private who were being attacked by Russian cavalry during the retreat. But he soon tarnished his reputation by leaving the regiment with one Rosa Maria Douglas – the wife of the commanding officer, Lieutenant Colonel John Douglas. Dunn died in 1868 while commanding the 33rd (Duke of Wellington's) Regiment during the Abyssinian campaign, apparently in a hunting accident, although it was later claimed that his valet had murdered him for a £300 inheritance.

The Light Brigade had been led by Major General the Earl of Cardigan, who survived unscathed. After the charge he returned to his yacht in Balaclava harbour for a champagne meal. He had been the unpopular commanding officer of the 11th Light Dragoons for several years.

Private John Bambrick, whose horse had been killed in the charge, was one of the survivors. But the battlefield would not be the only enemy in the coming months. The harsh winter took a heavy toll on the British Army, which was poorly supplied, with disease a bigger threat than Russian bombs and bullets. There was not enough food, clothing or shelter and horses were starving. One cavalryman reported: 'When a horse dropped dead in the lines, the others that could reach it would gnaw the hair off its skin. Saddlery, blankets, ropes and picket pegs all were eaten by them, and we had to be careful on going near them, or they would seize us by the beard and whiskers for the same purpose.'

On 4 February 1855 there was only one man in the 11th Hussars who was fit for picket duty. Troop Sergeant Major Smith reported: 'It was piteous to see him sitting on a frozen saddle, muffled up, looking perfectly helpless and the poor horse without mane or tail, eyes nearly closed, with lumps of ice hanging on his legs.' The once impressive Light Brigade was in a hideous state.

John Bambrick, who had originally enlisted in the Rifle Brigade, transferring to the 11th Hussars in 1849, was promoted corporal in 1855 but soon reduced back to private. The reason for his demotion is unclear. He had survived the Charge of the Light Brigade and the harsh winter, but on 5 July he died at the cavalry camp near Kadikoi, 2 miles from Balaclava, probably of disease.

His brother Valentine joined the army on 12 April 1853, one day before his sixteenth birthday. Described as a clerk, he did not follow the family tradition of the 11th Hussars, instead signing on with infantry, The 60th, The King's Royal Rifle Corps. He joined the 1st Battalion, which was stationed in India. In December 1855 the battalion went to the city of Meerut, some 40 miles north-east of Delhi. Meerut, which had a large garrison, would be the flashpoint for the Indian Mutiny. In August 1856 the 60th faced an outbreak of cholera, which claimed the lives of forty-eight men, women and children. On 1 January 1857 the battalion was armed with the long Enfield rifle but, bizarrely, the military authorities decided not to issue any ammunition. When the commanding officer protested, each man was allowed ten rounds and that was still the total amount when the mutiny broke out with a vengeance in May after discontent in several areas had been simmering for months.

On 24 April, eighty-five men of the 3rd Native Cavalry Regiment refused to drill at Meerut and were arrested. A court martial handed down jail sentences of up to ten years with hard labour. On 9 May the convicted men were paraded in front of British units, including the 60th Rifles, and the 11th and 20th Native Infantry. Only the British soldiers had loaded weapons and 'the least movement of insubordination would have been followed by instant death'. The condemned men were stripped of their uniforms and accoutrements, put in irons and taken to a local jail, pleading in vain for mercy.

Shortly before 6 p.m. the following day, a Sunday, as men of the 60th assembled for a church parade, an off-duty private ran up to the acting adjutant, Lieutenant Cromer Ashburnham, 'so breathless as to be unable to impart the evidently alarming message which he was struggling to utter. Before the man could find words Ashburnham heard behind him the sound of hurrying feet, and looking round saw to his surprise the riflemen running to their bungalows, with rifles, swords and the only ten rounds of ammunition which had as yet been served out to the battalion since the issue of the Enfield rifle. By this time Ashburnham had received the message of terrible import.'

Incensed at the humiliating treatment of their comrades, sepoys of the 11th and 20th Native Infantry had gathered in Meerut, some distance from the barracks, in open revolt, encouraged by angry locals. When a colonel tried to restore order he was shot in the back and cut to pieces. Other officers were murdered and then the sepoys massacred every white man, woman and child they could find, burning their homes. The gates of the jail were broken down and the eighty-five convicted soldiers freed, along with hundreds of other prisoners. At the barracks, Ashburnham pointed out to his commanding officer that the riflemen still had only ten rounds of ammunition each, and that the regimental magazine was in the sole charge of a native guard. A party was sent to seize the magazine and the guard fled, but the order to send a sizeable force to deal with the mutineers was given too late. That night most of the rebels left Meerut and headed to Delhi. When the 60th, 6th Dragoon Guards and horse artillery arrived in the centre of Meerut, they found scenes of devastation. Some mutineers were still there and the order was given to 'shoot them like dogs' – the first shots fired by British troops in the Indian Mutiny.

The revolt spread, enveloping Delhi, Benares, Allahabad and Cawnpore. Some garrison commanders acted quickly in disarming their native troops but those who hesitated paid a high price. The scenes in Meerut were repeated in many towns. There were no British regiments at Delhi, only native infantry – the 38th, 54th and 74th. The 38th soon joined the mutiny, killing its officers and hunting down Europeans in the city. Some of those who managed to escape reached Meerut in searing heat. On 15 May a battalion of native sappers and miners arrived and were welcomed as reinforcements, But the next day they mutinied and murdered their colonel – 'the riflemen and dragoons promptly turned out and shot fifty of them'.

On 27 May, sixteen officers and 450 men of the 60th, with dragoons and horse artillery, left Meerut to join a field force that was marching on Delhi, although Valentine Bambrick was one of the men who remained behind on garrison duty. When they were 9 miles from the city, the 700 troops fought and defeated mutineers seven times that number. On 6 June they joined the field force, with one observer noting: 'The Rifles in particular, though they had had a long march, came along stepping out merrily and singing in chorus.'

Two days later there was a successful battle against some 30,000 rebels at Budlee-ka-Scrai, north-west of Delhi. But, with only around 3,000 British and loyal native troops in place, an attack on the walled city of Delhi, with its formidable defences and 40,000 mutineers, was out of the question until the arrival of major reinforcements. On 14 September, with breaches in the walls, the assault was finally made.

Men of the 60th provided covering fire for the column advancing on the Kashmir Gate. A chaplain recalled their enthusiasm:

Carried away entirely with the excitement of the occasion, the Rifles, whose duty it was to cover, and who discharged that duty to the admiration of every beholder, could not withstand the temptation that now met them. Forgetting that being light infantry they were essentially skirmishers, they were among the very foremost to mount the walls of the city. Theirs were the first caps waved in token of victory, and theirs among the first human voices proudly raised to proclaim what we had gained and the enemy had lost.

That day twenty-eight men of the regiment were killed. Savage fighting continued until 20 September, when Delhi was finally recaptured. Major General Archdale Wilson paid a special tribute: 'The 60th Royal Rifles have shown a glorious example in its splendid gallantry and its perfect discipline to the whole force.' Seven men of the regiment were awarded the Victoria Cross for their bravery during the siege and capture of Delhi: Ensign Alfred Heathcote; Colour Sergeant George Waller; Colour Sergeant Stephen Garvin; Bugler William Sutton; Private John Divane; Private James Thompson; and Private Samuel Turner. Valentine Bambrick would win his Victoria Cross later.

Although Delhi had been captured, there were still thousands of rebels at large over a huge area, and a major operation to deal with them was necessary. However, it was recognised that the 60th and the Goorkhas, who also played a valiant part in the fighting, needed to rest and they were chosen to garrison Delhi, with the honour of being quartered in the city's palace. On 31 January 1858 the 1st Battalion returned to its base at Meerut, but by March it was on active service again, soon becoming part of the Roorkee Field Force, which would operate in a jungle region 'of fever and wild beasts'. Bambrick was one of the soldiers. The objective was the strategic city of Bareilly, some 150 miles north of Lucknow. After several engagements, rebels led by Kahn Bahadur were attacked near Bareilly on 5 May and defeated, many of them retreating to the city. The next day the British force advanced on Bareilly, which was taken after fierce street fighting. It was here that Bambrick won his Victoria Cross. He showed conspicuous gallantry in fighting off three Ghazees in a building, one of whom he cut down. The private was wounded twice. *The London Gazette* of 24 December 1858 announced the award, and the medal was presented to him in India the following year.

With the capture of Bareilly, the Roorkee Field Force was disbanded. Brigadier John Coke, who had been involved in the operations, saluted the 60th:

At Delhi I saw them when their discipline and gallantry under no ordinary trials showed them to be the elite of that army. On 17 April the attack on the enemy in the Hurdwar jungles and their subsequent skirmishing through many miles of heavy forest showed not only what perfect skirmishers they are, but their unwearied energy, which enabled them to work for eight hours through such a country and under such a sun. On 6 May at Bareilly the rush of Captain MacQueen's company on the guns and the advance up the street had a spirit and dash in it that was delightful.

The 60th would see some further fighting but by January 1859 its role in the Indian Mutiny had ended. Bambrick appears to have been a good soldier up until May that year, when his first punishment was recorded. He was jailed, possibly for insubordination. It would set a pattern. He was also jailed in July and November. The following year the 1st Battalion returned to England – without Bambrick, who remained in India, perhaps serving a sentence. He then transferred to the 87th Regiment, which later became the Royal Irish Fusiliers. The 87th did not stay in India for much longer and by 1862 it was stationed at the Curragh in Ireland. Bambrick found himself back in jail in July, and in March 1863 he received a sentence of 160 days for being absent without leave. At Aldershot in November he was discharged – and within hours found himself in trouble again.

He got into a fight with a soldier at an Aldershot brothel, 'a den of infamy', and was afterwards accused of assault and theft, but there are conflicting reports of the incident. Bambrick told a court the following month that he went to the aid of a woman screaming 'Murder' who was being attacked by Lance Corporal Henry Russell of the Commissariat, a corps engaged in supply duties. Russell was no match for the newly discharged soldier who had once beaten off three armed Ghazees. The lance corporal had been wearing four medals and during the struggle these fell off – and disappeared.

Russell's version of events was completely different. He said he had been walking past the 'private house' when he saw Bambrick at the entrance drinking beer and was invited in for 'a pot'. He claimed that when it was his turn to buy a round Bambrick, who was with a woman called Charlotte Johnson, suddenly grabbed him by the throat and tore off his medals. Johnson also took part in the attack. Bambrick said that after restraining Russell he picked up the medals and put them on a mantelpiece and that was the last he saw of them. He was still at the brothel with Johnson when a police officer turned up. Bambrick was disdainful of Russell's version, pointing out to the court that he had won the Victoria Cross – a medal more prized than all those possessed by his accuser – and he would never commit such a paltry robbery.

Russell's version was implausible. He was no doubt suffering from injured pride over his beating, and as a serving soldier he would have been reluctant to explain to his superiors how he had lost his medals in a brothel after attacking a prostitute. But Bambrick's manner may not have endeared him to the court. Despite the fact that Russell was the only prosecution witness, the jury found Bambrick and Johnson guilty. Bambrick was outraged and 'spoke most contemptuously of the court'. He declared: 'I do not care now if I am imprisoned for fifty years. I am the victim of perjury, and I will have my revenge on Russell.'

At Hampshire Winter Assize in Winchester, Bambrick was sentenced to three years' penal servitude. Johnson was jailed for twelve months. Following his conviction Bambrick forfeited the Victoria Cross under a royal warrant dated 3 December 1863. After a spell in Winchester Prison he was transferred to Pentonville in north London, continuing to protest his innocence.

On the evening of 1 April 1864, Valentine Bambrick VC was found hanged in his cell, aged twenty-six. He left a letter written on slate:

My dear, dear Friends and Family – Being quite tired of my truly miserable existence, I am about to rush into the presence of my Maker uncalled and unasked. To you I appeal for forgiveness and pardon for all the unhappiness I have ever caused you. I do not ask for mercy of God, I am doing that which admits of no pardon, but if He will hear my prayer, I pray to Him to grant you consolation in your hour of affliction, for I know that, notwithstanding all my faults, the love which you always manifested towards me is not withheld yet, and therefore the news of my unfortunate fate will make home sorrowful. Pray for your unfortunate son,

Val Bambrick

PS Before I close, I protest solemnly my entire innocence of the charge for which I was punished, all but the assault, and that was done under the circumstances before mentioned to you in my letter. God bless you all. Love to all my relatives. Pity even while you condemn.

Poor Val

The prison governor had given Bambrick special permission on 26 February to send the letter referred to in his last message. The governors of Pentonville and Winchester prisons both believed that he was innocent. Unknown to Bambrick at the time of his death, the Pentonville governor was trying to get the three-year sentence commuted.

A comment piece in *The United Service Gazette* demanded a 'searching inquiry' and accused the Winchester court of 'this melancholy miscarriage of justice'. The magazine asked: 'What we want to know is, whether the deceased had a patient and careful trial, whether the evidence was properly verified and sufficient, and whether, in short, as much patience was taken to arrive at the truth as if it were one of those cases in which a person of higher state is sometimes brought to the bar of justice on a charge of petty theft.'

The article continued: 'If Bambrick had been a sentenced member of gentlemanly position, whole counties would have risen on his behalf, and the Secretary of State would have been bullied into the timid remission of a more just sentence. As it is, he was only a poor private soldier known in his regiment better by his number than his name; and when he was wrongfully convicted of theft he had no friend or protector to seek a remission of his sentence.'

Valentine Bambrick VC was buried in an unmarked grave in St Pancras and Islington Cemetery. And there he lay forgotten until September 2002, when a King's Royal Rifle Corps plaque in his honour was unveiled in the cemetery's chapel. No picture of him is known to exist.

7

For the Love of Money
Evelyn Wood

There is no doubt that Evelyn Wood was exceptionally brave, though his courage sometimes bordered on recklessness. Twice he was recommended for the Victoria Cross during a career that saw him rise from midshipman to field marshal. But Wood had two flaws: he was vain, and he liked money. His quest for riches saw him engineer a divorce scandal that shocked Victorian society and led to the downfall of a prominent politician, Charles Parnell.

Wood was born in the Essex village of Cressing on 9 February 1838, the son of a clergyman, Sir John Wood. He was one of thirteen children but only six survived their early years. Wood's formal education was brief. At the age of nine, after his father decided he could no longer afford a governess, the boy was sent to Marlborough Grammar School, transferring two years later to the local college, which he came to hate. Discipline at the college was poor, with incidents of pupils setting off fireworks in the dormitories at night and burning teachers' desks.

Wood recalled: 'I gave no trouble while at the college, or at least escaped adverse notice, till December 1851, when unjust punishment made me anxious to leave the school for any place, or for any profession.' After he was flogged for being out of bounds he pleaded with his parents to remove him. Wood was so desperate that he suggested working in a merchant's office in London. However, he ended up sitting an exam for the Royal Navy, which was probably at the suggestion of his mother, Emma [Lady Wood]. She was the daughter of an admiral and had a brother in the service, a future admiral, and no doubt thought that her favourite son could do better than take a job in a merchant's office. In May 1852, aged fourteen, Wood joined HMS *Queen*, a 116-gun three-decker, as a cadet.

He quickly caught the captain's eye – for the wrong reason. Wood was spotted with his hands in both pockets. A sail-maker's mate was summoned and ordered: 'Sew this young gentlemen's hands up in his pockets.' But the captain relented as the first stitch went in. Wood was warned that if he did it again his hands would be sown in the pockets for a week. A couple of months later he was in for another surprise. His mother's brother, Captain Frederick Michell, took command of *Queen*. Michell's 'courteous, mild manner hid great determination and force of character', and Wood was worried that his uncle would be too strict with a relative. Messmates advised him to transfer to another ship. Wood made two unsuccessful attempts: 'My uncle asked me why I had volunteered, and I said frankly mainly to get away from him.'

Queen went to the Mediterranean. In April 1854 the Crimean War broke out, and the ship sailed for Odessa. Wood was about to experience his first conflict. And relations with his uncle did not turn out to be as bad as he had feared. Michell presented him with a certificate confirming his abilities, which allowed promotion to midshipman. *Queen* took part in the bombardment of Sebastopol, and by the October Wood found himself a member of the naval brigade, led by the charismatic Captain William Peel. Wood and Midshipman Edward St John Daniel, the future Victoria Cross winner whose naval career would end in disgrace, were later appointed Peel's aides-de-camp.

The brigade – sailors with heavy guns – had been formed to support the army on land, and Wood quickly saw how much the soldiers were suffering, not so much from Russian artillery and infantry but from starvation, lack of clothing and fatigue, factors that were costing some battalions around 70 deaths in every 100 men. Wood noted: 'In the Naval Brigade all casualties were replaced from the fleet, which is one of the reasons why our sick list showed such satisfactory results in comparison with that of the army.'

Wood had a number of narrow escapes. He and Daniel were keen to impress Peel, and they took chances in making sure their battery had enough ammunition and that parapets were repaired after being hit. For two teenagers, there were sobering sights from the battery:

> While Mr Daniels [*sic*] and I were sitting on the powder boxes, a mule being led up with two barrels of powder, one on either side, was struck full in the chest by a shell, which exploding scattered the body of the mule, but the powder remained intact. There was another remarkable escape, as the drivers of a waggon we had just emptied were mounting. The wheel driver was winging his right leg over the horse's back, when its hind quarters were carried away by a round-shot. Later in the afternoon another waggon which had been brought to the same place was exploded by a shell, one of the horses being thrown high into the air, on which the Russians, standing up on their parapets, cheered loudly. We did the same, however, when magazines in the Malakoff and in the Redan [key fortifications protecting Sebastopol] exploded in rapid succession.

It was not just horses, of course, that were killed. On another occasion, taking cover from a Russian shell, Wood found himself standing in the disembowelled stomachs of two sailors. On 18 October he performed an outstanding act of bravery after a shell set ablaze the roof of a magazine. As men took cover, fearing an explosion, Wood climbed up and put out the flames, with Peel's help. Both men were exposed to enemy fire. This act would see Wood's name put forward to the commander-in-chief, Lord Raglan, for the Victoria Cross.

A harsh winter and disease took its toll on British forces. Wood again distinguished himself on 18 June 1855 when an attack was launched on the Redan. Despite illness he insisted on taking part, with one officer betting 5 guineas that the midshipman would be killed. Men of the naval brigade carried 18-foot ladders so that soldiers could storm the fortifications. But it was a mission doomed to failure. At one point Wood was forced to take cover: 'I was lying next to Mr Parsons, a mate, when suddenly he knocked against me violently, and as I thought in rough play. I was asking him to leave off skylarking when I noticed he was insensible. He had been thrown over by a round-shot, which had killed another man and covered me in dust.'

The fire from the Russians was withering, but Peel, waving his sword, cheered on his men, shouting: 'Come on, sailors, don't let the soldiers beat you.' The men charged forward, along with Wood, who was also waving his sword 'invigorated by excitement'. He was soon hit and thought he had lost an arm. Looking again he decided it was only a flesh wound and carried on, 'fearing that anyone passing might think I was skulking'. Peel was also shot but Daniel took the captain to safety. With so many casualties and no realistic chance of storming the Redan, the operation was called off. A drained Wood returned to the nearest British parapet and grabbed a passing soldier's rifle to haul himself up. As the startled soldier turned round, a bullet missed the midshipman's right shoulder and struck the man. Wood stepped over the body 'so exhausted as to be indifferent to his death'.

Wood's wound was more serious than he had believed, and after persuading doctors not to amputate his arm he returned to England in the August to continue his recovery. He had made a name for himself, impressing Lord Raglan and his uncle among others, but he changed his mind about a career in the navy. No doubt influenced by the excitement of fighting on land, Wood applied to join the army, seeking a commission in a cavalry regiment. He was soon made a cornet in the 13th Light Dragoons. The switch cost him the Victoria Cross, as the navy did not press his case. His only award from Britain was the Crimea campaign medal with clasps for Inkerman [Inkermann] and Sebastopol. The French gave him the Legion d'Honneur and Turkey the Order of the Medjidie (5th Class).

Wood was an experienced rider and took to cavalry training in Dorset. Still seventeen, he returned to the war in the Crimea, arriving at Scutari in January 1856. But within a month the new cornet was taken to Florence Nightingale's Scutari hospital suffering from typhoid and pneumonia. With dubious care at the hands of a brutal nurse, his condition deteriorated, and his parents were warned that he was unlikely to survive. They sailed out and his mother, the first to see him, was shocked to find a living skeleton. Despite a warning that Wood would not survive the trip from the hospital to a ship, he was taken back to Britain, though various health problems would affect him for the rest of his life.

When he was well enough he rejoined the 13th Light Dragoons in Ireland as a lieutenant after a generous uncle bought him the commission. In June 1857, with the Crimean War over, he learned of the Indian Mutiny and, eager for more action, managed to negotiate a transfer to the 17th Lancers, one of the regiments being sent out as reinforcements. On the voyage to Bombay he decided it would be useful to learn Hindustani with the idea of acting as an interpreter. After arriving with no prospect of immediate action, he hired teachers to give him lessons for a gruelling twelve hours a day. The mutiny effectively ended in June 1858, but operations to deal with pockets of rebels continued for some time. Wood's request to join a squadron on active service was granted in the May, and he spent many months on patrols riding a horse called The Pig and travelling thousands of miles across difficult terrain and in a harsh climate. There were several engagements.

'We had nearly arrived at the limit of human endurance,' he wrote. 'Many officers had straps sewn on to the front of the saddle, by fixing their wrists in which they were able to sleep when on the march. I counted three lancers on the ground at one time, who had tumbled off while asleep. The horses became so leg weary that they would lie down before they were picketed on the lines, and many refused to eat.'

Wood's resilience impressed his superiors and he was appointed brigade-major of a native cavalry unit called Beatson's Horse. He took over when the commanding officer had to return to England soon afterwards. Renamed the 2nd Regiment Central India Horse, the unit did not impress Wood. The men were poorly trained and did not take care of their horses. But within a month he had transformed the regiment – and would go on to win the Victoria Cross.

In late December 1859 Wood learned that rebels had kidnapped an important landowner loyal to Britain near a place identified as Sindhara. The landowner, one Chemmun Singh, was taken to a jungle hideout and, according to local intelligence, faced execution. A villager who was a former rebel nervously agreed to lead Wood to the hideout after being offered £5 and a pardon. Believing that the group numbered around twenty-five, Wood set off on the night raid with fifteen men, soldiers and police, counting on a surprise attack. The operation soon had elements of farce. The guide was so jittery that he kept taking doses of bhang – opium – and at one point Wood was 'holding his hand to prevent his taking bhang, as I feared he would fall insensible'. The men had been told to be as quiet as possible as they approached the camp but they kept 'breaking sticks and branches'. Wood crawled to within 10 yards of the sleeping rebels and was shocked to discover that they numbered around sixty – it later emerged that the figure was more than eighty.

'The thought came into my mind to retreat,' he wrote. 'I reflected that failure might discredit the action of [General] Sir John Michel, who had been so kind in giving me the command, and I pictured in my mind newspaper articles on "The folly of appointing young English officers to command natives, who overtax their powers". Fortunately my men could not see my face and after a moment's hesitation I thought of Chemmun Singh's impending fate, and moreover realised that my only safety lay in attacking.'

The cocking of guns alerted a sentry and when challenged Wood answered: 'We are the government.' Turning to his men, he shouted: 'Fire! Charge!' Wood ran at the sentry but fell over two sleeping rebels and ended up in a hollow. Two of his soldiers also fell over. Wood was then involved in a comical sword fight with the sentry, their weapons getting caught in branches: 'We cut at each other three times in succession, the boughs intercepting our swords, and as he drew back the fourth time, I going close to him with the point of my sword behind my right foot, cut upwards, wounding him in the fleshy part of the thigh. He staggered to my left, which brought him before Burmadeen Singh [a sergeant] who twice cut in vain at him, his sword catching in the trees, when I shouted, "Point, give the point." Burmadeen Singh now disappeared, and I ran after him, tumbling into a drain, on top of my sergeant and the rebel, whom he was killing, using vituperation ...'

Fortunately for Wood most of the rebels had fled without their weapons, probably believing they faced a much larger force. The police officers had 'compensated for their want of activity in charging by the noise they made, which was perhaps more effective, shouting, "Bring up the horse artillery, bring up the cavalry."'

Wood had to deal with a soldier who 'behaved well, until having wounded a rebel, he saw blood flow, when he became idiotic at the sight, falling on the guide, whom he mistook for one of the enemy. Eventually, to save the guide, I had to knock the soldier down with my fist by a blow under the jaw.'

Chemmun Singh was found tied to a tree and rescued. The group returned to Sindhara, with the unfortunate soldier half unconscious and the guide 'speechless and dreamy from opium'. Chemmun Singh's wife was so grateful that she kissed Wood's boots. And the authorities were certainly pleased with the rescue. The Agent Governor General for Central India, Colonel Sir Richmond Shakespear, described it as a 'brilliant attack'. The Viceroy of India, Lord Canning, also thought Wood, who had saved the British from a lot of embarrassment, should be rewarded. The farcical side of the operation had apparently not been stressed in initial reports.

Wood's citation for the Victoria Cross also mentioned another act of gallantry. At Sindwaho on 19 October 1858, he had routed a group of rebels 'almost single-handed'. He had no doubt earned the Victoria Cross in the Crimea, so the award saw justice in the end.

Wood continued to improve the effectiveness of his regiment, although the training and discipline did not go down well with many of the men. During his command he dismissed all but 100 of the original 535, and at one point feared there would be a mutiny. In October 1860 a medical board in Calcutta decided that his campaigning in challenging conditions had taken too much of a toll on his health. He was invalided back to England. After a good rest and consultations about his increasing deafness – a legacy of the gun actions in the Crimea – Wood decided that a spell at the staff college, Camberley, would help his career. He discovered that there was already a likely candidate from the 17th Lancers and so transferred to an infantry regiment, the 73rd Regiment (Perthshire), buying a captaincy with money saved in India. And he finally received his Victoria Cross. It had been sent out to India and then returned. There was no special presentation. It must have been disappointing to receive the medal in a registered packet.

He was cheered, however, to win a place at the staff college and to be promoted brevet major, thanks to his endeavours in India. He finished staff college at the end of 1864 but continued to suffer health problems and left the 73rd, which was due to go to Hong Kong, because he disliked the new commanding officer. Wood ended up in the 17th Regiment (Leicestershire) based at Aldershot, spending much of his free time riding and hunting.

For several years he had been conducting a long-distance romance with one Paulina Southwell, who came from an Irish Catholic family. Her parents had died and her brother, Viscount Southwell, looked after her interests. Wood's early marriage proposal failed because the viscount insisted on his conversion to Catholicism. Wood made another approach in August 1867 with the less than romantic condition that his future wife should never object if he faced further war service. He also pointed out that he did not have much money. The viscount had softened his attitude and Paulina, declaring her love, accepted. The couple married shortly afterwards in a Catholic church, although Wood still did not convert to Catholicism. His mother's sister Maria was a wealthy widow who usually gave £5,000 each to her nephews and nieces when they married, but Wood was the exception. Always known to the nephews and nieces as Aunt Ben – short for Benjamin, her late husband's name – she objected to his marriage to an Irish Catholic. It was a bitter blow. Wood had been counting on the money. After marriage, increasingly, he lived beyond his means. And he would later be at the centre of a shameful struggle to get at Aunt Ben's fortune.

The thought of an alternative, more lucrative career occurred to him and he studied to become a barrister, showing once again his determination by rising at 4 a.m. to digest legal books for several hours before going on duty. His first son, also called Evelyn, was born in November 1869, adding to the financial pressures. He passed his final exams in 1874 but by that time his army career had flourished again and he decided not to turn to the law to make a living. However, his legal training would play a part in his battle with Aunt Ben.

In 1873 he was promoted lieutenant colonel and took part in the Ashantee campaign in West Africa, led by Major General Sir Garnet Wolseley. Wood raised a native regiment and distinguished himself on several occasions. In one action he was shot in the chest and a doctor gloomily decided that his patient would not survive.

Within days Wood was back leading his men. The campaign was judged a great success and he returned to England the following year, gaining promotion to full colonel and being made a Companion of the Order of the Bath. After a brief time with the 90th Regiment he went to Aldershot in a new role, focusing on officer training throughout the nation.

Conflicts in South Africa saw Wood returning to the continent in early 1878 as colonel of the 90th, initially helping to deal with the Galekas and Gaikas tribes in Cape Colony. As usual, he pushed his men to their limit, with long marches in testing conditions. One artillery commander, Lieutenant Colonel Arthur Harness, observed: 'Wood is the most ambitious man I ever met. He certainly is most energetic ... but he is a hard master to serve – everything must go straight, and success is everything.' Another officer, Lieutenant Henry Curling, complained that 'he wears himself out and everybody under him'.

Wood would later admit that he suffered. Of an attempt to confront 1,000 Gaikas on Gwili-Gwili Mountain, he wrote:

Fourteen days of very hard work combined with little sleep had brought a return of my neuralgic pains which, although not severe, obliged me to take doses of chloral and bismuth, and foreseeing that I might be on the mountain for three days, I took the precaution of getting a large bottle from a doctor in King William's Town, who enjoined me on no account to finish it until the third day. When we started my pain was worse, and it increased as I climbed, with the result that when we reached the top of the mountain and I sat down on a stone to rest, I had finished the bottle, and was tormented with acute thirst.

Unfortunately for Wood and his men, the Gaikas were not keen on open battle and disappeared down another side of the mountain.

The Zulus would later prove a much tougher enemy. That war saw the tragedy of Isandlwana and the heroics of Rorke's Drift – and the shredding of reputations, especially that of the British commander, Lieutenant General Lord Chelmsford. Wood was involved in a disastrous attack on a Zulu stronghold, Hlobane Mountain, on 28 March 1879. Encouraged by Lieutenant Colonel

Redvers Buller, he ordered a largely mounted force to head up narrow tracks to assault well-defended positions. Zulu marksmen found easy targets and two of his best men were soon among the dead. Wood was thrown to the ground when his horse was shot and killed. The Border Horse, which became isolated, was virtually wiped out. Wood and Buller, who won the Victoria Cross during the action, escaped, but they lost nearly 200 men. However, they redeemed themselves the following day when the main Zulu army attacked their base at Kambula and suffered a decisive defeat. Luckily for Wood, Kambula completely overshadowed Hlobane. On 4 July, commanding a 'flying column' in the rank of brigadier, he also took part in the Battle of Ulundi, which effectively ended the war.

Returning home with his reputation enhanced, Wood was knighted. After posts in Belfast and Chatham he went back to South Africa in early February 1881 after British reverses in the First Anglo-Boer War. There would soon be another reverse. Major General Sir George Colley, commander of the forces in Natal, was killed when Boers routed his men at Majuba. Wood, who was critical of Colley's tactics, took command, becoming acting governor of Natal and administrator of the Transvaal. He agreed a truce and ended up signing a controversial peace agreement, which even Queen Victoria criticised as 'very humiliating'. In fairness, Wood was largely carrying out the wishes of the British government.

A new campaign – Egypt – emerged in 1882. Britain wanted to protect its interests, especially the Suez Canal, after an army coup. General Wolseley, who led the Ashantee campaign, was given command of the expedition, which Wood, now a major general, was keen to join. Although Wood was a member of the Wolseley Ring of favoured officers, his mentor had grown to dislike him, noting his vanity. For example, Wood had insisted on having black borders around his many ribbons so that they stood out. And Wolseley had not been impressed with the Boer peace deal. Wood's lobbying eventually won the day, but he arrived in Alexandria to find that he would not be involved with the main force. The campaign ended in success with the battle of Tel el Kebir on 13 September. Soon afterwards Wood was given the job of forming a new Egyptian army. His last campaign was the attempt to relieve Khartoum in 1884–85. The rest of his career was spent in England, where he pushed for army reform with some success. After a spell at Colchester, reshaping the Eastern District, he secured one of the top posts, commander at Aldershot, the army's main training centre. He was now a lieutenant general.

Although he put his usual energy into the new post, he was also involved in another battle – to get at elderly Aunt Ben's fortune. She, of course, had snubbed him when it came to a generous wedding gift. Wood was determined not to miss out again.

Aunt Ben was extremely fond of Wood's youngest sister, Katharine, who had married another soldier, Captain William O'Shea, whom Wood had introduced to the family. Apart from army life, Wood and O'Shea had two things in common – a love of riding and poor finances. Over the years Aunt Ben and Katharine had developed a close relationship. The aunt bought her niece a house near her own grand home in Eltham, south London, and Katharine was a frequent companion. In her will she had originally left equal shares to her nephews and nieces, but twice she changed it to give larger sums to Katharine. This did not go down well with the other Wood children – Evelyn, his brother Charles and sisters Maria and Anna – and by the end of 1887 they were concerned about their inheritance. Aunt Ben had around £150,000, a considerable sum in those days, plus property.

Katharine was twenty-one when in 1867 she married twenty-seven-year-old O'Shea at St Nicholas, the parish church of Brighton, Sussex, which would become one of her favourite towns. To her aunt she appeared to be happily married, but from about 1880 she had been having an affair with Charles Parnell, the influential Irish nationalist politician who was pushing for home rule. Parnell was another concern for Wood. Did he have his eyes on Katharine's inheritance? O'Shea, of course, knew of Aunt Ben's fortune. For many years he was also aware of his wife's adultery, and no doubt refrained from divorce proceedings because of the money. And Dublin-born O'Shea, who had been a nationalist Member of Parliament after his army career and several business ventures, was no stranger to Parnell and even sought political favours from him.

Wood, Charles, Maria and Anna tried to persuade their aunt to change her will to its original form by casting doubts on Katharine's character. It is unlikely that they told her of the affair, but whatever they suggested had the opposite effect. The independent Aunt Ben did change her will, leaving everything to her favourite niece, apart from small bequests. With his training as a barrister, Wood decided there were two courses of action. They could wait until their aunt's death and then contest the will on the grounds that Katharine had unduly influenced her, or they could take immediate action and try to have her declared insane, with the aim of invalidating the will. At that time there were Lunacy Acts and relatives could petition the bluntly named Masters of Lunacy, who had the power to administer an insane person's estate until death.

It was clear that Aunt Ben would be shown no mercy. Wood and Charles decided on the second course and presented a petition to the Masters of Lunacy. The move shocked Katharine, who decided to fight on her aunt's behalf. She filed objections to the petition, which meant a court battle. Through her relationship with Parnell, Katharine had come to know the Liberal leader William Gladstone, who would serve four times as Prime Minister. She appealed to Gladstone for help and he arranged for her to see his personal physician, Sir Andrew Clark, who agreed to visit Aunt Ben. Clark produced a report saying that he found Aunt Ben 'attentive, capable of apprehension and reflection, to reply coherent and logical, free from illusions, delusions and hallucinations, full of old stories, able to quote largely from the French poets and sometimes seasoning her reminiscences with flashes of quaint humour'.

Her only defects were poor eyesight, occasional forgetfulness and a slight tendency to repetition. She was definitely not mad. But Wood and his brother refused to withdraw their petition, even briefing the attorney general. Katharine hired a famous barrister, Sir Charles Russell. She turned again to Gladstone, asking him to stress to Russell the importance of the case, and he agreed. The petition was dismissed in the summer of 1888.

On 19 May 1889 Aunt Ben died, much to the distress of her niece, who was at her bedside. 'She left a great void in my life,' Katharine recalled. 'Through all the years in which I waited on my aunt I never heard her use a clipped word, or use a sentence not grammatically perfect and beautifully rounded off and although I sometimes felt impatient when chided for some swallowed pronunciation or ignored g's, I look back upon the years of my life spent in that old-world atmosphere as a very precious memory.'

With Katharine set to inherit the fortune, Wood and his brother and sisters went on the attack again, applying to the probate court to contest the will. It is more than likely that a decision was taken to blacken Katharine's name to strengthen their case. This married woman, a mother, had been carrying on an affair for years and was obviously a bad influence on her ageing aunt. In O'Shea they found an ally. He decided that the last change in the will contravened his marriage settlement, and on Christmas Eve he filed for divorce on the grounds of adultery. There is a suggestion that Katharine was willing to pay a large sum to her husband to drop the case, but because of the probate setback this was not possible. It also appears that she and Parnell, surprisingly, were confident that O'Shea would not win. They were both denying adultery despite the fact that Parnell had fathered three of Katharine's five children, one of whom died.

After various delays the case, *O'Shea* v. *O'Shea and Parnell*, began before a jury at the High Court on 15 November 1890. Parnell declined to be represented. Katharine submitted a statement making counter-claims, but she weakened her case from the outset. Far from denying outright that there had been an adulterous relationship she claimed that her husband had 'constantly connived at and was accessory to the said alleged adultery from the autumn of 1880 to the spring of 1886'. O'Shea had 'induced, directed and required' her to form the relationship with Parnell so that he could seek favours from the nationalist leader. He had also put pressure on her to get large sums from Aunt Ben.

O'Shea was accused of neglect and misconduct and being absent from the marital home for long spells. According to Katharine, he was a serial adulterer, having sex with various women, including prostitutes, in Britain, France and Spain. In 1875 he had seduced a parlour maid working at the family home in Mortlake, south London. O'Shea denied all the charges. Katharine did not give evidence or produce any witnesses. In reality, she was not defending the case.

O'Shea had witnesses who confirmed that Parnell visited Katharine on many occasions over the years. He was sometimes known as 'Mr Smith' or 'Mr Stewart'. Caroline Pethers, who worked as a cook at a Brighton home rented by Katharine, told the court that the couple 'were nearly always in a room together'. She related a comical episode in which Katharine and Parnell were in the upstairs drawing room when O'Shea rang the front doorbell. Ten minutes later the doorbell rang again – it was Parnell asking to see O'Shea. Parnell had apparently disappeared using a fire escape.

The jury quickly returned its verdict. Katharine was guilty of adultery, but her husband had not connived at it. O'Shea had won. The judge pronounced a decree nisi, which allowed newspapers around the world to report the case. It was a major scandal, and Parnell and his home rule cause were the big losers. There was also ridicule, with music hall comedians finding rich material. Toy models of the Brighton fire escape, complete with a Parnell figure, went on sale. One of the visitors to the court during the two-day hearing was Lieutenant General Sir Evelyn Wood VC. He must have sensed victory in the battle over Aunt Ben's will.

Katharine and Parnell married at Steyning register office in Sussex on 25 June 1891 and settled in Brighton at Walsingham Terrace. But Parnell's health deteriorated sharply as he fought for political survival. Confined to bed at their home, he died of a heart attack on 6 October, aged forty-five. According to Katharine, his last words were, 'Kiss me, sweet Wifie, and I will try to sleep.'

In 1892 Katharine, with growing financial problems, was forced to settle the dispute over Aunt Ben's will out of court. Wood, his brother and sisters received 50 per cent of the estate. For many years the public remained in the dark about the bitter family feud. Wood did not mention it in his two volumes of memoirs, nor did Katharine in a book she wrote about Parnell, *The Uncrowned King of Ireland*, which touched only briefly on her divorce. Curiously, the book appeared under the name Katharine O'Shea, despite the fact that she was Parnell's widow.

Wood continued to enhance his reputation, rising to full general and then field marshal. He died on 2 December 1919, aged eighty-one, and was buried with full military honours at Aldershot, a hero to the end.

8

The Deserter
Thomas Lane

Private Thomas Lane narrowly escaped death when a 12lb shell was dropped on his head from the ramparts of a Chinese fort. Lane's wicker pith helmet cushioned the blow as he collapsed to the ground. Although stunned, he was soon on his feet only to feel the steel of a bayonet. He carried on, battering at the breached stone-and-mud wall with a length of wood until it was breached enough for soldiers to enter.

Lane was among the storming party that attacked one of the Taku forts in north-east China on 21 August 1860. The attack had started at dawn with a British and French artillery bombardment, supported by gunboats. Then Lane's 67th (South Hampshire) Foot, along with the 44th (East Essex) Foot, crossed 2 miles of swampy ground before reaching an area covered with iron and wooden stakes. Musket fire from the fort was continuous, with men 'falling to be impaled upon the stakes like butterflies'.

The fort, with its high walls, was surrounded by a moat, which soldiers started swimming across. The defenders, whose main guns had been knocked out, hurled down blocks of stone dislodged by the bombardment. The 12lb shell struck Lane as he joined Lieutenant Nathaniel Burslem of the 67th, who had been shot in the chest, in battering the weakened wall. Soon men were swarming through the breach. Others used scaling ladders. Ensign John Chaplin rallied the 67th with the regiment's colour. He was shot in the forearm and shoulder but went on, with Lane in support. Despite being wounded again, badly, in the stomach, the ensign reached

73

a high point and replaced the enemy flag with the colour. The fort surrendered after hand-to-hand fighting. Some 1,800 Chinese had been killed, including two generals, one of whom refused to surrender and was shot dead by a Royal Marines captain, who took his hat adorned with a peacock feather as a souvenir. British and French losses totalled about 300 killed and wounded.

The fort had been chosen for attack because it was the most strategically placed of five forts on both banks of the Peiho River [Hai River]. The others capitulated without a fight after being given a two-hour ultimatum.

Lane, Burslem and Chaplin were all awarded the Victoria Cross. Andrew Fitzgibbon, a fifteen-year-old hospital apprentice with the Bengal Subordinate Medical Service, who was attached to the 67th, also received the medal for going to the aid of two wounded men under fire. He was himself severely wounded. As well as his other injuries, Lane may have received a gunshot wound to the face. He would no doubt be long grateful for his wicker pith helmet. The Chinese had ridiculed the headgear, dismissing their enemy as The Hats.

The Taku victory was a defining moment of the Second China War, also known as the Second Opium War. Hostilities had broken out in 1856 after China's rulers refused to agree to British demands for greater trading rights, legalisation of the sale of opium and diplomatic representation in Peking.

The Taku forts were well known to British forces. Gunboats had captured them in May 1858. A treaty appeared to signal peace, and the Chinese reoccupied the forts. However, relations soon broke down. The forts were attacked again, in June 1859, but the operation was an embarrassing failure. The successful attack in August 1860 opened the way to Peking. Tientsin, some 40 miles up the Peiho River, surrendered, and there were decisive actions at Chang-kia-wan and Pa-li-chiao. Peking was occupied in October, and Emperor Xianfeng's old summer palace was looted and burned down in revenge for the torture and execution of European prisoners. Private Lane may have taken part in the palace's destruction or witnessed it. That month the conflict ended, with the Chinese agreeing to new treaty terms.

The 67th would remain in China until July 1865. After the war the climate proved the biggest challenge. Winters were harsh. One soldier wrote home: 'We have been given greatcoats lined with the fur of some shaggy beast, and there we sit huddled at nights, sleep being difficult, with braziers of coke to make us cough and beer that we have to chop up with axes as if it were floes of ice before we can melt it.' Summer saw dysentery, cholera and diphtheria, and the soldier preferred 'a foe you can stick a bayonet in'. Each year the regiment lost men to sickness and death. Lane had several spells in hospital – and the cells, a familiar punishment. In Shanghai on 28 February 1863, Brigadier Charles Staveley, who had taken part in the capture of the Taku forts, presented him with the Victoria Cross.

Lane, 'a wild Irishman', enjoyed fighting and like a number of other winners of the Victoria Cross he had a poor disciplinary record in peacetime. He was born in Cork in May 1836. Little is known of his early life, though his family most probably struggled to survive, and he was illiterate. On 21 February 1853, aged sixteen, he enlisted in the 47th (Lancashire) Foot, which was recruiting in Cork. The bounty of £3 10s must have been an attraction. He was sent to a depot at Limerick for training, but over the next six months he spent twenty-eight days in hospital and went absent without leave for two days. In February 1854 he was jailed for two months at Nenagh, County Tipperary, for an offence that is no longer known.

But Lane was soon heading off to war. He arrived in the Crimean peninsula on 14 September and six days later the 47th fought at the Battle of Alma, when British and French troops routed the Russians from an entrenched position. Lane also took part in the Battle of Inkerman on 5 November. Private John McDermond was awarded the Victoria Cross for saving the life of the regiment's wounded commanding officer, Lieutenant Colonel William Haly. The 47th suffered nineteen dead and forty-seven wounded.

The harsh winter was spent besieging Sebastopol in terrible conditions, as *The Times* reported: 'The condition of our army was indeed miserable, pitiable, heartrending. No boots, no greatcoats – officers in tatters and rabbit skins, men in bread bags and rags; no medicine, no shelter; toiling in mud and snow week after week, exposed in open trenches or in torn tents to the pitiless storms of a Crimean winter.'

In 1855 Lane ended up in the cells on two occasions for being absent without leave. He also spent fifteen days in Florence

Nightingale's hospital at Scutari. Eight officers and 300 men of the 47th were part of the force that captured the Russian position known as the Quarries on 7 June 1856 and held it against repeated counterattacks. The Russians evacuated Sebastopol three months later, but the 47th remained in Crimea until May 1857.

In the October Lane was in Britain with his regiment, based in Portsmouth, but there had been several further brushes with authority – and then he deserted. He was caught the following month, and a court martial sentenced him to eighty-four days' hard labour. After his release he was given cooking duties but again went absent without leave. The officers of the 47th were no doubt exasperated with Lane's conduct and in September 1858 he was transferred to the 67th Foot, though it is unclear if the South Hampshires were made fully aware of his record. Days later the 67th sailed for India, where it had spent twenty-one years in the early part of the century, arriving in Calcutta on 14 December. There were thirty-one officers and 764 other ranks. The Indian Mutiny had effectively ended, with only small-scale actions continuing. In September 1859 the regiment was on the move again, destination northern China. For Lane, the Taku forts and Peking lay ahead, as well as the Victoria Cross.

After its five challenging years in China the 67th was posted to South Africa, where the fine climate was a welcome contrast. Once again Lane found himself in the cells, and he was even imprisoned on board ship when the regiment sailed for home twelve months later. In Belfast on 25 June 1866, the difficult soldier was discharged, receiving a ration allowance of 5s and the train fare to Cork. Lane's whereabouts over the next few years are something of a mystery. At some stage he went to New Zealand and fell on hard times, pawning his Victoria Cross and campaign medals, according to the *Otago Witness* of 27 March 1875. The newspaper stated that 'a gentleman' had seen the Victoria Cross in the window of a Dunedin pawnshop and bought it 'for a few shillings'.

Lane would have been thirty-eight at the time, and the report went on:

He came to the colony about six months ago. He applied to Major Atkinson for a situation in the militia office, but there was no vacancy; in fact, if there was, it was questionable whether he could have been taken on, as he was an unlettered man, being unable to read and write. Application was also made by him at the gaol and police, and in either force he would have been gladly taken on, had he been able to read and write. Being, like most pensioners, useless for almost every employment, he had difficulty in getting work. A gentleman, however, gave him temporary work; but it seems he afterwards got 'hard up', and rather than ask anyone for money he pawned his medals.

He bears the reputation of being a man of the strictest honesty, and of the best character. While, from one source we learn that he was a little given to drink when he got his [Victoria Cross] pension remittances, we find from the same quarter that he made it his first duty on such occasions to pay the tradesmen whatever little he owed them, and then to visit the publican. From enquiries, we have reason to believe that he pawned his medals for actual necessities, and not to satisfy a craving for stimulants, and therefore we think there is the more reason why his medals should be reclaimed and sent to him.

The report added that Lane was married and had recently gone to Boston, Massachusetts, 'where he has friends that are doing well, and where he is likely to have better prospects than here'. He travelled there by working his passage as a ship's cook. It is not known how he fared in the United States, but by 1879 he was in South Africa again – and back in uniform. Border disputes with the Zulus had led to war, and Lane joined the 3rd Natal Native Contingent, which recruited European officers and NCOs. The British commander, Lord Chelmsford, did not think much of the fighting ability of the native troops and was reluctant to use them in battle, though some lost their lives in the massacre at Isandlwana. Lane's unit went to Rorke's Drift after 150 British and colonial troops famously defended the mission station against thousands of Zulus. When the unit was disbanded during hostilities, Lane transferred to the Natal Horse in the rank of sergeant. The war ended in December 1879.

Lane next surfaced in 1881 as a sergeant in Landrey's Light Horse, which had been raised to help deal with small-scale tribal opposition in Transkei and Basutoland. A farmer, John Landrey, led the unit, and poor discipline soon became a problem – probably not helped by Sergeant Lane himself. Fighting among the soldiers, drunkenness, venereal disease and desertion all combined to undermine morale. And there was no guarantee that the men would be paid on time. On 7 April 1881 Lane disappeared from the unit near the town of Ladybrand in the Orange Free State, taking his horse, carbine and other equipment, valued at around £59. He was owed £13 6s in back pay.

There had been twenty-eight desertions between February and May, but Landrey appears to have taken particular exception to the disappearance of the Victoria Cross winner. He complained to the Colonial Secretary, urging that Lane, 'much addicted to drink', should be stripped of his pension. The *Natal Government Gazette* of 14 June listed the sergeant as a deserter. That month he appeared at Kimberley Criminal Court charged with desertion and theft. He was subsequently sentenced to four months' hard labour. The following year Lane found himself in trouble again. He tore down the flag of Transvaal, a symbol of Boer independence, from its pole outside public offices in Pretoria while 'under the influence of liquor'. He was apparently serving with the King William's Town police. The punishment was six months' jail.

By this time the War Office in London had learned of his conviction for desertion and theft. The commander of the British forces in South Africa was asked for details, and he sent an extract from Kimberley's criminal record book. In December 1882 it was decided to prepare a royal warrant to remove Lane's name from the Victoria Cross Registry and to stop his pension from the date of desertion, 7 April 1881. Queen Victoria approved the warrant.

Lane's jailing in Pretoria attracted the attention of a Transvaal artillery commander, Henning Pretorius, who was recruiting for the Mapoch campaign, which would involve Boers seizing tribal land. Pretorius thought the veteran soldier 'could be useful'. The magistrate who had dealt with Lane reflected that the sentence was 'slightly harsh' and agreed to an early release. Lane served in the campaign for about nine months. Once again he courted controversy when, for 'mere devilry', he put the decapitated head of an African on a pole outside the tent of the Boer leader General Petrus Joubert. Lane was sentenced to two years' hard labour, but the punishment was dropped two hours later after protests from other soldiers, who then 'carried him shoulder high round the laager. Their appreciation of his courage was great, and to this day it is a fruitful source of inspiration to the older men to relate stories to youngsters of their first commando of the deeds of derring-do performed by the gallant Irishman.'

Lane presumably left the artillery unit after this escapade. In September 1884 he was back in Pretoria prison – but this time as a warder. His pregnant wife Elizabeth was appointed the jail's matron. Weeks later Lane fell out with the chief warder, accusing him of improper behaviour with Elizabeth. He had seen his wife coming from the chief warder's quarters, where she had been drinking gin. Lane must have made his protest too forcefully – entirely in character – because he was locked in a cell and sacked the next day. He complained to a magistrate without success. The Lanes left Pretoria and went to Kimberley, where a daughter, Anne, was born. In August 1885 Thomas Lane was once again in uniform after joining the local police force. When in uniform he always wore his medal ribbons, including that of the Victoria Cross, despite being stripped of the honour.

On 13 April 1889 he died in a Kimberley hospital, aged fifty-two. The cause of death was given as inflammation of the lungs. He was buried the next day with military honours at the local Gladstone cemetery. A procession included the Victoria Rifles, the Diamond Fields Horse and several police units. Even the municipal fire brigade turned up and several hundred civilians followed the cortege. After so many turbulent years Thomas Lane had won the respect of many.

A report in *The African Review* was headed 'A Wild Irishman', and commented: 'Old Kimberley men were most of them well acquainted with old Tom Lane, a veteran VC man who loved fighting for its own sake … News has come to hand that he is dead and has at last got the peace which he tried to avoid all his life.' The article recounted one of Lane's actions during the Mapoch campaign, when Boers surrounded natives in a cave:

The Kaffirs were good shots, as six Boers one fine day found to their cost. Of the attacking party only three were left alive, one being Tom Lane. They had been firing at the enemy at a distance of five yards, and the Kaffirs kept up a brisk reply, sending shot for shot at the three white men. After some hours Tom Lane saw the head of a Kaffir through a crevice in the rock, and resorted to stratagem. Holding out a bottle of 'Cape smoke' [brandy] to the native, he invited him to *puza* [to drink, Xhosa language]. The native grasped the opportunity and put his hand out, when Tom shot him dead on the spot.

It was this native that Lane decapitated, taking the head back to camp to display outside General Joubert's tent.

Lane struggled financially for most of his life, but it appears that he acquired some wealth during his time in Kimberley. He owned two properties, though it is not clear, as a low-ranking police officer, how he obtained them. His will made no mention of his Victoria Cross or his campaign medals. When Lane's name was removed from the Victoria Cross Registry, the War Office asked for the return of the medal. The request led to a great deal of correspondence with authorities in South Africa, with Lane either unwilling to give up the decoration or no longer having it in his possession. It will be recalled that in New Zealand the *Otago Witness* of 27 March 1875 reported that 'a gentleman' had bought Lane's Victoria Cross from a pawnshop in Dunedin for a few shillings. The newspaper suggested that the medal should be returned to Lane, so perhaps he did have it when he went to South Africa.

The War Office hunt even led to sixteen magistrates and other officials being asked if they had Lane in their prison and, if so, to try to find his medal. Eventually the British commander in South Africa, no doubt exasperated and wishing to end the matter, sent a Victoria Cross to London. It was almost certainly not Lane's but probably a medal that had been sent out earlier for possible award.

There is an unsubstantiated story that the Lane Victoria Cross was bought for a few pounds from a pawnshop in Pietermaritzburg in 1909. The museum of the Royal Hampshire Regiment in Winchester has not one but two Victoria Crosses named to Thomas Lane, and both are regarded as genuine. One of the medals had appeared at auction or on dealers' lists several times between 1953 and 1985. There is no record of a second decoration being issued to Lane, so the mystery may never be solved.

9

Suicide at Dunedin
Duncan Boyes

At the age of seventeen, Duncan Boyes became a Victoria Cross hero. Four years later he was in such despair at being stripped of the honour that he killed himself.

Boyes was born in Cheltenham, Gloucestershire, on 5 November 1846, the son of John and Sabina Boyes, who seem to have been well off. He went on to be educated at Cheltenham College and another school before joining the Royal Navy as a cadet, aged fourteen. There was no apparent family connection with the service, but tales of adventure told by a next-door neighbour in Cheltenham, retired naval captain Robert Madehaw, could have influenced the teenager in his choice of career.

Midshipman Boyes's first ship was HMS *Euryalus*, a thirty-five-gun frigate, which he joined on the East Indies Station in 1862. *Euryalus* had served in the Baltic campaign and in the Mediterranean, and on 14 September that year she arrived at Yokohama, Japan. As Vice Admiral Augustus Kuper's flagship, the frigate took part in the bombardment of Kagoshima, on the southern island of Kyushu, in August 1863 after coastal forts attacked Royal Navy vessels. *Euryalus* had ten crew killed, including the captain, John Josling, and his second-in-command, Edward Wilmot, who were both decapitated by the same cannonball. The ship withdrew as her band played 'Oh Dear, What Can The Matter Be'. Hundreds of homes in Kagoshima were destroyed, but casualties were low because the town had been largely abandoned.

The action stemmed from an attack on four British subjects at the village of Namamugi the previous year. Samurai of Satsuma province thought the party, out riding, had not shown respect to their leader by dismounting, and one merchant, Charles Richardson, was hacked to death. Two others were badly wounded. The British charge d'affaires, Lieutenant Colonel Edward Neale, demanded an apology and compensation, which Satsuma province initially rejected. Kuper's squadron was sent to reinforce the demands. Neale was on board *Euryalus* during the bombardment of Kagoshima.

Like China at that time, the Japanese were reluctant to engage in trade and diplomacy with western countries. Although Japan had an emperor, the country was fragmented politically, with some 300 clan chiefs, called daimyo, exercising power mostly in their own interests. Japan's isolation had been breached in July 1853 when an American naval officer, Matthew Perry, appeared in Edo Bay with four ships intent on opening relations between the two countries. This led to a treaty the following year, paving the way for Britain and Holland, as well as Russia. However, Japanese resentment grew.

A year after the Kagoshima bombardment there was another punitive expedition, with Britain being backed by France, Holland and the United States. The Choshu clan had fired on foreign ships in the Straits of Shimonoseki between Kyushu and the island of Honshu, and on his own initiative diplomat Sir Rutherford Alcock decided that retaliation was necessary.

Once again Vice Admiral Kuper in *Euryalus* was given the mission, and he led a squadron of British, French, Dutch and American ships, which bombarded Shimonoseki shore batteries on 5 September 1864. The next morning marines and sailors, seventeen-year-old Midshipman Boyes among them, landed to destroy the enemy guns and blow up ammunition. This task was accomplished relatively easily by late afternoon. But a large force of Japanese that had gathered in thick bush launched a surprise counterattack. The naval brigade, led by Kuper's flag captain, John Alexander, forced the attackers back along a valley where a large fort was discovered. The fort needed to be silenced because it could train its guns on the sloop HMS *Perseus*, which had run aground during the previous day's bombardment. With Boyes carrying the Queen's Colour of the leading company, the sailors continued to advance along one side of the valley, with the marines on the other flank.

Commander John Moresby recorded: 'They were met by hot fire from the parapet of a ditch in front of the battery and from the top of an 8-foot wall protecting the palisade. Seven seamen were killed and another twenty-six were wounded. Captain Alexander was hit by a musket ball in the ankle.' Moresby added: 'Our men never checked, and rushing on swarmed over the wall and won the stockade, the enemy disappearing into the bush.'

Despite the withering fire, Boyes had pressed ahead with the colour. Two colour sergeants were with him. One was killed, the other badly wounded. Only Captain Alexander's direct order stopped Boyes from going further. Afterwards it was found that six musket balls had peppered the colour. The fort, along with its magazine, was destroyed, and days later the Choshu clan sued for peace.

Boyes's bravery impressed Alexander, who recommended him for the Victoria Cross. The award was announced in *The London Gazette* of 21 April 1865. Two other men from *Euryalus* were awarded the Victoria Cross: Thomas Pride, the colour sergeant who was badly wounded, and Ordinary Seaman William Seeley, who had been wounded carrying out a daring reconnaissance mission. Seeley, a merchant seaman before joining the Royal Navy, was the first United States citizen to be awarded the decoration. At the time American nationals were forbidden from joining British forces and he could have faced arrest. In 1866 he was invalided out of the navy and returned to the United States to take up farming in Massachusetts, the authorities apparently unaware of his service with the crown.

Euryalus returned to England, and on 22 September 1865 the Commander-in-Chief, Portsmouth, Admiral Sir Michael Seymour, pinned Victoria Crosses to the uniforms of Boyes, Pride and Seeley at an impressive parade on Southsea Common. The *Hampshire Telegraph* reported: 'Not only did the ceremony take place in the presence of a strong muster of officers, whose breasts were already decorated with the Cross, and of seamen and marines serving on board the vessels in the harbour and at Spithead; but so large a number of civilians have rarely assembled on Southsea Common.'

The crew of *Euryalus* were present to hear Admiral Seymour speak of the 'noble daring' of the three recipients. Tellingly, as he presented the medals, the admiral said: 'I earnestly hope that in your future career you will persevere in the same course of duty which has gained for you this signal mark of Her Majesty's approbation.' Those words would no doubt come to haunt Boyes who, still only eighteen, must have found the occasion overwhelming. The ceremony drew to a close with HMS *Victory* firing a salute, the presentation of arms – and three cheers. The next day *Euryalus* was paid off.

Later Boyes served in the corvette HMS *Wolverine* on the North America Station. On 9 February 1867 his naval career ended abruptly. He and Midshipman Marcus McCausland, both serving in the brig HMS *Cadmus*, were court-martialled for breaking into the naval yard in Bermuda at night after a run ashore. The pair had been turned away from the main gate because they did not have passes. It may well have been a prank, fuelled by alcohol. They pleaded guilty but the penalty was severe – the midshipmen were dismissed the service. Naval historian John Winton described it as 'an astonishingly harsh punishment', adding 'but obviously there was more to the story than appears'.

Indeed, there was more to the story. Admiralty papers have revealed that Boyes had been warned on several occasions about his conduct. In July 1865, two months after his Victoria Cross was gazetted, he left his post ashore while on duty, returning drunk. Vice Admiral Kuper was informed. In December that year he again disappeared and was warned that any further misconduct 'may lead to immediate dismissal'. Three months later he was severely reprimanded for being impertinent to a commander. By the time of his fourth offence, the Bermuda fiasco, senior officers had clearly lost patience. There is no record of Boyes being a problem before the award of the Victoria Cross, so his fall from grace suggests that he found it hard to cope with his role of young hero. Perhaps arrogance took root. Perhaps jealous superiors gave him a testing time.

Whatever the cause, a misleading explanation for Boyes's dismissal was passed down through generations of the family, as this story from one member, Esme Harman, blaming a party on board a ship, shows:

Uncle Duncan's heroic achievement was celebrated by his friends and shipmates for some time afterwards, as you can well imagine, and all the praise and champagne toasts and congratulations went to his poor little head a bit. Remember he was only seventeen! An awful part was that if only the party had been confined to his own wardroom, the matter might have been toned down, but there were guests on board that night from other ships in port.

As it was, a quarrel arose among the bright spirits, and Duncan, after too much champagne, struck a superior officer with devastating results from the discipline angle. The captain of the ship was a family friend, and as sympathetically inclined as was possible under such circumstances. So instead of a court martial, followed by dismissal and a lot of unpleasant publicity, it was all hushed up and Duncan was allowed to resign quietly on the plea of ill health.

Certainly Boyes's mother was never told that he had been court-martialled and dismissed the service. The punishment left him shattered. Severe depression and heavy drinking took over. Adding to the pressure was the fact that his sister Louisa had married another naval hero, Captain Thomas Young, who won the Victoria Cross during the Indian Mutiny. Young would have taken a dim view of his brother-in-law's behaviour. Boyes went to New Zealand in the hope of recovery. One of nine children, he joined his brothers Charles and Frank, who ran a 32,000-acre sheep station at Kawarau Falls in Otago province. But he did not take to his new life as a sheep farmer and was 'too miserable to settle to anything'. During this time his father died, and he had a complete breakdown.

On 26 January 1869 Duncan Boyes VC jumped to his death from the Criterion Hotel in the centre of Dunedin. He was twenty-two. Strangely, Captain Young died less than two months later. The fact that Boyes committed suicide may have been covered up officially. No inquest appears to have been held, and the cause of death was given only as delirium tremens, the DTs. His brothers Charles and Frank, prosperous settlers, no doubt had influence in the community. They told their mother that he had died of 'fever'. Local newspaper reports of Boyes's heroism fail to mention suicide.

Duncan Boyes did not leave a will, and Charles was appointed administrator of his estate. After a no doubt painful search of the sheep station and the Criterion Hotel Charles produced an inventory of his brother's belongings, which included a gold watch, two gold chains, a gold ring, a writing desk, 'wearing apparel', and a saddle and bridle. Duncan Boyes also had a share in the sheep station and he left £116 in cash. But there was no mention of his Victoria Cross, and no article to suggest that he had served in the Royal Navy. Before leaving Britain Boyes had apparently given his decoration to another brother, George, who joined the navy and went on to reach flag rank and to be knighted.

Dunedin has another Victoria Cross connection – Thomas Lane, whose decoration was reportedly sold by a local pawnshop 'for a few shillings' in 1875 after he fell on hard times. He had won the Victoria Cross while serving with the 67th (South Hampshire) Foot during the Second China War in 1860. The much-travelled Lane was later stripped of the honour after being convicted of desertion from a unit in South Africa and theft.

Boyes was buried in Dunedin's Southern Cemetery. In May 1907 an army chaplain, Daniel Dutton, took a group of cadets to the graveside and gave 'a stirring address' about Boyes's heroism. The *Otago Witness* carried a colourful report of Dutton's speech:

A party of sailors and marines was put ashore from the *Euryalus*, and was ordered to take a formidable stockade, which was strongly held by the Japanese. On the order being given the storming party rushed forward but were subjected to very heavy fire from the Japanese. Many of the British went down, and among them several colour-bearers one after another. Then Midshipman Boyes seized the colours and carried them forward at the head of the stormers. The stockade was quickly won, and the shot-torn flag hoisted over the captured stronghold. Before the fight was over Boyes came near to paying for his valour with his life. Two Japanese rushed to cut him down, but he beat them off with his flagstaff and, needless to say, he became the popular idol of his comrades, and their gratification was immense when he was mentioned in the despatches and recommended for the VC, which he obtained, though he did not live long to wear it.

Dutton, who served in the Second Boer War, had firm views on the British Empire as well as heroism, which he was keen to pass on to the cadets. The newspaper report continued:

He had no doubt that now attention had been called to the facts that had been briefly stated this grave would henceforth be to them a shrine of valour which they would often visit, and which they would at least annually decorate with flowers. They had been hearing a great deal about the greatness of the British Empire. It was not necessary to enlarge on the subject except to impress upon them the responsibility that rested upon them all to maintain the integrity of the empire. He used the word integrity not only to signify that the various parts of the empire must be held together, and that those who were rash enough to attack any parts of it would have to count with the whole empire in the defence. He used the word to express their responsibility to uphold the integrity of the empire as it applied to national character. They must, as a people, cultivate a true sense of national honour and uprightness in all their dealings with each other and with outside nations, remembering that all history showed that when a nation lost its moral integrity all its fibres were weakened and its decay was certain.

Clearly, Dutton was unaware of Boyes's dismissal from the navy and the tragic circumstances of his death, or the irony of the plea for 'uprightness'. Perhaps Boyes turned in his grave. Dutton went on to serve in the First World War, and one wonders how many of those cadets also responded to the call to defend the empire, patriotism that might have led to the horrors of Gallipoli.

Boyes's grave was also the focus of attention in 1954, when the remains were reinterred in the military plot at Dunedin's Anderson's Bay Cemetery. The Dunedin Returned and Services' Association had thought this was a more fitting location and obtained official permission. However, the following year a newspaper called *Truth* claimed that the association failed to consult the public and had, in fact, desecrated the original grave because 'Midshipman Boyes was given a Viking funeral for brave seamen by which his last resting place should remain inviolate for ever'.

The front-page report went on:

An Englishman who has spent a lifetime at sea recently made a pilgrimage to the grave and was shocked to find the earth disturbed. He was not mollified by the information that the grave had been transferred officially, and pointed out that the two stones raised at the head and foot were symbolic of the dogs which Vikings burned at a funeral. He said that until comparatively recent times it was customary when sailors were buried at sea to place a stone at each end of the shroud signifying the dogs. Similarly on land, a 'dog at the head and a dog at the foot', more often than not marked the graves of seamen and this was considered particularly important in the case of anyone who displayed heroism in his lifetime.

The association stressed that it had acted with 'the very best intentions'. The Southern Cemetery was full, choked with weeds and 'an eyesore'. Following the criticism the association consulted naval historians and 'tradition-minded navy men' and 'none has heard of any tradition that a sailor's bones must not be removed'.

Surprisingly, Anderson's Bay Cemetery also has the grave of another disgraced Victoria Cross winner, Horace Martineau. The Englishman joined the 11th Hussars in 1891, aged seventeen, and went on to serve in South Africa and India before purchasing his discharge. The outbreak of the Second Boer War saw him serving as a sergeant in the Protectorate Regiment. He won the Victoria Cross in an action near Mafeking on 26 December 1899, when he rescued a comrade under heavy fire despite being wounded three times, one of the wounds resulting in the amputation of his left arm near the shoulder. Civilian work and militia service in South Africa followed.

Martineau was in New Zealand when the First World War broke out, and he enlisted as a lieutenant in the Otago Infantry Battalion. As part of the New Zealand Expeditionary Force, the battalion served in Egypt and at Gallipoli, where Martineau fell ill with gastroenteritis. It was serious enough for him to be sent to Alexandria for treatment and recuperation.

At a local café, the Pallotta Court, on the evening of 7 September 1915, he was involved in an argument with a Captain Hunt of the Royal Army Medical Corps. The next day he was arrested and accused of drunkenness and using insubordinate language. Shortly afterwards a hearing was held at Sidi Bishr camp, where soldiers from New Zealand and Australia were based. Hunt had been with a Lieutenant King and an Egyptian civilian at the café when Martineau sat behind them. 'While sitting there he commenced swearing [at the Egyptian],' said Hunt, who may not have been in uniform. 'His remarks were so offensive that I spoke to him about the matter and asked him to behave like a gentleman. He immediately turned on me and told me that he was a Colonial and asked who the bloody hell I was and to mind my own bloody business. He continued his remarks then came down in front of me and was again offensive. Amongst other things he threatened to punch my face.'

Martineau walked away but later Hunt heard him say loudly 'bloody bugger' and 'bloody bastard'. The Victoria Cross hero told the hearing that Hunt had mocked his disability, saying: 'Because you have only one arm you can do as you like.' The captain denied this, stating that when Martineau threatened to punch him, he replied: 'You are taking advantage of the fact that you have only one arm.' Asked if he thought the lieutenant was drunk, he said: 'In my opinion the accused was under the influence of liquor.' Lieutenant King said Martineau had made 'disparaging remarks' because he thought the Egyptian's chair was blocking his way.

Martineau denied being drunk or insulting the Egyptian 'for I am always courteous to these people'. But he admitted: 'I did insult Captain Hunt, which I regret exceedingly but it was done in the heat of temper and undue provocation.' Another witness said that Martineau had returned to camp 'sober' but 'very upset over this matter'. The camp's commanding officer decided there was only enough evidence to charge Martineau with using insubordinate language. The recommendation went up the chain of command, and Brigadier C. R. McGregor decided it was 'a case of disgraceful conduct of an officer in a public place'. But he noted that Martineau was a holder of the Victoria Cross and added: 'Under the circumstances I recommend that his services be dispensed with without trial and that he be sent back to New Zealand.' Another senior officer pointed out that the lieutenant was 'not physically fit for service at the front'.

Martineau had a further spell in hospital in Egypt before boarding a ship for Auckland, where he arrived on 31 December 1915. Within days Minister of Defence James Allen was informed that the officer would be 'gazetted out of the Expeditionary Force'. Curiously, a minute sheet listed the alleged offences as drunkenness and using insubordinate language, even though the original inquiry had not found enough evidence to justify a charge relating to the former. Martineau's army service was ended swiftly. On 24 February 1916 the *New Zealand Gazette* announced: 'Lieutenant Horace Robert Martineau, V.C., attached to 14th (South Otago) Regiment, is struck off the strength of the N.Z. Expeditionary Force, under the provisions of paragraph 11 (1), Expeditionary Force Act, 1915, with effect from 1st January, 1916.' Serious stomach problems returned and Martineau was admitted to Dunedin Hospital, where he died on 8 April 1916.

It is bizarre that one place in New Zealand – Dunedin – should have links with three disgraced Victoria Cross heroes in Duncan Boyes, Thomas Lane and Horace Martineau.

10

Condemned by the Church
Robert Jones

Robert Jones won the Victoria Cross during one of the British Army's most remarkable actions, the defence of the mission station Rorke's Drift in Natal, South Africa, in 1879. Nineteen years later he died in an English garden on a summer's day in circumstances that remain controversial to this day.

The heroics of Rorke's Drift on 22 and 23 January came hours after the disaster at Isandlwana, when a Zulu army overwhelmed a British camp that was unprepared for a major attack.

A force under the command of Lieutenant General Lord Chelmsford had invaded Zululand in several columns earlier that month following King Cetshwayo's rejection of an ultimatum over border disputes. On 20 January Chelmsford's main column set up camp at the base of the Isandlwana rocky promontory. The general did not order defensive positions, believing they would take too long. He also seriously underestimated the strength and fighting capability of his enemy, who had some rifles but were mostly armed with spears [assegais] and clubs [knobkerries]. His force included Royal Artillery and colonial units as well as native troops, but his key soldiers were well-disciplined men from two battalions of the 24th (2nd Warwickshire) Regiment [renamed the South Wales Borders in 1881], who were armed with the powerful Martini–Henry rifle. Scouts were sent out and there were skirmishes with groups of Zulus.

At dawn on 22 January, Chelmsford left camp with about 2,500 men, including half his British infantry, believing that he would soon make contact with the Zulu army and fight a decisive battle.

In fact, he was being lured away by diversionary tactics. Lieutenant Colonel Henry Pulleine, an administrator who had no fighting experience, was left in command of the camp. During the morning some 500 men of the Natal Native Horse and the Natal Native Contingent arrived from Rorke's Drift, taking the total number of soldiers at the camp to around 1,700, of whom 950 were Europeans. There were two artillery pieces.

Various reports of Zulu movements were given to Pulleine, who was under the impression that, if confronted, the enemy might number around 400. By noon he would be made painfully aware that he was about to face an army of more than 20,000 warriors, which had been spotted in a nearby ravine. Pulleine was soon out of his depth on the battlefield. The Zulus surged towards the exposed camp, aiming to encircle it with their 'two horns' strategy. They were humming and buzzing 'like a huge swarm of bees'. The 24th were in advanced positions and managed to slow the attack. But Pulleine's defenders were scattered and in danger of being outflanked, and he ordered a retreat to the camp, where there was little cover. Many of the native troops, poorly trained and armed, fled. By the middle of the afternoon the British position was desperate, groups of soldiers fighting back-to-back using bayonets and rifle butts to defend themselves. Although there was plenty of ammunition at the camp, distribution had become a problem. Two copper bands and nine screws held down each lid on the wooden ammunition boxes, and quartermasters tended to be methodical when handing out cartridges from their wagons. In the end, the waves of Zulus could not be stopped. Isandlwana became the scene of a massacre.

The British force lost more than 1,300 men, including 590 from the 24th, which did not have a single survivor. Pulleine was among the European officers killed, an assegai thrust into his chest as he sat writing at a field desk in his tent, possibly a report for Chelmsford. Tellingly, 400,000 rounds of ammunition were not used. Zulu deaths may have been as high as 3,000.

Reports that a large enemy force was heading towards Isandlwana had reached Chelmsford early in the day, but he was slow to react, even when told that an attack had started. His troops returned to the camp at sundown after the battle to find shocking scenes. British soldiers had been mutilated, when wounded and after death. Bodies were stripped of uniforms in a looting frenzy. And the attackers had gone, apart from a few stragglers intoxicated by the spoils of alcohol.

At about 2.30 p.m. that afternoon, two shocked lieutenants of the Natal Native Contingent, named Ardendorff and Vane, had arrived on horseback at Rorke's Drift, which was being used as a supply base and temporary hospital, with news of the overwhelming attack 10 miles away and a warning that a large force of Zulus was on its way to the mission station. The officers had clearly left the battle early and soon rode away from Rorke's Drift; they were later accused of desertion. The news stunned Lieutenant John Chard of the Royal Engineers, who was in temporary command. Then, realising that time was not on his side, he conferred with Lieutenant Gonville Bromhead of the 24th, who was there with 109 of his men from the 2nd Battalion's B Company, although twenty-two of them were ill.

It was decided that the only realistic option would be to stay and defend the post rather than attempt an escape. In total, there were some 350 soldiers, including men of the Natal Native Contingent and a newly arrived troop of the Natal Native Horse, which had been fighting at Isandlwana. Chard thought they had a reasonable chance of holding out, although at that stage he did not know that the Zulu force heading his way numbered around 4,000. The mission station had two buildings about 30 yards apart, which were being used as a storehouse and the hospital. Doors and windows were barricaded, and a perimeter wall was quickly built, using wagons, mealie bags and biscuit boxes. Wisely, ammunition cases were unscrewed. By 4.30 p.m. it was confirmed that the Zulus were on their way.

Without warning the mounted natives, who were positioned outside the post, rode off. A lieutenant shouted that they were refusing to obey orders – and he, too, disappeared. Soon afterwards all the men of the Natal Native Contingent scaled the barricades and ran away, along with their commanding officer, Captain George Stephenson. Chard's force of 350 was suddenly reduced to 139, with thirty-five of them incapacitated. Chard realised that he could not defend the original perimeter and another defensive line was set up around the storehouse. A shout from the hospital roof alerted the defenders to the arrival of the Zulus, a reserve force that had not fought at Isandlwana but were no doubt fired up by the day's events. The warriors charged in huge numbers and the first of many Martini–Henry volleys rang out.

Private Robert Jones, aged twenty-one, was one of the men stationed in the hospital to protect the patients. It was a building that had a number of rooms, not all of them connected. Only three of the patients were suffering from wounds. Most of the others were down with fever or the victims of wagon or riding accidents. One of the patients, oddly, was a Zulu. Years later Jones gave this account:

I and another soldier of the name of William Jones were on duty at the back of the hospital, trying to defeat and drive back the rebels, and doing our endeavours to convey the wounded and sick soldiers out through a hole in the wall, so that they might reach in safety the small band of men in the square. On retiring from one room into another, after taking a wounded man by the name of Mayer, belonging to the volunteers, to join William Jones, I found a crowd in front of the hospital and coming into the doorway. I said to my companion, 'They are on top of us', and sprang to one side of the doorway. There we crossed our bayonets, and as fast as they came up to the doorway we bayoneted them, until the doorway was nearly filled with dead and wounded Zulus. In the meanwhile, I had three assegai wounds, two in the right side and one in the left of my body. We did not know of anyone being in the hospital, only the Zulus, and then after a long time of fighting at the door, we made the enemy retire, and then we made our escape out of the building. Just as I got outside, the roof fell in – a complete mass of flames and fire. I had to cross a space of about 20 or 30 yards from the ruins of the hospital to the leagued company where they were keeping the enemy at bay. While I was crossing the front of the square, the bullets were whishing past me from every direction. When I got in, the enemy came closer and closer until they were close to the outer side of our laager, which was made up of boxes of biscuits on sacks of Indian corn. The fighting lasted about 13 hours or better. As to my feelings at the time, they were that I was certain that if I did not kill them they would kill us, and after a few minutes' fighting I did not mind it more than at the present time; my thought was only to fight as an English soldier ought to for his most gracious sovereign, Queen Victoria, and for the benefit of old England.

In his account, Jones neglected to say that he and Private William Jones had run out of ammunition, which is why they resorted to using their bayonets. The pair managed to get six patients out of a window. Robert Jones also tried to save Sergeant Robert Maxfield of the 24th, who was delirious with fever and refused to move from his bed. Maxfield was speared to death.

Outside, along the barricades, soldiers stood shoulder to shoulder and kept up a withering fire. Zulus who got too close were bayoneted. After an hour there were piles of the enemy dead and dying, which attackers clambered over, only to meet a similar fate. Chaplain George Smith was busy handing out cartridges from a haversack, and admonishing anyone he heard swearing. But the noise was almost deafening – the firing, the clash of spears and bayonets, and the chanting of thousands of warriors. Chard's last bastion was a circle of mealie bags near the storehouse. Donald Morris recorded in his book, *The Washing of the Spears*: 'The men had lost all count of the furious charges and all sense of time. They existed in a slow eternity of noise and smoke and flashes, of straining black faces that rose out of the darkness, danced briefly in the light of the muzzle blasts, and then sank out of their sight. It was long after midnight before the rushes began to subside, long after two o'clock in the morning before the last of them was over.' The Zulus had not retreated and from sheltered positions they flung assegais for a further two hours.

It was remarkable that only fifteen soldiers had been killed. Two others were dying and eight were seriously wounded. The rest of the men were exhausted and, as daylight broke, they must have known that they would not be able to hold out for much longer. But the Zulu force – what was left of it – had gone. Scattered around Rorke's Drift were hundreds of bodies. The defenders had used 20,000 rounds of ammunition. At about seven o'clock that morning there was a shock – the Zulu army reappeared in the distance. Then they vanished again. They, too, were exhausted and hundreds of them were wounded. Their leader, Dabulamanzi, had disobeyed King Cetshwayo, his half-brother, in carrying out an attack across the border in Natal. Shortly afterwards Chelmsford and his remaining force arrived at Rorke's Drift to hear tales of remarkable bravery.

The Victoria Cross was awarded to Robert Jones and ten of the other defenders, including William Jones, Private Henry Hook and Private John Williams who had helped to defend the hospital and save patients. Chard and Bromhead also received the decoration. Lieutenant General Sir Garnet Wolseley, commander of British troops in South Africa, presented Robert Jones with his medal at Utrecht, Natal, on 11 September 1879.

Jones had been born at Raglan, Monmouthshire, on 19 August 1857, one of seven children to Robert and Hannah Jones. His father was a local farmer. By the age of fourteen Robert junior was working as a farm labourer. Four years later, apparently to his father's annoyance, he joined the army at Monmouth, sailing to South Africa with the 2nd Battalion 24th Regiment in 1878. That year the battalion was involved in frontier fighting against the Galeka tribe. In the July Jones tarnished his record, accused of being drunk on duty. A court martial sentenced him to fifty-six days' hard labour, but he was released from prison at Pietermaritzburg after serving less than two weeks. In January 1880 he left South Africa to serve in Gibraltar. Jones also saw service in India before returning to Britain in November 1881, soon afterwards transferring to the army reserve. In January 1885 he married Elizabeth Hopkins at Llantilio, Monmouthshire, and they went on to have five children. By 1898 the family were living in the village of Peterchurch, Herefordshire, and Jones was working as a farm labourer on a local estate belonging to Major William Delahay, a retired officer. On 6 September 1898 Robert Jones was found shot dead in the major's garden. He was forty-one.

A few days later a local newspaper reported that the 'quiet and peaceful village' in the Golden Valley had been 'thrown into a state of considerable alarm on Tuesday morning when the report was circulated that Robert Jones, a well-known personage on account of his brilliant connection with the army, had shot himself'. The report continued: 'Some people seemed to hold the opinion that the affair might have been an accident, but all doubt was set at rest when the position in which the deceased held the gun became known. He had been acting in a rather peculiar manner of late, but the idea of his committing suicide was never dreamed of.'

An inquest with a jury was held at the Boughton Arms pub in Peterchurch the day after Jones's death. His widow Elizabeth told the coroner that they had argued on the Monday. Jones, who had a small plot of land, went to a local fair with a sheep he owned, selling it for £2 5s – the same amount he had paid for the animal twelve months earlier. He was found 'the worse for drink' after visiting the Boughton Arms, and his wife confronted him about the price, complaining that he should have got more. She told him to go back to the fair, return the money and retrieve the sheep. This he did. Mrs Jones actually followed him to the fair to make sure he carried out her wishes, and she resold the sheep for £2 9s. Jones returned home at about six o'clock that evening and had 'a good supper' before going to bed. Asked by the coroner if they had argued again, Mrs Jones said: 'No, sir. I had no quarrel with him.'

But the next morning, Tuesday, Jones appeared 'very hot and very wild in his appearance'. Mrs Jones told the inquest: 'I asked him to sit down and I would get him some tea. He would insist on going out, and then I fastened the door but he went out another way afterwards.' However, he returned about half an hour later, drank two cups of tea, changed his clothes and left for work. 'He seemed all right,' said Mrs Jones.

She was asked about his army service, and replied: 'He served in South Africa and was wounded in five places.' The coroner asked: 'At times he complained of his head?' Mrs Jones: 'Yes, sir. He has this past summer very much. He had been wounded close to the eye.' About three weeks earlier Jones had suffered a fit, collapsing in his employer's garden. Mrs Jones added: 'He has been very quiet at times, and if he got in a passion he seemed very wild. He was a kind husband and a good father.'

Louisa Wellers, a maid at the Delahay home, told the coroner that Jones had greeted her on Tuesday morning and asked for the major's shotgun. He often went out shooting birds. The maid heard the gun go off and later went to fetch some wood. In the garden she saw Jones's hat and then a lot of blood. She ran back to the house. Major Delahay had heard her scream and went to investigate. He said he found Jones's hat in the middle of the path 'covered in brains' and the body lying face down about 10 feet away. The gun was underneath him.

A policeman found the top of the head almost blown off. Jones's left hand was close to the muzzle, with the right hand near the trigger. There was an empty cartridge in the gun and a loaded cartridge in one of his pockets. A doctor said there was a large hole in the back of the roof of the mouth. The muzzle of the gun must have been in the mouth when it went off. With his long arms, Jones would not have had any difficulty in firing the gun in such a position. The coroner told the jury that it was 'pretty clear from the doctor's evidence' that Jones had killed himself, and they returned a verdict of suicide while temporarily insane.

Jones was buried in the local churchyard the next day. However, it appears that the church authorities initially refused to allow the burial in consecrated ground because of the sin of suicide. The decision angered villagers who thought the Victoria Cross hero deserved better. A compromise saw the burial going ahead – but the coffin had to be lifted into the churchyard over a wall and it was not allowed into St Peter's Church. The authorities also insisted that Jones's marble headstone should face away from the other tombs to signify the nature of his death. The headstone still remains in that position. It would also appear that the church covered up the controversy because the only reference to him in official documents is the burial register, which simply lists 'Robert Jones VC', his abode, date of burial, age and the minister who performed the ceremony. Suicide is not recorded, unlike an entry on 5 August for one Frederick Jones, aged fifty-four. This man apparently killed himself and was not allowed the usual service. His burial involved a non-conformist minister.

In September 1998 *The Sunday Telegraph* carried a report suggesting that Jones had not committed suicide. It quoted Alan Baynham-Jones, a former soldier and firearms expert, as saying: 'Jones was shot in the side of the head as well as under the chin which must surely rule out suicide. The reach of the barrels alone would have made it virtually impossible for him to have killed himself. He probably accidentally shot himself as he tripped, then as he hit the flagstones the weapon discharged a second time. I have seen written evidence from Jones's employer, a Major De La Hay [Delahay], who said that the gun was faulty and prone to go off at the slightest knock. For some reason he was never called as a witness at the coroner's inquest.' The Regimental Museum of the Royal Welsh, guardian of the old 24th, has also queried the suicide verdict, echoing Baynham-Jones: 'There is a great deal of debate as to whether or not he shot himself or was killed accidentally when the double-hammered shotgun he was carrying fired as he tripped on a garden path. Jones was shot in the side of the head as well as under the chin, which probably rules out suicide. The reach of the barrels would have made it almost impossible for him to have killed himself.'

Of course, the medical and police evidence given to the inquest – reported in detail three days later – clearly contradicts these claims. Witnesses told of only one shot being fired. Jones apparently had two cartridges and one was still in a pocket. He suffered a massive wound to the top of his head via the back of his throat, and he was judged to be capable of inflicting the injury. Major Delahay was, in fact, called as a witness. And there was also a great deal of evidence about Jones's mental state.

The attitude of the church was raised again in 2010, when another former soldier, Pete Winner, discovered that Robert Jones's headstone was facing the wrong way because of the suicide verdict. 'I owe it to this brave soldier to try to right a wrong that has existed for well over a century,' said Winner. 'If soldiers back then suffered mental problems it was largely ignored or dismissed as battle fatigue. Fortunately we are more enlightened now. But I believe there is no doubt that Robert Jones was suffering from classic symptoms of post-traumatic stress disorder. I live near to the churchyard in Peterchurch and when I went in search of Private Jones's grave I was appalled at this insult to a man who was a hero to his country. I am determined to try to do something about it – to get the authorities to re-site the gravestone so it faces the church, just like every other one in the churchyard.'

But Jones's descendants decided they did not want the headstone moved. Gillian Evans, a great-granddaughter, said: 'We were very pleased that Mr Winner took an interest but the headstone has been placed that way for over a hundred years and we can see it from the road and everything. It is a rather sensitive point. We were always told it was put that way because the family had requested it. We were never told about the suicide.'

A similar controversy surrounds Joseph Trewavas, who won the Victoria Cross during the Crimean War in July 1855. Under heavy Russian fire the seaman sabotaged a strategic bridge at the Genitchi Strait. Trewavas, who was also awarded the Conspicuous

Gallantry Medal, left the navy in 1862 after serving nearly ten years and returned to his native Cornwall, becoming a fisherman. He led an active life but in 1905 he was badly affected by a stroke. On 20 July, in the living room of his home at Mousehole, he cut his throat with a bread knife, dying the next day, aged sixty-nine. An inquest jury returned a verdict of suicide 'whilst of unsound mind'. A funeral service was held at the parish church, St Pol de Leon in Paul village, but Trewavas was not allowed a Christian burial. The hero was left in an unmarked grave on the other side of the churchyard wall.

Major Charles Lumley appears to have been an unusual exception when it came to canon law in Victorian times. As a captain with the 97th (Earl of Ulster's) Regiment, he also won the Victoria Cross during the Crimean War. He showed his bravery in the attack on the Redan, the Russian defensive position, on 8 September 1855, but he was shot in the mouth as he rallied his men, a wound that left him disfigured. Later he joined the 2nd Battalion 23rd (Royal Welsh Fusiliers) Regiment and was given command of a detachment stationed in Brecon. On 17 October 1858 he shot himself in the head at his quarters after his wife Letitia had gone to a Sunday church service. An inquest heard that Lumley had been in 'very low spirits and very absent in his manner'. He was discovered fatally wounded in a water closet with a pistol in his left hand. The inquest jury 'found that the deceased had destroyed himself while labouring under temporary insanity'. The major was buried with full military honours three days after his death at the local parish church, which later became Brecon Cathedral. An imposing tomb was erected at his grave. There seems to be no evidence that his burial in consecrated ground caused any controversy. In 1882 canon law was changed, allowing a Christian burial for those who committed suicide 'while of sound mind', which would appear to be a contradiction.

In 2015 the Dean of Brecon, the Very Reverend Dr Paul Shackerley, commented: 'According to my colleagues, his rank would not have mattered. However, him receiving a VC could possibly have been. At the end of the day, there is no way of knowing. We have a greater understanding now of post-traumatic stress disorder. If only we had such understanding, treatment and support for our predecessors.'

11

A Disastrous General
Redvers Buller

The courage of Redvers Buller on the battlefield was never doubted. As Field Marshal Sir John French once noted: 'Had a thunderbolt burst at his feet he would merely have brushed from his rifle jacket the earth it had thrown upon him without any break in the sentence he happened to be uttering at that moment.'

There was, however, another view of him: 'He was an admirable captain, an adequate major, a barely satisfactory colonel and a disastrous general.' His first name was pronounced 'Reevers', and after major setbacks during his campaign against the Boers in 1899 he became known as 'Reverse Buller'. He lost his command and was eventually sacked.

Buller was born at the family estate, Downes, at Crediton, Devon, on 7 December 1839. He was one of eleven children, and grew to love his surroundings, an estate of some 5,000 acres. An outdoor life suited him. He appreciated country crafts, and took to riding. His parents were comfortably off but did not flaunt their wealth. From his father James, who dabbled in politics and part-time soldiering as well as being a landowner, he inherited a degree of shyness, but there were contradictory elements in his character. He became highly opinionated and sometimes found it difficult to control his temper. The young Buller was sent to a prep school and then Harrow, which he soon left under a cloud. Eton accepted him. At the age of sixteen, he had a harrowing experience. He went to meet his mother Charlotte at St David's railway station in Exeter in December 1855 on her return from a shopping trip. She suffered a lung haemorrhage on the platform and was taken to the waiting room, where she remained for three days, too ill to be moved. Buller stayed at his mother's side and she died at the station.

In July 1858 the well-built teenager joined the army after buying a commission in the 60th, The King's Royal Rifle Corps. His father presumably met the high cost, £450. Such a payment avoided the rigours of Sandhurst training. The following January Ensign Buller sailed for India to join the regiment's 2nd battalion. Mopping-up operations stemming from the Indian Mutiny were drawing to a close, and the battalion later went to Hong Kong. Buller also caught the tail end of the Second China War, when an Anglo-French force successfully attacked the Taku forts in August 1860 and swept on to Peking for an orgy of looting and destruction. The ensign wanted to see action, but not at any price. He was among those who wondered if the war was justified, and for a long time he refused to wear his China campaign medal. There was a brief return to England before a posting to the 4th battalion in Canada in 1862 and promotion to lieutenant. Several years of peacetime soldiering followed, and fortunately for the adventurous Buller the country's forests provided a distraction, allowing him to hone his outdoor skills, trekking, canoeing and hunting. At one point he wondered if he should continue with his army career.

In 1867 Canada became a dominion. Buller returned to England in the summer of 1869 but soon found himself back in Canada with the 1st battalion in the rank of captain. That December the Hudson Bay Company sold its territory in the west to the new government, a decision resented by the local inhabitants, the Metis, who objected to new settlers. The leader of the Metis, Louis Riel, with some 500 armed men, seized the Hudson Bay Company's headquarters, Fort Garry, on the Red River, and imprisoned British subjects. One of the prisoners, Thomas Scott, who tried to escape, was executed, which caused outrage in the English-speaking provinces. Colonel Garnet Wolseley was ordered to lead an expedition to retake the fort, a daunting task because it meant covering more than 1,100 miles across lakes, rivers and mostly wilderness. His force of the 1st battalion and Canadian militia left Toronto on 14 May 1870, acquiring a large number of boats and supplies.

It was tough going, as Wolseley later acknowledged:

All the officers with expeditionary force soon became expert in making portages and in mending boats, no one more so than my very able friend and valued comrade Redvers Buller. It was here I first made his acquaintance, and I am proud to feel that we have been firm friends ever since. He was a first-class axeman, and I think he was the only man with us of any rank who could carry a hundred pound barrel of pork over a portage on his back. He could mend a boat and have her back in the water with her crew and all her stores on board whilst many, under similar circumstances, would have been still making up their minds what to do. Full of resource, and personally absolutely fearless, those serving under him always trusted him fully.

The 1st battalion reached Lake Winnipeg on 19 August in driving rain, and learned that Riel and his men would stand and fight, which was pleasing news. At last Buller would see action. Five days later, with downpours continuing, the 60th were within sight of Fort Garry. But no shots were fired at the approaching troops and the south gate was open. Riel and his followers had fled, heading for the United States border. The Red River campaign was over. A disappointed Buller observed: 'It does so disgust one to have come all this way for the band to play God Save The Queen.' Five days later Wolseley began the return journey, leaving militia units at the fort. In 1885 Riel staged another rebellion, also short-lived. He was captured and executed.

Although Buller had not been able to prove himself in battle he impressed those around him with his determination and willingness to share hardship. He returned to England and gained a place at the staff college, Camberley, in 1872. During the course Buller learned that Wolseley was leading an expedition to west Africa to confront the Ashantis, who were launching attacks in the Gold Coast protectorate and threatening trade. Wolseley, who had been knighted, was happy to take his 'resourceful friend'. He and his staff arrived in October 1873, and he placed Buller in charge of intelligence, a challenging task as the local language had many dialects. There would be other challenges – dense bush and disease.

That month a force of marines, seamen and soldiers of the West India Regiment defeated Ashantis at Essaman. Buller was involved in the fighting. More troops arrived and there were several clashes, but the first major action was at Amoaful on 31 January 1874, a success for Wolseley despite difficult conditions. The town of Bekwai was captured the next day. On 4 February the Ashantis were defeated at Ardahsa. The Ashanti capital of Coomassie [Kumasi] was also taken, and before the month was out King Kofi Karikari had accepted peace terms. The campaign, which saw the award of four Victoria Crosses, was thankfully short. Fighting and sickness had taken a heavy toll, and Buller admitted: 'I shall be very glad to get back home.' He had gone down with fever and was still seriously ill when he sailed away from the 'white man's grave'. Wolseley, who returned to Britain a popular hero, acknowledged that Buller had been 'an excellent staff officer'. Promotion to brevet major and a CB were Buller's rewards.

He convalesced at Downes, where he immersed himself in the countryside and literature. Tragedy struck on 12 October 1874 when his dearest brother James died. Buller inherited the Downes estate, but he decided to continue with his army career, although it meant a desk job in the adjutant general's department at the War Office. In early 1878 he jumped at the chance to go to South Africa with Major General Frederic Thesiger – soon to become Lieutenant General Lord Chelmsford – to deal with tribal unrest. In the April Buller, a brevet lieutenant colonel, was given his first independent command, the Frontier Light Horse, 250 men of dubious quality, whose regimental sergeant major was a deserter from the 80th Foot. Leading by example and enforcing discipline, he transformed the unit. As one young trooper put it: 'If we were lying in the rain, so was Buller. If we were hungry, so was he. All of the hardships he shared equally with his men.' The lieutenant colonel became 'the idol of all'. The Frontier Light Horse was involved in several engagements, losing some men. In August Buller learned that war with the Zulus was likely, and in January 1879 Chelmsford went on the offensive in Zululand, only to face disaster at Isandlwana. At the time Buller was serving under Colonel Evelyn Wood at Kambula, mounting patrols over long distances and skirmishing, with a shrinking unit because many of his men had served their time. Like Buller, Wood was noted for his stamina and a thirst for action.

In March Chelmsford ordered Wood to create a diversion in an attempt to draw away Zulu forces besieging Eshowe. For some weeks Wood and especially Buller had been itching to strike at the belligerent abaQulusi Zulus camped about 20 miles north east of Kambula on Hlobane Mountain, a natural fortress with lower and upper plateaus, rising to 1,500 feet with steep cliffs and only a few narrow trails. Buller had actually launched an assault on the mountain earlier, admitting: 'I have several times asked Colonel Wood to let me attack it and I did one day attack it without leave, but I had only 70 white men and had to leave the strongest part of it untouched. There are now about 1,000 Zulus there and they are getting cheeky.' It was a serious underestimate of the enemy. Hlobane was hardly a suitable target for cavalry, and there was confusion whether Wood intended a reconnaissance mission or an all-out attack. The colonel decided on a pincer movement using Buller, who was now in command of all mounted units, including the Frontier Light Horse, and a force led by Lieutenant Colonel John Russell of the 12th Lancers. Buller and Russell also had hundreds of native troops.

In the early hours of 28 March Buller set off to scale the mountain on the eastern side, but riding on rocky ground soon proved difficult and his cavalry, some 400 men, were forced to dismount and lead their stumbling horses, several falling on to rocks below as darkness and a storm added to the problems. And Zulus were waiting for them, hiding behind boulders and in caves. Shots rang out, claiming the lives of two officers and a trooper of the Frontier Light Horse. Russell, who had set out later, found progress difficult on the western side. Wood, with a small escort, also went up the mountain. Buller and his men fought their way to the mile-wide upper plateau, land where the Zulus kept cattle and dotted with thick bush. It had been thought that most of the Zulus were on the lower plateau, but then Buller discovered that the opposite was true. Many of them were on the upper plateau and moving to cut off escape routes. There was an even worse discovery – in the distance was the main Zulu army of around 22,000 warriors 'in five dense columns, glistening black masses speckled with bobbing white shields, with the sun sparkling on the assegais'.

Charles Hewitt, a trooper in the Frontier Light Horse, later wrote of the moment he spotted them:

We were plugging away at the Zulus and they were at us for several hours till a comrade stationed next to me told me he could see something on some mountains a long way off, which looked like shadows caused by clouds passing between the sun and the mountains, and asked me to look. I used to carry with me a small telescope. I looked through it and saw what looked like a vast mass of Zulus swarming down the sides of the mountains and while I was looking Colonel Buller came along my way and I called his attention to it, and he at once levelled his field glasses, much better than mine of course, and after a minute or two he said, 'Yes, that's an impi of Zulus all right.'

Leaving the mountain and getting back to Kambula became a priority. Buller sent vague orders to his second-in-command, Captain Robert Barton of the Coldstream Guards, who rode off in the wrong direction with thirty men and joined up with the fifty-strong Border Horse. Most of these soldiers were massacred. Buller would later confess: 'Alas for the use of careless words!' With his position becoming more difficult by the minute, he decided that the only feasible escape route was to cross to the lower plateau and use Russell's steep boulder-strewn trail, fittingly called Devil's Pass. He sent his native troops and many of the mounted men ahead, with the Frontier Light Horse covering the retreat. Buller and seven troopers were the last to leave. He may have been an inept commander but there was no questioning his bravery.

The retreat became a rout as Zulus pursued the soldiers, shooting and stabbing them. Some troopers had large rocks dropped on them as they descended. Horses were killed and soldiers found they were unable to outrun Zulus. An unfazed Buller repeatedly went to the aid of his men. He saved Lieutenant Henry Cecil D'Arcy and two other members of the Frontier Light Horse by taking them to safety on his horse after they had lost their mounts. For these acts he was given the Victoria Cross, one of four awarded for that day of disaster.

Trooper Hewitt was among men who managed to get down the most difficult part of the mountain to a wide ledge. He recalled:

While I and the others were looking up at the struggling mass of horses, Zulus and volunteers, I saw the Zulus fling some man clean over the end of the mountain down among the mass of rocks and bushes. I saw him come tumbling over and over and his arms and legs flying in the air while the struggling mass was still making its way down towards the ledge we had already gained.

While all this was going on and we were waiting for as many of the others to get down as was possible, I saw Colonel Buller rendering assistance to a Captain [then lieutenant] D'Arcy, whose horse I understood had got its legs smashed by a rock pitched down from above. Then he, Colonel Buller, gave his attention to a Lieutenant Everitt. Then when we were all down the mountain ... and just before giving the final orders to retreat, Colonel Buller spotted a crowd of our volunteers on foot racing for life with crowds of Zulus chasing them and all but on top of them and he asked some of us who still had horses fit to ride to go and give some of those poor beggars a hand to get away from the Zulus.

So five of us [Buller leading them] rode back and each man managed to pick up one of the poor chaps onto his horse behind him and with two others hanging on to the stirrup straps, we managed to dash out from the crowd of Zulus, who were hotly chasing us, and thus saved a dozen or more, who but for our timely assistance must have perished in a very few minutes by the hands of the Zulu savages. I know I brought out three and I have no doubt that my four comrades did equally well – but there was no time just then to stop and take stock.

The long trek back to Kambula began. On the way Hewitt picked up another man:

I carried him a good distance when I told him I did not think my horse could carry both of us back to Kambula camp. I suggested that we should have to take turns at riding or walking, or running, as the camp was still a long way off. He reckoned he was fairly knocked up and couldn't run, so I got off and hanging on to my stirrup leather ran alongside my own horse, and was getting a bit tired. I found just along the track we were following several knocked up horses fairly played out, the riders evidently finding them no more use had jumped off them and ran and left them, with saddles on, to the tender mercies of the Zulus who would presently come along after us. Well I tried three or four of them but could scarcely get a move out of them, so I had to abandon the idea and run after my own horse and its rider.

When I caught up with him I managed to persuade him to dismount and give me a chance. He got off but made such a job of running and had almost to drag him along that I got disgusted with it and once more got off myself and put him on again. By this time the Zulus were slackening off a bit.

They came to a watercourse and Hewitt lay down for a long drink. When he stood up he discovered that the man he saved had ridden off with his carbine and ammunition. 'I was defenceless. Well I trotted along as best I could in the hopes of overtaking him, but with no success.' Later a group of officers, including Buller, rode up:

> Colonel Buller asked about my horse and why I was on foot, as he had seen me with my horse and carrying the man on my saddle with me. So I told him what had happened and saw him look very savage and utter a word or two which sounded very unlike anything I ever heard at Sunday school, and wondered how any fellow could play such a low game to a comrade, especially to one who had done him a real service and probably saved his life. Then taking his left foot out of his stirrup, he said to me, 'Come here Hewitt, put your foot in that and climb up behind me and I'll give you a lift. I think there is a kick in old Punch yet', referring to his horse.

They rode on for several miles and reached a rocky spot where soldiers were resting. Veterinary surgeon Francis Duck asked Hewitt about his missing horse and was also appalled at the explanation. Duck insisted that Hewitt take his horse and find the missing mount and 'the scoundrel', which he did. The remaining stragglers reached Kambula late that night.

Wood's force had lost nearly 200 men, including seventeen officers. It was a high price to pay for a diversionary tactic, although Buller had another aim – stealing Zulu cattle for prize money. This proved to be a lucrative sideline during his earlier patrols. Buller's men were in the process of rounding up cattle on the upper plateau when they were taken by surprise and forced to retreat.

There was little rest for the survivors. The next morning, 29 March, the Zulu army moved on Kambula. Wood's camp was well defended with regular troops and artillery, and it seemed that the Zulus might skirt round it and head for softer targets as their king, Cetshwayo, had forbidden attacks on fortified positions. But the camp was too tempting for warriors emboldened by the success at Hlobane. They began preparing their 'two horns' formation to encircle the camp. Buller saw a chance to disrupt the right horn and took out a mounted force. Dismounting about 300 yards from the enemy, the troopers fired a volley and fell back, repeating the manoeuvre until the Zulus came within range of the camp's 7-pounder guns. Surging forward, they took heavy losses. The left horn and centre charged, and fighting raged for most of the afternoon. Then the Zulus retreated, with Buller's men in pursuit and showing no mercy. Trooper Hewitt was once again in action: 'We chased them back to their strongholds for an hour or two, accounting for a good many besides those we had finished off at camp.' According to Lieutenant D'Arcy, Wood was 'like a tiger drunk with blood'.

British losses that day were only twenty-eight. The Zulu toll was probably more than 2,000. Kambula proved to be a turning point, and the decisive battle of the war was fought near the Zulu capital, Ulundi, on 4 July 1879. Buller and Wood played major roles. As at Kampala, the retreating Zulus were shown no mercy by Buller's horsemen. It was a much-needed victory for Chelmsford, who was days away from losing his command to Lieutenant General Sir Garnet Wolseley. Buller and Wood, who became members of the Wolseley Ring of favoured officers, returned to Britain the following month 'pretty worn out'. There were rewards, however. Buller was appointed ADC to Queen Victoria with the rank of colonel and awarded the CMG. The queen, who presented him with the Victoria Cross, liked Buller despite finding him 'reserved and shy, with rather a dry, gruff manner', adding: 'He also, though naturally averse to talking, told me much that was very interesting. He is downright when he does speak and gives a very direct answer. Colonel Buller is very modest about himself, saying he had got too much praise.'

After postings to Scotland and Aldershot Buller found himself back in southern Africa in February 1881 as second-in-command to Wood, who had been given the task of dealing with a revolt by Boers in the Transvaal. After several reverses the British government had little appetite for a costly and protracted war, and Wood and Buller were involved in peace negotiations, which led to a provisional treaty in March. Buller spent months as a desk warrior, helping with administrative matters. It suited him because he had some sympathy for the Boer cause. Further conflict would have involved 'harrying their farms and burning their homesteads – cruel work at the best of times ... So on the whole I am really glad it is over.'

He returned to Britain in early 1882, and, at the age of forty- two, married a cousin's widow, Audrey Howard, who had four small children. But he was soon off to another campaign, Egypt, at the invitation of Wolseley, who had been given command of a large expeditionary force to protect the Suez Canal and other British interests after an army coup. Buller took part in the battle of Tel el Kebir on 13 September, which he 'thoroughly enjoyed'. It was a victory that led to Cairo. Buller was knighted (KCMG) and appointed assistant adjutant general at the War Office, under Wolseley. He was sent to the Sudan in February 1884 to deal with an uprising, and distinguished himself during two spells there, winning the battle of Abu Klea in January 1885. A major general, he returned to the War Office. In 1886 he accepted, reluctantly, his strangest appointment – special commissioner to restore law and order in large parts of Ireland, where peasants had tired of being exploited by English landlords. He had some success but was happy to go back to the War Office in October 1887 as quartermaster-general, soon suggesting major army reforms. From 1890 to 1897 he was in the powerful post of adjutant general, and during that time became a lieutenant general and then a full general. He would have been made the army's commander-in-chief, but the Liberal government fell and the Conservatives preferred the less liberal Wolseley. In 1898 Buller was given command of the large force at Aldershot. But he would soon face his greatest challenge: the Second Boer War.

Tensions between the Boers and Britain had been growing for years. The British desire to control the Transvaal and the Orange Free State, the future of the goldmining industry and voting rights for the rising number of uitlanders – foreigners –were key factors. Negotiations failed and in October 1899 the president of the South African republic, Paul Kruger, gave Britain a forty-eight-hour ultimatum to remove troops from the borders of the Transvaal and the Orange Free State. The ultimatum was rejected and the Boers declared war. This did not come as a surprise to the Secretary of State for War, Lord Lansdowne, who months earlier had decided that Buller was the man to lead an expeditionary force.

It was a strange decision. They disliked each other, and Buller made it clear that he was not the best choice. The general was nearly sixty and had spent a long time behind a desk. He was fond of good living and drank large quantities of champagne. More importantly, he had never been a commander-in-chief. But Lansdowne insisted, even though he thought Buller 'pro-Boer'. The expeditionary force landed in Cape Town on 31 October, and Buller had further misgivings, not least about troop numbers and equipment. And he was about to fight a new type of war, with a well-armed and often mobile enemy who knew the terrain and employed skilful tactics, the first commandos.

There were early setbacks. The commander in Natal, Lieutenant General Sir George White, was trapped with his troops at Ladysmith after defeats at Lombard's Kop and Nicholson's Nek. Kimberley was also besieged. Then came Black Week in December, with three successive defeats, Stormberg, Magersfontein and Colenso on the 15th, when Buller himself directed an attack on well-prepared Boer positions.

The general had decided to go to White's aid. A force under Louis Botha along the Tugela River guarded the southern route to Ladysmith. The obvious crossing point was at Colenso, about 12 miles from Ladysmith, and Botha hid men and artillery in hills north of the river, so well concealed that British officers wondered if the position was even defended. Buller's plan was a three-pronged assault but it was poorly thought out, based on little intelligence and inadequate maps. Nevertheless he had 18,000 troops against Botha's 4,500 men.

The attack began in the early hours, but the soldiers on the left flank were led in the wrong direction and met devastating fire from hidden positions on the opposite bank of the river, with the British suffering more than 500 casualties in less than two hours. The assault in the centre saw confusion, with the artillery racing ahead of the infantry and getting cut off. The picture on the right was brighter and then advances were made in the centre, but Buller, with eight battalions in reserve, failed to send reinforcements that might have secured victory. He became obsessed with retrieving the artillery. But only two field guns were saved, and with mounting deaths, including that of Lieutenant Frederick Roberts, the only son of Field Marshal Lord Roberts, the remainder were abandoned. Soon afterwards Buller, wounded by shrapnel, ordered a general retreat. The Guns of Colenso would be a controversial topic for many years. No attempt was made to retrieve them after darkness fell, and a senior officer later wrote: 'To this day every Gunner is indignant at what evolved.' British losses totalled 1,139 dead, wounded or missing. The Boers reportedly had eight men killed and thirty wounded. Surprisingly, Buller regarded Colenso as 'a reverse' rather than a defeat.

He told Lansdowne: 'Colenso is a fortress which I think if not taken in a rush could only be taken by a siege. There is no water within 8 miles of the point of attack. The place is fully entrenched. I do not think either a Boer or a gun was seen by us all day, yet the fire brought to bear was very heavy. Our infantry was quite ready to fight, but were exhausted by the intense heat.' He added: 'My view is that I ought to let Ladysmith go...' Buller would later say that this comment referred to a suspension of military operations, though he conceded it was badly worded. A shocked Lansdowne and others in government decided it was a move to surrender – and totally unacceptable. Buller also sent a message to White a day after the retreat at Colenso, saying: 'The enemy is too strong for my force, except with siege operations, which will take one full month to prepare. Can you last so long? If not, how many days can you give me to take up defensive position, after which I suggest your firing away as much ammunition as you can, and making the best terms you can.' Again, Buller insisted he was misunderstood. The ageing White, who had won the Victoria Cross in Afghanistan, was another senior officer out of his depth in South Africa. He had a substantial force at Ladysmith but was reluctant to go on the offensive. However, he did not take Buller's advice and refused to surrender.

Lansdowne's reaction to Colenso and the 'surrender' messages was swift. He decided that Field Marshal Lord Roberts, who was in Ireland, should be commander-in-chief, with Buller as second-in-command. Following setbacks at Spion Kop and Vaal Krantz, 'Reverse Buller' relieved Ladysmith at the fourth attempt on 28 February 1900 after victory at Tugela Heights. There were further successes for Buller and Roberts, who was given significant reinforcements. But Buller's reputation was too tarnished by his early failures and he was reappointed to the Aldershot post, though there was another honour, GCMG.

He was still popular with soldiers and the British public, but his bluntness had made too many enemies in high places, including the future King Edward VII. He had long shown his disdain for the press, and *The Times* war correspondent Leo Amery was one of his fiercest critics. At a formal lunch in London on 10 October 1901, attended by Amery, Buller's temper got the better of him and he lashed out at his detractors, possibly fuelled by too much drink.

St John Brodrick had replaced Lansdowne as Secretary of State for War, and he was no friend of Buller. Nor was Roberts, who had become commander-in-chief of the army. Brodrick suggested that Roberts should remove Buller from his command. Their letters crossed, with Roberts writing: 'Buller's speech yesterday is really an extraordinary help to us, and I am strongly of the opinion that we should take advantage of his indiscretion and remove him from his command ... and I am under the impression that the king would approve of our taking the action I now suggest. Buller has brought this on himself.' Brodrick replied: 'I am very glad we are at one over the Buller question.' Buller refused to resign and was sacked. His request for a court martial was declined.

Buller retired to his Downes estate and avoided further controversy. The war in South Africa did not end until May 1902. The general died on 2 June 1908, aged sixty-eight. A scapegoat? Or, as the military historian Richard Holmes put it, 'one of the bad jokes of Victorian military history ... his campaign in South Africa in 1899 is often regarded as the very epitome of bull-headed stupidity'.

12

The Sympathetic Queen
Edmund Fowler

It is curious that four Victoria Cross heroes who tarnished their names – Field Marshal Sir Evelyn Wood, General Sir Redvers Buller, Captain Henry D'Arcy and Colour Sergeant Edmund Fowler – all fought at the disastrous battle of Hlobane Mountain during the Zulu War in 1879.

Several years after distinguishing himself Edmund Fowler faced a court martial, but he was fortunate to win the sympathy of Queen Victoria. The Irishman was born at the village of Crooke, 6 miles south-east of Waterford city, in 1861. The village had gained some notoriety in the 1798 rebellion when prisoners were held at its military barracks in brutal conditions. Little is known of Fowler's early life. Even his date of birth is uncertain. Aged fifteen or sixteen and giving his occupation as servant, he enlisted in the 90th Regiment of Foot (Perthshire Volunteers) [later the Cameronians (Scottish Rifles)] at Waterford in March 1877. After spells at Limerick and Portsmouth the regiment was posted to southern Africa. The Zulu War saw the 90th assigned to Evelyn Wood's column, and Private Fowler, with the 2nd battalion, was among the colonel's small mounted escort at Hlobane.

On the morning of 28 March 1879, Wood set off to check on the progress of Lieutenant Colonel Redvers Buller's force, which had approached the mountain from the east. Another force under Lieutenant Colonel John Russell was attempting to scale the western side. Wood soon encountered the problem that Buller and Russell faced – the narrow, rocky trails were unsuitable for mounted troops. It was a poorly planned operation. The officers had seriously underestimated the strength of the enemy position, its natural defences and the number of Zulus camped on the upper and lower plateaus.

On the way to the mountain Wood came across the Border Horse, which was supposed to link up with Buller but had got lost. The unit, some fifty strong and commanded by Lieutenant Colonel Frederick Weatherley, was mainly made up of English settlers, who were reluctant to join the fight after hearing gunfire coming from the mountain. Wood and his men, including Fowler, rode off in disgust, ascending part of the mountain and dismounting when the rocky terrain made riding impossible. Some 100 yards from the summit a Zulu sniper, hidden among boulders, opened fire. Llewellyn Lloyd, Wood's political agent and interpreter, was fatally wounded, crying out, 'My back is broken!' Wood tried to lift him on to his horse but the weight was too much, and Captain Ronald Campbell of the Coldstream Guards, the senior staff officer, carried him down to the safety of a stone kraal. Wood moved on, only for his horse to be shot and killed, the animal knocking him to the ground. Shaken but unhurt, he went to find Campbell.

Surprisingly, the Border Horse had turned up. Zulu fire was coming from a cave, and Wood ordered Weatherley's men to storm the position, but they refused. Campbell called them cowards and said he would go. Lieutenant Henry Lysons of the 90th and four other members of the escort, Fowler among them, volunteered to attack the cave. After clambering over boulders the men went up a narrow trail in single file. At the mouth of the cave Campbell was shot in the head, dying instantly. Lysons and Fowler rushed forward and opened fire as the enemy fled down subterranean passages. Campbell's body was taken to the kraal.

The deaths stunned Wood, who had lost two friends within minutes. Zulus were firing down from several positions but Wood seemed oblivious to the danger. Fearing that the bodies might be mutilated, he decided that Campbell and Lloyd must have a proper burial. The bodies were taken to a suitable spot. Then Wood remembered he had borrowed a prayer book from the captain before leaving his base at Kambula and it was in the saddle of his dead horse. He told his bugler, Alexander Walkinshaw, to retrieve the prayer book.

Walkinshaw 'walked erect through a hail of fire to the dead horse, tugged the saddle out from under the carcass, and returned with it on his head'. Wood would describe the bugler as 'one of the bravest men in the army', and he was awarded the Distinguished Conduct Medal. Native troops accompanying the escort dug the graves with their spears. As the battle raged on, and with Zulus closing in, Wood read an abridged version of the burial service.

The Border Horse were ordered to join Buller's force on the upper plateau. This time they obeyed, but another order sent them in the wrong direction and they were virtually wiped out. Meanwhile, Buller and his men were in danger of being surrounded, and a disorderly retreat began. Then came the shock of seeing the main Zulu army in the distance.

After the burial of Lloyd and Campbell it is not clear what part Wood played in the battle. He may have been in a state of shock for several hours. He would claim that he stayed on the mountain until early evening, but Fowler recorded that the colonel and his escort fled earlier. Writing to his mother two weeks later, the private stated, 'After we had ridden 3 miles we saw on our right front the whole of the Zulu army. The old man [Wood] says, "Gallop for your lives men", which we did, and a hard run we had of it for 25 miles ... We had a lucky escape, and when we reached camp [Kambula] and told the news it caused a great sensation.' Buller may have tried to cover for Wood by stating that he had arrived at Kambula before him. But Buller had spotted the Zulu army when he was still on the mountain, and Fowler's comment that 'it caused a great sensation' clearly suggests that Wood and his escort were the first to arrive at the camp.

If Wood had failed to show his usual aggressiveness in battle after the deaths of his friends, he was a changed man the following day, when the main Zulu army made the mistake of attacking his well-defended camp. With the help of Buller and his mounted men, he seized the initiative, eventually routing the enemy. Fortunately for Wood, the victory at Kambula, with relatively few casualties, overshadowed the disaster of Hlobane, which saw the loss of nearly 200 men. There was no respite for Fowler, who found himself in the thick of the fighting at Kambula and, once again, coming to the attention of his commander.

In his autobiography, *From Midshipman to Field Marshal*, Wood recalled how he succeeded in killing a Zulu chief after a plea from Fowler: 'Private Fowler, one of my personal escort, who was lying in the ditch of the fort, had asked me, "Would you kindly take a shot at that chief, sir? It's a quarter of an hour I am shooting at him, and cannot hit him at all!" Fowler handed over his carbine, but Wood failed to put it fully to his shoulder and the first shot sent him reeling backwards. His second shot was on target. On three further occasions he killed Zulus who foolishly tried to taunt him by waving a red flag.

On the evening of 29 March, Wood sat down in his tent and wrote a misleading report of the two actions which appeared in newspapers at home, including *The Times* and the *Daily News*:

Despatch from Colonel Wood. Kambula Camp.

March 29th 9.00pm. We assaulted the Kholobana [Hlobane] successfully yesterday and took some thousands of cattle but while on top about 20,000 Zulus coming from Ulundi attacked us, and we suffered considerable losses, the enemy retaking the captured cattle. Our natives deserted. Our camp was attacked today from 1.30pm to 5.30pm in the most courageous manner by about 20,000 men. We have lost about seven officers and seventy killed and wounded, but we have entirely defeated the enemy who were pursued for a considerable distance.

Buller and Major William Leet (13th Foot) were awarded the Victoria Cross for saving lives at Hlobane, as was Lieutenant Edward Browne (24th Foot) for showing similar courage at Kambula, although his citation wrongly stated Inhlobana [Hlobane] but gave the correct date, 29 March 1879. These awards were listed in *The London Gazette* of 17 June 1879. Lieutenant Lysons and Private Fowler also received the Victoria Cross, but they had to wait more than three years for their *Gazette* announcement, which came on 7 April 1882. Wood had not originally recommended them, but Lysons's father, General Sir Daniel Lysons, thought his son deserved the honour and lobbied on his behalf – and the general had some influence with the commander-in-chief at Horse Guards, the Duke of Cambridge. It was felt that Fowler should get equal treatment.

Fowler also took part in the battle of Ulundi on 4 July 1879, which was the last major engagement of the war, ending the power of the Zulus. He was still only a teenager, but he appears to have become disillusioned with the army, possibly because his courage had not been officially recognised. Back in England in January 1880 he purchased his discharge, handing over the large sum – for a private – of £18. He had served less than three years. But in February 1882 he re-enlisted, this time in the 2nd Battalion Royal Irish Regiment. Perhaps he had been told he was being awarded the Victoria Cross – and civilian life did not have that much appeal after all. At Windsor Castle on 13 May, Queen Victoria presented him with his decoration, and in August he sailed off to take part in the Egyptian campaign. By the end of the year he had been promoted sergeant.

Fowler returned to England in May 1883, and at Aldershot a few weeks later he married a woman from County Donegal, Mary McGuire. Later that year he was posted to India. Enteric fever and a bad case of varicose veins took a toll on his health, and he was sent home after a medical board recommended a change of climate. There was a posting to Ireland, and his career during that time appeared uneventful until December 1886, when he was accused of embezzling money 'from a comrade'. After a spell in detention he faced a court martial at Devonport the following month. He was sentenced to be reduced to the ranks and to forfeit his Victoria Cross and campaign medals. The War Office asked Queen Victoria to confirm the forfeiture, but she refused. Her secretary, Sir Henry Ponsonby, wrote: 'The Queen cannot bring herself to sign this submission ... He is still considered fit to serve the Queen and Her Majesty thinks he should retain his Victoria Cross.' The queen may have remembered the young face at the Windsor investiture a few years earlier.

Fowler kept all his medals and one year after the court martial he had his good conduct pay restored. By September 1891 he was back in the rank of sergeant. There were various postings in Ireland, but in 1896 he transferred to his old regiment, the Cameronians, and went to Scotland. However, severe leg ulcers and varicose veins continued to trouble him, and the colour sergeant was given a medical discharge in February 1900. His character was recorded as 'good'.

Fowler settled in the garrison town of Colchester, Essex, with his wife and six children, four daughters and two sons. He took a job running a pub called the Live and Let Live, but it was not long before he was in trouble with the authorities. In February 1901 he appeared in court accused of selling alcohol after licensing hours. A constable had spotted him giving a gallon of beer to a sergeant in the Essex Regiment eighteen minutes after closing time. Fowler was clearly advised by his solicitor to make the most of his heroism. He turned up in court with his breast 'covered with medals', and the lawyer proceeded to read a 'thrilling description' of how he had won the Victoria Cross. The court heard that Sir Evelyn Wood 'declared that the deed was the bravest he had ever seen'. The hero, perhaps not surprisingly in an army town, was acquitted. It was deemed a technical offence, and 'the bench hoped Fowler would be more careful in future'. He may have run another pub in the town and also a greengrocer's shop, which was apparently damaged by fire, but by February 1906 he was so short of money that he sold his Victoria Cross, which fetched £42 at a Sotheby's auction. Little is known of his life from this point up to his death on 26 March 1926, at the age of sixty-five or sixty-six.

Fowler may have been a forgotten hero in his last years, but his death was marked by 'most impressive' military honours in Colchester. It is worth recording the tribute:

Not only was every unit in [the] garrison represented, but [the] deceased's old regiment – the Cameronians (Scottish Rifles) – was represented by Colonel Ferrers, DSO, Captain Carroll, a veteran of the Zulu war, as well as by a special detachment of men to furnish [the] firing party, bearers and mourners.

Quite a crowd of civilians watched the assembly of the units at West View, Berechurch Road, the late residence of the deceased, and the body having been borne to the Royal Artillery gun carriage, with the RSM as outrider in charge of the team, and sergeant majors from the 78th, 83rd and 85th Batteries riding the three pairs of fine black horses, the imposing procession passed slowly and solemnly along Meyrick Crescent, the pipes of the Scottish Rifles under Pipe Major Eady, skirling *The Flowers Of The Forest*. As chief mourner walked Colonel Ferrers, who was accompanied by Captain G. D. Melville, garrison adjutant (in charge of the parade) and other officers; then followed one warrant officer and five NCOs from the 3rd/6th Dragoon Guards, 11th Field Regiment, RA, 4th Division Signals, 2nd Norfolk Regiment, 1st Suffolk Regiment, details 2nd Royal Scots, 2nd Battalion The Leicestershire Regiment and the 1st Battalion The Essex Regiment, with one WO and three NCOs of the RASC, RAMC and RAOC. The regimental mourners carried many wreaths, and among the complimentary visitors were ex-Sergeant Kershaw (late deceased's regiment), Mr W. O. Rippier (Norfolk Regiment OCA), Mr Mark Mills (Royal Artillery OCA) and Mr F Hayter, a former colleague of [the] deceased's during the war [presumably the First World War] in the Transport Office.

The 'most impressive' tribute came less than eight years after the end of the First World War, when a nation weary of conflict had seen so much sacrifice. Edmund Fowler VC was buried in the local cemetery, where 'a large crowd had foregathered' at the entrance.

13

A Faked Death?

Henry D'Arcy

For many years it was believed that a skeleton found at a cave in the wilderness was all that remained of Captain Henry D'Arcy, a hero of the Zulu War. Then came the intriguing possibility that the officer who was twice recommended for the Victoria Cross might have faked his death.

D'Arcy, usually known by his second name, Cecil, was born at Wanganui, New Zealand, on 11 August 1850, the son of Major Oliver D'Arcy, who was stationed there with the 65th Regiment (2nd Yorkshire, North Riding) of Foot. He would be one of nine children. Six years later the family went to England. D'Arcy's father, an Irishman, transferred to the 18th (The Royal Irish) Regiment of Foot and was posted to southern Africa in 1859. The family were given quarters in King William's Town on the banks of the Buffalo River in the Cape. The outdoor life suited D'Arcy and his older brother Richard:

They were never to know the meaning of the word fear and lived their comparatively short lives to the full. They were born leaders, the instigators of many a wild escapade and, no doubt, a constant source of anxiety to their parents and the despair of the parents of other boys who followed their example. They roamed the countryside on foot and on horseback, swam the rivers and became expert shots and horsemen. These activities developed in them exceptional powers of endurance ...

Major D'Arcy's service with the 18th was short-lived and he transferred again, this time to a local unit, the Cape Mounted Riflemen, probably because he had decided to remain in the country after retirement. When it came to a career the young D'Arcy seems to have lost his adventurous streak, opting for a position as a government clerk at Grahamstown. However, the Galeka conflict in 1877 saw him giving up the desk job and joining the Albany Mounted Volunteers as a trooper. He was soon promoted sergeant major. After a few months he switched to the Frontier Light Horse in the same rank, and promotion to lieutenant followed.

In April 1878 Lieutenant Colonel Redvers Buller was given command of the Frontier Light Horse, and D'Arcy was involved in long patrols and several tribal engagements before the year was out. D'Arcy's first major test came on 28 March 1879 during the disastrous attack on Hlobane Mountain, when Zulus routed Colonel Evelyn Wood's troops. The twenty-eight-year-old lieutenant, along with Buller and a handful of men, played a key role in trying to hold back the warriors as soldiers stumbled down the mountain through the steep, boulder-strewn Devil's Pass. A crashing boulder 'about the size of a small piano' crushed one of his horse's legs and he put the animal out of its misery with a revolver shot. Soon afterwards a falling horse knocked him over, almost crushing him. With Zulus surging forward, he managed to jump to a lower level and struggled on in his heavy boots, with a carbine and seventy rounds of ammunition. A trooper from his unit caught a loose horse and D'Arcy mounted it, but he had not gone far when he heard a wounded soldier shouting for help. D'Arcy dismounted and put the man on the horse.

A report noted this act of bravery: 'The officers could not imbue the men with their calm spirit, and the retreat soon became a wild stampede. The Zulus were soon among the struggling horses, and their riders fell victims to the stab of the assegai. In this fearful scene a trooper was dismounted and cried aloud for help. D'Arcy gave up the horse he was riding to this man, and continued his flight on foot.' Buller and Lieutenant Alfred Blaine of the Frontier Light Horse went to D'Arcy's assistance. With difficulty, the weary officer climbed behind Buller, who took him a short distance before returning to the fight. Blaine and then Major Edmund Tremlett made sure that he reached the safety of Wood's camp at Kambula. D'Arcy was among Wood's recommendations for the Victoria Cross, but it was not approved on the grounds that he was a member of a volunteer unit – a decision that angered the colonial authorities.

D'Arcy was back in action the next day, 29 March, when the main Zulu army attacked Wood's men at Kambula. The Frontier Light Horse, with the lieutenant second in command, galloped out of the camp before the Zulus could form their 'two horns' attack and tricked a large body of them into advancing, which led to high casualties from artillery fire. The battle was a decisive defeat for the Zulus, and Buller's mounted men, avenging Hlobane, showed no mercy as they fled. In a letter to his parents, D'Arcy told of the high death toll:

> We have buried 800 of them that were killed close to the camp, but there were hundreds and hundreds of men some miles off, that are being eaten by dogs and vultures. We got about twenty or thirty of the 24th rifles, some carbines belonging to the men from the day before, and a number of little things from the general's camp, beside some 500 odd rifles of various descriptions.

The '24th rifles' and the 'little things from the general's camps' were grim reminders of the massacre at Isandlwana on 22 January.

In the weeks that followed, the mounted men carried out more patrols, checking on Zulu movements. D'Arcy was gaining a reputation for being 'rather reckless'. On one occasion he was setting fire to native huts while smoking a pipe 'with the utmost calm' as bullets threw up dust all around him. Another officer rushed forward and reportedly said: 'For heaven's sake, D'Arcy, give me a light and let me die smoking too.' D'Arcy 'burst into a hearty fit of laughter'.

Promoted captain and taking over command of the Frontier Light Horse from Buller, he had another lucky escape on 3 July, the day before Lieutenant General Lord Chelmsford's attack on Ulundi, the Zulu capital. Buller led a mounted force, including the Frontier Light Horse and the Transvaal Rangers, on a scouting mission. Small groups of Zulus were spotted and as the soldiers neared a grassy hollow Buller slowed his men, suspecting a trap. Moments later some 3,000 Zulus rose from the grass in a semi-circle and opened fire. Buller's heavily outnumbered force retreated. Most of the Zulu shots were high, but three troopers and six horses were hit. With great difficulty, Captain Lord William Beresford and Sergeant Edmund O'Toole rescued a wounded trooper who was so dazed he did not know he needed saving. Beresford threatened to 'punch his head' if he did not obey and get on the captain's horse.

D'Arcy went to the aid of another trooper, a large man called Raubenheim, who had fallen from his horse and could not stand. Dismounting, D'Arcy managed to lift him on to his horse. They were about to ride away when the horse threw them to the ground. In trying to repeat the process D'Arcy strained his back so badly that he found he could no longer lift the now unconscious man. With Zulus yards away he remounted and had a 'miraculous' escape. Raubenheim was captured and mutilated during the night, his cries being heard by some of Chelmsford's men. In a despatch two days later, Buller wrote: 'Commandant D'Arcy, Frontier Light Horse, reckons neither inconvenience nor danger in the execution of any order, determined and bold, he has frequently shown great personal gallantry, and has always given a fine example to his men.'

D'Arcy, Beresford (9th Lancers) and O'Toole (Frontier Light Horse) were awarded the Victoria Cross for their actions that day. But again there was controversy. Beresford's award was the only one announced by the War Office on 23 August. To his credit the captain indicated he would not accept it if the bravery of D'Arcy and O'Toole went unrecognised. And D'Arcy may have made the case for O'Toole. The War Office relented and a further announcement was made on 9 October. In D'Arcy's case, it was widely felt that justice had been done at last in light of his bravery at Hlobane and the recommendation that was not approved. Lieutenant General Sir Garnet Wolseley, Chelmsford's successor, presented D'Arcy with his decoration in Pretoria on 10 December. The general is reported to have said:

Commandant D'Arcy, I have today to perform a very pleasant duty. It has been my great pleasure to affix the Victoria Cross, the honour most coveted of all by a soldier and the highest which

Her Majesty can bestow, upon the breast of many a brave soldier since I arrived in South Africa. But on no former occasion have I experienced greater pleasure or satisfaction in doing so than in now affixing this Victoria Cross upon the breast of one who has conducted himself in the distinguished and signal way in which we have just heard. I am sure, Mr D'Arcy, that not only in South Africa, but in every other colony of the British Empire, it will now be understood, from the gift of this decoration by Her Majesty, that Her Majesty does not reserve this honour for imperial troops alone, but is anxious to distinguish the courage and devotion of the soldiers of her colonial empire.

Disenchanted colonials no doubt welcomed the general's message, but how sincere was Wolseley? In his diary, he wrote, 'I gave away the VC to Captain D'Arcy today on parade. I don't think he was a good case for the citation, as he did not succeed in saving the life of the man he dismounted to assist.'

D'Arcy had hurt his back so badly on 3 July that he was unable to take part in the battle of Ulundi. The Frontier Light Horse was disbanded after the Zulu campaign, and he joined his father's old regiment, the revived Cape Mounted Riflemen, commanding a squadron. Another conflict arose in 1880, this time involving Basutoland after the Cape authorities tried to disarm the Basutos and reduce the power of their chiefs. In July D'Arcy left King William's Town with 165 men, and they fought in several engagements. He continued 'to uphold the brilliant reputation he had so well earned'. But by April 1881, shortly before a peace agreement, he was forced to resign his commission, apparently because of drunkenness and depression.

D'Arcy told a newspaper that he left the Cape Mounted Riflemen for 'private' reasons. He may have been unhappy with the way his unit was being led. But campaigning had taken a toll on his health, and he was suffering from malaria and bilharzia, a tropical disease associated with contaminated water. He bought a farm north of King William's Town, but his condition did not improve and he would go for long solitary walks, which failed to help his mental state. On 4 August he went to stay with the Reverend Charles Taberer and his wife, friends of his parents, at St Matthew's mission station,

Keiskammahoek. They had suggested that the mountain air might help him. A few evenings later D'Arcy retired early, complaining of tiredness. The next morning the clergyman took him a cup coffee, only to find the room empty. The bed had not been slept in, and there was no sign of their guest.

A relative would write later: 'What drove Cecil out that night will never be known. Several theories may be considered. It can be accepted that he drank too much. Several members of the family have been asthma sufferers, a hereditary complaint, and he may have been driven out in search of fresh air. He had been exposed to bilharzia and malaria, infections which debilitate a constitution and bring about spells of morbid depression.'

Thinking that his guest would return later, Taberer did not raise the alarm immediately. The next day 200 natives helped in a search of the surrounding area. A few days later a coat belonging to D'Arcy, who would have been thirty-one on 11 August, was found on a boulder, but a further search proved fruitless. It was assumed that the Victoria Cross hero was no longer alive. Taberer was mortified to find himself accused of gross neglect in letters to newspapers. However, in one paper there was a fine tribute to D'Arcy:

With all with whom he came in contact he was a great favourite, and especially so with his men, none of whom ever sought redress in vain from him. Such was their confidence that if D'Arcy was to command, everyone rested assured that, come what may, they were in the hands of a skilful and daring leader. Since 1877, with scarcely any intermission, he has served his country most faithfully and gallantly. As a private gentleman he was much esteemed, and many will never forget the many happy hours spent in his company. The beau-ideal of a soldier, a gentleman in the truest sense of the word, and a sincere friend, his loss will long be mourned by those who knew him well, as well as those who have watched with so much interest his very brilliant military career.

D'Arcy's disappearance took a new turn on 28 December 1881, when a native reported finding the remains of man in a cave in the

Amatola Forest some 6 miles from St Matthew's mission station. A party led by Taberer went to the scene, and found a ring and a pocket watch belonging to D'Arcy, along with shreds of clothing. Curiously, the skeleton was in a sitting position with the back against the rock wall and the legs stretched out, as if it had been placed there. It was assumed that the remains were those of D'Arcy and he had died of exposure, prompting speculation he intended suicide. On 3 January 1882 D'Arcy was given a military funeral at King William's Town cemetery. Taberer took part in the service.

But was it the body of the Victoria Cross hero? It has been suggested that D'Arcy faked his death to start a new life, changing clothes with a body he found in the forest during bad weather and planting his ring and watch. There were unconfirmed reports that he went to Kenya and settled near Mount Kilimanjaro. Papers given to the Killie Campbell Africana Library claim that D'Arcy was spotted at a cricket match in Newcastle, Natal, in 1925. One of the cricketers, V. G. Sparks, recognised him from a photograph. Sparks approached the man, who pleaded that he should tell no one as 'he wished to remain dead to the world'.

14

The Womaniser
James Collis

James Collis won the Victoria Cross during one of the British Army's worst defeats, the battle and retreat from Maiwand in Afghanistan in July 1880. Fifteen years later he was stripped of his decoration. Women were his downfall.

The Second Afghan War had been launched in November 1878 after the country's amir, Sher Ali, rejected peace overtures from Britain and signed a treaty with Russia, which was seen as a threat to India. The British saw a succession of victories – Ali Musjid, Peiwar Kotal, Charasia, Kabul and Ahmed Khel. Sher Ali fled after the Peiwar Kotal defeat to be replaced by his son, Yakub Khan, who soon abdicated. Abdur Rahman, a nephew of Sher Ali and pro-British, became ruler but Ayub Khan, brother of Yakub Khan, claimed the throne and headed for the strategic city of Kandahar with a force estimated at 10,000.

It fell to Brigadier George Burrows with some 2,700 men, mostly Indian soldiers, to stop Ayub Khan. The brigadier's column – one infantry brigade, one cavalry brigade and a Royal Horse Artillery battery – left Kandahar on 3 July 1880, expecting to be joined by around 6,000 friendly tribesmen. But in a country of shifting allegiances, the tribesmen suddenly decided they preferred to be friends with Ayub and swelled his ranks. Unknown to Burrows, he was heading towards an enemy that, in fact, numbered at least 25,000, including many religious fanatics known as ghazis. The decisive encounter would be near the village of Maiwand, 45 miles from Kandahar. In the early hours of 27 July, the Anglo-Indian force left its camp on empty stomachs and already tired. By nine o'clock the heat was intense as the soldiers headed along a wide valley covered with stones and scrub. The shimmering haze made it difficult to see far ahead.

James Collis was a twenty-four-year-old gunner in the Royal Horse Artillery's 'E' battery, commanded by Major George Blackwood. At about 10 a.m. small groups of enemy cavalry were spotted in the distance. Shortly afterwards an officer of the 3rd Bombay Light Cavalry saw 'dark masses which I first took for belts of tress'. This was the main body of Ayub Khan's army heading west towards Maiwand. Burrows's force was on an open plain, and Collis soon found himself in action. There was an artillery duel. 'We began firing from the right of the battery,' Collis recalled. 'After we had fired a few rounds their artillery replied. The first shot struck the near wheel of my gun, killing a gunner, wounding another and Lieutenant Fowler [Lieutenant Newton Fowell]. The limber box upon my gun was smashed by a shell, which also killed the wheel horses, but did not touch the driver. Several riding horses of my battery were killed, and a good deal of damage done to the guns and carriages. Four gunners and Sergeant Wood, the No 1 of my gun, were killed, leaving only three men to work the gun. I took Sergeant Wood's place.'

The enemy used a ravine as cover and then moved forward on both flanks. Despite taking heavy casualties, they pressed on with their superior numbers. And the toll on Burrows's small force continued to grow.

Collis recorded:

About half past one some of Jacob's Rifles [30th Bombay Native Infantry], who were lying 10 yards in the rear, began to be panic-stricken and crowding round our guns and carriages, some getting under the carriages. Three got under my gun. We tried to drive them away but it was no use. About that time we ceased firing for a little. The enemy on the left got pretty close up. To check them General Nuttall [Brigadier Thomas Nuttall, the cavalry commander] formed up the 3rd Bombay Cavalry and the 3rd Scinde Horse to charge. Gunner Smith of my gun, seeing what was going to be done, mounted his horse and joined the cavalry. After going about 300 yards, the enemy being about 200 yards off, the whole line, with the exception of the general, the European officers and Gunner Smith, turned tail. General Nuttall with the officers, finding themselves deserted, returned. General Nuttall was actually crying from mortification. Gunner Smith dashed on alone and was cut down.

Burrows should have ordered a retreat to the village of Mundabad, which his force had passed through earlier and where he could have set up a defensive line. His reserve ammunition and other supplies were there, along with water, which his men desperately needed in the unyielding heat. But he left it too late. Instead, the troops were trapped in the open as the enemy pushed forward in a pincer movement. At about 4 p.m. Major Blackwood ordered the Royal Horse Artillery battery to retire, although Lieutenant Hector Maclaine shouted, 'No, no. Let's give them another round.' Some of the guns, with Collis, were taken away. At one point Blackwood was shot in the thigh and ended up with men of the 66th Regiment [later the Royal Berkshire Regiment], the only British infantry unit at the battle. The 66th were in the open fighting on two sides, and some 100 men managed to retire to Khig, where houses and garden walls offered some protection. The soldiers, along with Blackwood, fought on until only two officers and nine other ranks were left in a garden, completely surrounded. Rather than surrender, they charged out and were cut down. There were no survivors.

Burrows was left with only one option: a general retreat towards Kandahar, with the enemy in pursuit, supported by harassing artillery. Captain John Slade of the Royal Horse Artillery, who took command of the battery from Blackwood, told of their plight:

All over the wide expanse of desert are to be seen men in twos and threes retreating. Camels have thrown their loads, sick men, almost naked, are astride donkeys, mules and camels. The bearers have left the wounded to their fate. The guns and carriages are crowded with the helpless wounded suffering the tortures of the damned, horses are limping along with ugly wounds and men are pressing eagerly to the rear in the hope of finding water. Hordes of irregular horsemen are to be seen amongst our baggage animals, relentlessly cutting our men down and looting. A few alone remain with Brigadier Burrows to try and turn the rout into an orderly retreat.

And so it goes on for five or six miles, till the sun begins to sink into the horizon. The cries for Water! Water! become more frequent and louder. Most suffer in silence for they can hardly speak. After a long search in the dead of night a deep well full of muddy water is found in the village of Hauz-i-Madat. There is just sufficient to satisfy the wounded and those in severe distress, but none can be spared for the already worn out and exhausted horses. Everyone's hand is against us. Villagers from all sides creep up behind the low mud walls and fire on us, and many a gallant fellow who had battled against the trials of the night fell victim to the jezail [Afghan musket].

Collis remained remarkably calm during the retreat:

A shell burst open our treasure chest. Many of the troops and camp followers stopped to pick up the money and were overtaken and killed. Just after that some of the enemy's cavalry caught up the guns. One of them wounded me on the eyebrow as he passed. He wheeled round and came at me again. I took my carbine, waited till he was four or five yards of me, then let drive, hitting him on the chest and knocking him off his horse. As he fell his money came out of his turban, and trumpeter Jones jumped off his horse and picked it up. It was now dusk, and I got off to walk beside my gun. Seeing a village close by, and some men at a well, I followed them and got some water. Just as we reached the well the enemy charged and drove us off, killing a good many.

Collis found around ten sick and wounded soldiers of the 66th lying by the road and put them on his gun and limber. Thirst and fatigue tormented the retreating force throughout the night. On the afternoon of 28 July they reached a village called Kokeran, some 7 miles from Kandahar. As Collis went to find water for the men he had saved, he spotted about a dozen enemy cavalry heading towards his gun. Hiding in a ditch, he opened fire with a rifle to draw them away, shooting two men and probably saving many lives. 'I fancy they thought that a number were hid there, for they stopped and fired at me from the saddle,' said Collis. 'After firing about 35 rounds General Nuttall came up with some native cavalry and drove them off. General Nuttall asked me my name, saying,

"You're a gallant young man." He entered it in a pocket book, and then rode off. I then followed up my gun, which I found some 500 yards distant, by the side of a river. The enemy's fire, which had been going on all the way from Maiwand, now became hotter, the surrounding hills being full of them. Some of the garrison of Kandahar met us about four miles out and escorted us in.'

Burrows lost nearly 1,000 men, but the cost to Ayub Khan was more than 5,500. Ayub's weakened force besieged Kandahar, but he was finally defeated on 1 September after an epic 300-mile march from Kabul by Lieutenant General Sir Frederick Roberts's army.

Collis had also distinguished himself in August when he took a message to the officer in charge of a village about 200 yards from Kandahar, where fighting was raging. The gunner was lowered some 35 feet down a city wall by rope and then hauled back up after successfully completing his mission. 'When half way up I was fired at again, one bullet cutting off the heel of my left boot,' he said. 'General Primrose congratulated me, and Colonel Burnet gave me a drop out of his flask, for what with not having recovered from the fatigues of Maiwand and the exertion and excitement of this trip, I was a bit faint.'

On 17 May 1881 *The London Gazette* announced the award of the Victoria Cross to Collis: 'For conspicuous bravery during the retreat from Maiwand to Kandahar, on the 28th July, 1880, when the Officer commanding the battery was endeavouring to bring on a limber, with wounded men, under a cross fire, in running forward and drawing the enemy's fire on himself, thus taking off their attention from the limber.' The Victoria Cross was also awarded to another member of the Royal Horse Artillery battery, Sergeant Patrick Mullane, who had rescued a soldier yards from the enemy. He also obtained water for wounded men from a village where 'so many men lost their lives'. Collis and Mullane were presented with their medals at Poona, India, in July 1881.

Collis was born in Cambridge on 19 April 1856, the son of a coal porter. He had two brothers, both of whom joined the army, and a sister. Collis worked as a groom at Newmarket before enlisting in the 46th Regiment in 1872, transferring to the Royal Horse Artillery five years later. He was discharged from the army in the year he received his Victoria Cross and joined the Bombay police, rising to the rank of inspector. During his time in India he married a widow, one Adela Skuse, and they had three sons and a daughter. In 1884 Collis returned to Britain, apparently without his family. Three years later he re-enlisted in the army, this time joining the Suffolk Regiment. The following year Collis found himself serving in India, but it is not clear if he was reunited with his wife. Health problems emerged and in 1891 he was invalided home with rheumatic fever and discharged, his wife remaining in India.

In 1893, working as a park keeper for London County Council, he married a cook, Mary Goddard, who was unaware that he already had a wife and children. Goddard discovered the deception in March 1895, and it led to Collis appearing at the Old Bailey in November, charged with bigamy. The second Mrs Collis no doubt took exception to his attitude. When she announced that she planned to leave him, he 'told her to clear out as he had another girl to take her place'. After his arrest Collis said he thought he was free to marry again as he had not seen his first wife for years. He asked police 'not to stir up dirty water'. The court heard that he had been involved with a third woman, whom he abandoned after she gave birth to a disabled child. He had treated all the women with 'the greatest cruelty'. The judge told Collis that the Victoria Cross had saved him from 'a severe sentence of penal servitude' – but still jailed him for eighteen months with hard labour.

At the end of the trial the prosecution pointed out that a woman who gave evidence had been sacked from her job in a pub in Woolwich, south London. The judge told police to inform the licensing justices – 'he was sure that the justices would take a very serious view of the matter unless the young woman was restored to her employment'. It is not clear if this was Mary Goddard or another woman involved with Collis.

The War Office learned of the conviction and set in motion a royal warrant to deprive Collis of his Victoria Cross. The Home Office was also asked to locate the medal and send it. This request generated months of correspondence between the War Office, the Home Office, New Scotland Yard and Peckham police station. It emerged that a hard-up Collis had pawned his Victoria Cross and Afghanistan campaign medal for 8s before the court case. He gave the pawn ticket to a Miss Ada Price, living in Dulwich, who may have been another of his conquests. Police obtained the ticket, but when they went to the pawnbroker, a Mr Humphreys, of Peckham, he refused to hand over the medals without payment of 8s, saying he would consult a solicitor. Police went away empty-handed. The War Office eventually obtained the medals after giving a written promise to refund the money to New Scotland Yard.

After his release from prison Collis settled in Bury St Edmunds, Suffolk, working for a time delivering goods using a horse and cart. In July 1912 he was discovered in the infirmary of a Cambridge workhouse. A local newspaper journalist interviewed him, and an article appeared under the headline 'Cambridge Veteran's Pitiable Plight'. Collis, lying on a bed in the male ward, was described as 'well past his prime'. The report went on:

As soon as the visitor had made himself known the old soldier entered readily into conversation – now and then, as he recalled some of the thrilling events which are associated with active service, and as he told once again the touching story of how he won the Victoria Cross, he raised himself on to his elbows, slightly flushed with excitement, and there sounded the note of tragedy as he sank back for a moment to regain his breath. One felt a pang of commiseration for the brazened survivor, who had served his Queen and country well, but had been allowed in the later days of his life to find his shelter in the workhouse.

Collis gave a lucid account of his exploits during the battle and retreat from Maiwand. But there was no mention of his conviction for bigamy or the fact that the Victoria Cross had been taken away from him.

After the First World War broke out he once again volunteered for army service, re-enlisting in the Suffolk Regiment. At fifty-eight, he was considered too old for active service and remained on the home front as a drill instructor. But he continued to suffer from poor health and was medically discharged in 1917. He obtained a job as a gatekeeper at a bus depot in Battersea, south London, but heart trouble resulted in him being admitted to a local hospital, where he died on 28 June 1918, aged sixty-two.

Deservedly, the Victoria Cross hero was given a military funeral, his coffin borne on a gun carriage to a cemetery in Wandsworth.

However, no members of his family attended, and no money was available for a proper burial plot or a headstone. James Collis was buried in an unmarked pauper's grave. In May 1998 a headstone in his honour was unveiled at the cemetery in a short ceremony. The headstone displayed the regimental badge of the Suffolk Regiment and the design of the Victoria Cross, giving the impression that he had won the decoration with the infantry and not the Royal Horse Artillery. But at least, after eighty years, one unit of the British Army was proud to be associated with the man who had been convicted of bigamy, perhaps not the most serious of criminal offences.

Collis's family unexpectedly took an interest in the hero two years after his death. His sister, Hannah Haylock, asked the War Office to reinstate his award. As it involved a royal warrant the matter was referred to King George V, who took a sympathetic line: 'Even were a VC to be sentenced to be hanged for murder, he should be allowed to wear the VC on the scaffold.' However, Secretary of State for War Winston Churchill opposed the move, suggesting that Collis had placed little value on the decoration because he had pawned it. Churchill also questioned why the family were showing such interest when they had shunned Collis for years. With some irony, the minister had earlier approved amendments to the original royal warrant for the Victoria Cross so that only the most serious crimes such as treason would lead to forfeiture. Bigamy was not included.

Churchill's opposition saved the War Office from embarrassment because officials would not have been able to produce the Collis Victoria Cross if it had been decided to hand back the decoration. Perhaps Churchill was advised that it had long ago disappeared from War Office safekeeping. In 2014 the collector Lord Ashcroft stated: 'The precise whereabouts of the Collis VC between late 1896 and 1938 are not known although it would seem that it went initially, as was required at the time, into the possession of the solicitor general, a later holder of which office had an interest in gallantry medals. When that solicitor general died unexpectedly and the VC was found at his home it was decided to sell it.' The solicitor general at the time of the confiscation was Robert Finlay, later Viscount Finlay. But whether the medal ended up with another solicitor general must be open to question because its whereabouts were certainly known in 1911 – and none of Finlay's successors died that year.

The Collis VC was in the possession of Lieutenant Colonel J. B. [James Bellhouse] Gaskell, an obsessive collector of medals, paintings, books and Japanese ivories. He was wealthy, thanks to his father, who had founded a chemical business that later became part of the giant United Alkali Company. The colonel, who served as a militia officer with the South Lancashire Regiment, was a director of this and other companies. Gaskell was described as 'a man of refined instincts who found it possible to combine commercial activities with an earnest pursuit of art'. He was a well-known figure in Liverpool, where he had a splendid home, Roseleigh, at Woolton. In 1911 Gaskell decided to dispose of his medal collection, including the Collis VC, which went for £52 at a Glendining's auction in London in the May. How had Gaskell, a magistrate, obtained the Cross in the first place? It is not known, but he would have had contacts in the collecting world and in military circles. There is a suspicion that the medal was stolen from the War Office. Collis, who fell on hard times after his bigamy conviction, was probably unaware of the sale. Gaskell died in 1925, aged seventy-seven, leaving a fortune.

The Collis VC appeared at another Glendining's auction in 1938, when it was bought by Colonel H. J. P. Oakley for his collection. After Oakley's death his daughter asked Sotheby's to sell it, and in 1979 the Cross, along with a renamed Afghanistan campaign medal, fetched £5,800. But questions were raised by 'various sources' about the true ownership of the Cross. The sale was cancelled, and the Ministry of Defence carried out 'exhaustive' inquiries. 'In due course it was solidly established that there was no outstanding official claim on the Cross,' said James Morton, of auctioneers Morton & Eden, who worked for Sotheby's at the time. 'Accordingly it could be sold with clear title.' The question of a family claim does not appear to have been raised. The two medals went back on sale in late 1980, fetching £7,200. In 2014 Lord Ashcroft acquired Collis's Victoria Cross for an undisclosed sum in a private sale. In 2015 the Ministry of Defence was unable to locate the file on its 1979 investigation.

Collis had pawned his Victoria Cross but never sold it. Perhaps he hoped for better times and the possibility of raising those eight shillings to redeem his medals. Eight shillings is equivalent to 40 pence today.

15

A Real Bad Hat
Frederick Corbett

Frederick Corbett was 'a real bad hat, and it is a pity that he was ever awarded the Victoria Cross'. That was the view of Canon William Lummis, the respected Victoria Cross researcher.

Corbett was not his real name. Until his twenties he was David Embleton. Born on 17 September 1853 in Maldon, Essex, he was the son of William and Jane Embleton. His father was a baker, and there were many mouths to feed – the couple had twelve children. David Embleton's early life in Maldon, a town recorded in Domesday Book, is something of a mystery. As a teenager, presumably after little schooling, he became an apprentice metalworker. During that time he enlisted in the Essex Rifle Volunteers, based locally. At the age of twenty-five, he decided to join the regular army, enlisting in the 3rd Battalion The 60th, The King's Royal Rifle Corps in 1879, the year of the Zulu War. But he signed on as one Frederick Corbett, and it is not known why he chose a different name. It was not unusual for men to join the Victorian army using a false identity, though it was often an indication that they were trying to escape from something – perhaps a crime, or a pregnant woman. Or maybe there had been a rift with his large family and Corbett wanted to sever links.

In any case, Corbett was soon out of the country, with his regiment heading to southern Africa among reinforcements to fight the Zulus, who had inflicted the early humiliation of Isandlwana. Private Corbett did not see any action in that conflict, which barely lasted six months, and he does not appear to have taken part in the

First Boer War the following year, even though the 3rd Battalion fought in several engagements – Laing's Nek on 28 January, Ingogo on 8 February (five companies) and Majuba on 27 February (three companies). Ingogo was a costly defeat, the battalion losing five out of thirteen officers and 119 of its 295 other ranks. It is known, however, that Corbett was in Cape Town in February 1882 and sailed with his regiment, which had dropped The 60th from its title, to Malta in the troopship HMS *Orontes*. Another conflict was looming and in July the soldiers went on to Cyprus.

The focus was Egypt and its jewel, the Suez Canal, which Britain wanted to protect at all costs in the face of growing nationalism, led by a rebellious Egyptian army that had weakened the ruling Khedive. British nationals and other investments were also at risk. The first major engagement was the naval bombardment of Alexandria on 11 July 1882. Vice Admiral Sir Beauchamp Seymour, commander-in-chief of the Mediterranean fleet, had arrived off the port with a squadron and warned the Egyptians to stop fortifying Alexandria. When the work continued and batteries refused to surrender, he gave the order to open fire. The bombardment lasted more than ten hours. A white flag appeared the next day, and marines were landed, taking up key positions in the city, which had seen much destruction, some of it by retreating Egyptian troops. On 17 July Major General Sir Archibald Allison arrived with reinforcements, including the 3rd Battalion. But the force was missing cavalry, and it was decided to form a mounted infantry company from soldiers who could ride, using fine horses from the Khedive's stables. Corbett was one of the men picked, and he was soon in action. The unit was sent to Mallaha junction, 8 miles from Alexandria, on 22 July to protect an armoured train that had been sent to blow up the railway line. The mounted infantry stopped Egyptian cavalry attacking the train.

Corbett had been appointed batman to Lieutenant Henry Howard-Vyse and accompanied him when a force of mounted infantry and men of the 38th and 46th regiments, along with marines and naval artillery, went on a reconnaissance mission to Kafr Dowar on 5 August. They reached a canal and the force split to patrol both sides. Suddenly the enemy opened fire with artillery and then 'a discharge of musketry so vigorous and well sustained that the colonel of the 38th spoke of it as one of the heaviest fires he remembered to have witnessed'. A small group comprising Major Henry Parr, Howard-Vyse, another officer and six other ranks, including Corbett, rode on, only to encounter hundreds of Egyptians. Dismounting, they returned fire, expecting to be reinforced, but they became isolated. Howard-Vyse took a rifle from Corbett 'and stood erect on the canal bank to take a shot at the enemy'. He was hit and fatally wounded. Corbett went to his aid, and it was this action that led to him receiving the Victoria Cross. *The London Gazette* of 16 February 1883 carried this citation:

> During the reconnaissance upon Kafr Dowar, on 5th August, 1882, the Mounted Infantry, with which Private Corbett was serving, came under hot fire from the enemy and suffered some loss, including Lieutenant Howard-Vyse, mortally wounded. This officer fell in the open, and there being no time to move him, Private Corbett asked and obtained permission to remain by him, and though under constant fire, he sat down and endeavoured to stop the bleeding of this officer's wounds, until the Mounted Infantry received orders to retire, when he rendered valuable assistance in carrying him off the field.

According to Major Parr, Corbett 'sat down quite contentedly with the poor boy's head on his lap'. The twenty-three-year-old lieutenant, who had been hit in the thigh, severing the femoral artery, bled to death within minutes. Private Solomon Howes was also shot dead. The main force regrouped and the enemy retreated. The dead men were buried the next day in coffins made from the wood of a barracks shed. Howard-Vyse, who had gone to Egypt 'full of buoyant spirits and ardent hope for the future', was the first army officer to be killed in the campaign. The army showed its appreciation of Private Howes's sacrifice by deducting his funeral expenses from his 'effects and credits'. In January 1883, Major Parr recommended Corbett for the Distinguished Conduct Medal, pointing out that he was 'a soldier of whose steadiness and gallantry under fire I have been frequently a witness'. The commander-in-chief, Lieutenant General Sir Garnet Wolseley, saw the recommendation and wrote: 'In my opinion this gallant soldier is well deserving of the Victoria Cross.' Arrangements were made to substitute the DCM for the VC.

Corbett had also taken part in the battle of Tel el Kebir early on 13 September 1882, when 38,000 Egyptians were driven from their positions by a much smaller force in an hour's intensive fighting. Some 2,000 Egyptians died. Fifty-seven British soldiers were killed. The victory opened the way to Cairo and the enemy's unconditional surrender. In October Major Parr became commander of the Military Foot Police, based in Cairo, and he had Corbett, 'a very nice little chap', transferred as his orderly. Promotion to corporal followed, and Corbett received his Victoria Cross from Field Marshal Lord Napier at a parade in Cairo on 2 March 1883. He returned to England, rejoining the King's Royal Rifle Corps, but he was suffering from a large varix on his thigh and given a medical discharge.

According to his family, Corbett 'lived for the army' and his character changed over the next few months. He headed to his home town of Maldon a hero but still known as David Embleton. A younger brother was recorded as saying: 'Dave came back to Maldon and was feted by everyone, including strangers, who just wanted to buy him a drink, but he was teetotal. In the end he got tired of saying he didn't drink and began to accept these. He got embarrassed that he didn't have any money and couldn't stand his corner, so he sold the Cross to a London dealer for 15 guineas. That began a rift with his elder brother, John.'

A return to civilian life does not appear to have held much attraction, and Corbett applied to rejoin the army. A medical board turned him down but he was successful at the second attempt, in December, enlisting as a driver in the Royal Horse Artillery. He kept his false name but, bizarrely, gave his place of birth as Camberwell, south London, and stated that his father was dead, even though both his parents were alive. Plainly, there was something going on with his family. In February 1884 he found himself returning to Egypt with the horse artillery. Britain had inherited Egypt's problems, which included its provinces in Sudan. The threat this time was a revolt led by Sheik Mohamed Ahmed, the self-proclaimed Mahdi, who had thousands of Muslim fundamentalist followers. Egyptian forces suffered two defeats, Kashgil and El Teb, and one of the Mahdi's military commanders, Osman Digna, put the important port of Suakin on the Red Sea under siege. A naval brigade landed by Vice Admiral Sir William Hewett, a Victoria Cross holder, saved the port from capture. There were further reinforcements, and the British inflicted serious losses on Osman Digna's forces at Tamaai. Suakin, however, continued to be menaced, and it is believed that Corbett took part in operations around the port.

Corbett returned to England in June, and here his troubles began. On 31 July he appeared before a court martial at Aldershot charged with being absent without leave and stealing goods and embezzling money, 'the property of an officer'. Found guilty, he was given twenty-eight days' hard labour. The prison governor was told to confiscate his medals but, of course, Corbett had sold his Victoria Cross after being discharged the previous year. He did, however, have a VC in his possession, as well as an Egypt campaign medal and a Khedive's Star. It is believed that at some stage he had an unofficial copy VC made, with similar name and date engraving to the original.

After serving his sentence he was allowed to remain in the army, and in October he was posted to India. His conviction had been reported to the War Office, which wrote to Queen Victoria on 10 December asking her to approve the removal of Corbett's name from the Victoria Cross Register and the loss of his pension. The queen was clearly unhappy about taking this step. Noting that he had not been dismissed from the service, she asked if he might regain his decoration 'by good and faithful conduct'. Nevertheless, Corbett's name was removed. In 1887 the queen would refuse to strip Edmund Fowler of his award. He too had been convicted of embezzlement and was allowed to continue serving in the army.

Corbett encountered more trouble in India. In February 1887 a court martial convicted him of neglecting his equipment and stealing from a comrade. The sentence was eighty-four days' hard labour. On 17 September 1889 he faced a court martial again and received another eighty-four days' hard labour for striking an NCO. Corbett returned to England in December 1890 and was 'constantly in trouble with the authorities'. Just over a year later he was finally discharged as medically unfit, again because of a varix. He had also received treatment for alcoholism and sexually transmitted diseases. There was no pension because of his poor disciplinary record, with nine entries in the regimental defaulters' book and seventeen in the battery defaulters' book.

In another twist, Corbett became David Embleton on returning to civilian life. For a time he worked as a housepainter, but he spent sixteen years at the sprawling and challenging Greenwich Union Workhouse in London. In March 1896 he was remanded at the local police court for refusing to work there. In September 1904 he appeared before Bow Street magistrates after smashing a glass panel at the War Office, apparently in protest at not having an army pension. He was given twenty-eight days' hard labour. His remaining years were spent back in Maldon – at the local workhouse, where he died on 25 September 1912, shortly after his fifty-ninth birthday. He was buried in an unmarked pauper's grave in the town's London Road cemetery. In April 2004 the officers' club of the King's Royal Rifle Corps arranged for a headstone commemorating Corbett to be erected at the grave.

Corbett certainly had his run-ins with authority, but he may have got away with one offence – making or commissioning fake Victoria Crosses with his name and selling them as genuine. Hancocks of London, the official maker of the Victoria Cross, never produced a replacement for him. However, there are known to be at least three other 'Corbett Crosses', all believed to be copies. According to Hancocks's records, the original medal has *Pte. F. Corbett, 60th Royal Rifles* [author's italics] inscribed on the reverse of the suspension bar, with *5 Aug. 1882* on the reverse of the cross. A Corbett Cross held by the Royal Green Jackets (Rifles) Museum in Winchester has *3804 Pte. F. Corbett* and *5 Aug. 1882*. The Royal Artillery Mess at Woolwich acquired a Corbett Cross with *Pte. Frederick Corbett 3rd Bn. King's Royal Rifle Corps* and *5 August 1882*. Another Corbett Cross was known to be in circulation in 1903 with the wrong date inscription *5 August 1882*. This medal came into the possession of a Middlesex council official, W. T. Mansfield, who thought it was original. With some irony, he wanted to return the Cross to Corbett and contacted the War Office for advice. Back came the reply that he should keep the medal and that it 'should not be delivered to him [Corbett] or his representatives'. The real Cross seems to have disappeared.

Canon Lummis, the Victoria Cross researcher, made some interesting comments about the decoration in a letter to a friend in 1956:

> Hancocks claim to be able to identify whether any Cross has been made by them. They are not always sure about the earlier ones; but now they have a secret mark. By the way they do not make them themselves; but contract out, and again there is a sub-contract to a little man in Clerkenwell who actually does the work! This was told me by a *News Chronicle* journalist.
>
> You are quite right about the racket in VCs. Old Glendining [a leading London auctioneer] told me personally some years ago that in the 'good old days' of Queen Victoria some dealers would come round to VC recipients and offer to buy their Crosses for £10 each. Of course they sold them at about five times this figure and made a huge profit. In those hard times men often pawned or lost their Crosses, some had them stolen. They were replaced sometimes officially – some on payment, others a free issue – while some men had duplicates made themselves. This accounts for there being two or three Crosses belonging to the same individual in existence.

Corbett had not been able to resist selling his original Cross for 15 guineas, a tidy sum then for a penniless man. Had the sale given him ideas? He was, of course, a one-time metalworker.

16

The Hungry Mouths
George Ravenhill

George Ravenhill was so short of money to feed his family that he felt he had no choice but to give up three of his children to foster care, never to see them again. His plight had been raised in the House of Commons. Help did not come, and the hero of Colenso resorted to stealing some metal worth 6s. Magistrates took a dim view of this crime, and he was sent to prison.

Ravenhill was born in the Nechells district of Birmingham, a densely populated area with poor housing, on 23 February 1872. He was the son of Thomas and Mary Ravenhill. His father, originally from Whaddon, Gloucestershire, worked as a wood turner. There would be nine children.

In May 1889, aged seventeen, Ravenhill joined the army. Unusually, the Englishman was in Ireland when he enlisted in a Scottish regiment, the Royal Scots Fusiliers, which could trace its origins to 1678 and a revolt that followed the restoration of King Charles II. He was soon on his way to India, where he spent five years with the 1st Battalion, returning to England. When the Second Boer War broke out in 1899, he sailed to South Africa with the 2nd Battalion. That conflict would see the downfall of another Victoria Cross winner, General Sir Redvers Buller, who had been reluctant to lead an expeditionary force that landed in Cape Town on 31 October. The fusiliers were among reinforcements sent to the Cape in November and they went to Durban, forming part of the 6th Brigade under the command of Major General Geoffrey Barton. There was little time to familiarise themselves with the territory or conditions, and they were in action at Colenso as early as 15 December, the British Army's Black Week, which had already seen defeats at Stormberg and Magersfontein.

Buller had decided to go to the aid of the commander in Natal, Lieutenant General Sir George White, who was trapped with his troops at Ladysmith. Boers led by Louis Botha were in well-prepared positions along a 7-mile stretch of the Tugela River, guarding the southern route to Ladysmith. The obvious river crossing was at Colenso, 12 miles from the besieged town. Buller was a brave man on the battlefield but no strategist, and his plan to advance lacked good intelligence and proper maps. He had no idea where some of the Boer positions were located. But with a force of at least 18,000 against the enemy's 4,500 he no doubt thought – or hoped – he could bludgeon his way through. The three-pronged attack began in the early hours but the left flank was soon in trouble after getting lost and taking heavy casualties.

Buller's artillery, two batteries of twelve field guns and six naval 12-pounders, was in the centre under the command of Colonel C. J. Long of the Royal Horse Artillery. The guns, escorted by two companies of the Royal Scots Fusiliers, moved off to support the infantry assault. But the army gun teams were soon galloping too far ahead of the infantry, and they did not stop until they were about 1,000 yards from the southern bank of the Tugela – to the astonishment of Botha. The 15-pounders and their crews were on an open plain and within easy range of Botha's concealed artillery and his riflemen on the northern bank. Long's charge also astounded the lieutenant responsible for the naval guns, which had lagged behind because they were being pulled by oxen. The firing from the enemy was so intense that it 'gave the British the impression they were facing 20,000 Boers'. One of the first to be hit was Long. The gunners fired back until they had exhausted their ammunition wagons. These were removed and more ammunition was brought up. But by that time a third of the gunners had been killed or wounded, and the acting commander ordered the men to abandon the guns and take shelter in a hollow nearby. Two officers rode away to get help.

Buller called off the main attack, saying, 'I'm afraid Long's guns have got us into a terrible mess.' The naval guns were still firing – to Buller's approval – but the African drivers of the oxen had fled early on, with most of the animals stampeding later. Artillery horses took the naval guns to safety. Twice Buller went to the spot where the gunners were sheltering, on the second occasion asking for volunteers to save the guns. It took a minute for the first dazed volunteer, a corporal, to stand up. He was joined by six others, and then Buller, who had a shrapnel wound, turned to his own staff and three officers volunteered, including Lieutenant Frederick Roberts of the King's Royal Rifle Corps, the only son of Field Marshal Lord Roberts. Other volunteers included George Ravenhill, 6 feet tall and well built, who went several times to the guns as the Boers kept up a withering fire. Only two of the twelve guns were saved, and Ravenhill was involved in one of the successful attempts. He was wounded in the shoulder. When casualties continued to mount in the oppressive heat, Buller decided it was a hopeless task and ordered a withdrawal.

Lieutenant Roberts was awarded the Victoria Cross, the first time it had been given posthumously. Colenso was the third defeat of Black Week, and with some irony the grieving Field Marshal Roberts, a Victoria Cross winner himself, replaced Buller as the commander-in-chief in South Africa. In 1901 the field marshal was instrumental in getting Buller sacked. In a special tribute, the War Office presented the field marshal with the gun that Lieutenant Roberts tried to save and it carried the coffin at his own funeral in 1914. A remarkable seven Victoria Crosses were awarded for Colenso.

Only four companies of the Royal Scots Fusiliers took part in the fighting that day, the rest of the battalion being kept in reserve. The fusiliers had twelve men killed and twenty wounded. Some of the men found themselves cut off after Buller's retreat, and forty-five were taken prisoner. The battalion subsequently took part in a number of engagements, and Ravenhill showed his bravery again at Frederikstad, Transvaal, winning the Distinguished Conduct Medal (DCM). Later he was taken prisoner. Freedom came after the capture of Pretoria in June 1900. His Victoria Cross was announced in *The London Gazette* of 4 June 1901, and it was presented to him by the Duke of York, later King George V, at Pietermaritzburg, Natal, in August. However, the authorities decided that one award was enough for Ravenhill, and his DCM was cancelled, even though it was for a separate act of bravery.

Little is known of Ravenhill's remaining service with the army. He had married one Florence Langford at Aston register office in Birmingham in December 1898, and after his discharge he struggled to provide for his wife and their three children – two sons and a daughter. They ended up in their local workhouse, Erdington. In April 1906 Ravenhill appeared at Aston police court for refusing to work. A report of the case said: 'The authorities felt sorry for him as they knew his history. He was an ex-army man and holder of the Victoria Cross. He was treated with the greatest consideration, various kinds of work being offered to him, but as he refused to comply with all requests there was no alternative but to bring him before the court.' It transpired that Ravenhill was making a protest to draw attention to his claim for a bigger army pension. He was getting £10 a year but thought he was entitled to £50. He had hoped that the guardians of the workhouse would help him to press the claim. The master of the workhouse told the court that a meeting was arranged but Ravenhill had missed it. The master said he would raise the matter again. The case was adjourned after Ravenhill promised to work.

In 1908 Ravenhill's plight came to the attention of the Liberal MP for Droitwich, Worcestershire, Cecil Harmsworth. The MP raised the case with the Secretary of State for War, Richard Haldane [later Viscount Haldane], in the House of Commons on 30 April. Harmsworth asked 'whether he is aware that George Ravenhill VC is at present an inmate of Erdington workhouse, and whether he can see his way to relieving this soldier of the necessity of availing himself of charitable relief'. Haldane replied: 'This is the first intimation we have received on this matter. The case is being investigated.'

Harmsworth brought the matter up again on 13 May: 'I beg to ask the Secretary of State for War if he is now in a position to say what action, if any, is proposed to be taken by the War Office to relieve George Ravenhill VC, who is, or was recently, an inmate of Erdington workhouse, of the necessity of taking advantage of public charity.' Haldane's reply: 'The case is still under investigation. As soon as a decision has been reached, it shall be communicated to my honourable friend.'

No help came, and by August Ravenhill, whose wife had given birth to another girl, resorted to stealing some iron to make money. He was soon arrested and made another appearance at Aston police court, this time with two other men, Lot Galeford and John Toye. They were charged with taking the iron, valued at 6s, from a spot near the entrance gates of Bromford Mills. All three were described as labourers. The iron was sold to a dealer for 5s 7½d, 'the market price'. Toye told the court he helped to move the iron but had no idea it was stolen. He said Galeford and Ravenhill told him it had been found in a brook. Toye was discharged. Galeford, 'who had been in trouble before', was sentenced to three months' hard labour.

Referring to Ravenhill, a detective inspector said 'he could not say much in the man's favour'. The ex-soldier had appeared at the court for 'refusing to perform his allotted task' at the workhouse, and he had been keeping company with Galeford for the past month. Ravenhill, who wanted a job, told the court he believed he was entitled to an army pension of £50 a year but the authorities had so far failed to pay it. If he had received the money, he would not have stolen the iron. A local newspaper reported: 'The bench said they had no other course but to send Ravenhill to gaol for a month, they had tried to help him but he would not help himself.' So there was no sympathy for a jobless hero who had a wife and four children to support.

It is to Ravenhill's credit that despite his financial misery he had refused to pawn or sell his Victoria Cross. But if War Office bureaucracy had moved slowly to help him, especially with regard to his pension claim, it acted swiftly to dishonour him. His decoration and two campaign medals for South Africa were confiscated, and his name was removed from the Victoria Cross Register. The medals should have been kept by the War Office but, shockingly, they were offered for sale at a Sotheby's auction in December – little more than three months after Ravenhill's conviction – and fetched £42. The seller remains a mystery. The sale has echoes of the disposal of the Victoria Cross awarded to James Collis, the bigamist whose decoration was confiscated by the War Office but subsequently ended up in the medal collection of Lieutenant Colonel J. B. Gaskell, who sold it at a Glendining's auction in 1911 for £52. There is more than a suspicion that the Ravenhill and Collis VCs were stolen or obtained by fraudulent means. At the very least, the sales reflect shameful conduct on the part of the War Office.

At the time of the 1911 census, Ravenhill and his wife and children were still in the workhouse. Another child, Alfred, had been born, but such were the family's dire circumstances that three children, Lily, eleven, George, nine, and Raymond, five, were sent to Canada to be fostered by wealthy families. A girl, Nellie, was born in 1912 but she lived for only a year.

On 14 September 1914, soon after the outbreak of the First World War, the patriotic Ravenhill volunteered again for the army, serving initially in the Oxfordshire and Buckinghamshire Light Infantry. At the time of his re-enlistment the family were living at Chipping Norton, Oxfordshire. He is thought to have transferred to the 10th (Service) Battalion Hampshire Regiment, sailing from Liverpool on 7 July 1915 and landing at Gallipoli the following month, although he may have been sent to Lemnos from where 300 men joined an attack on Turkish trenches at Cape Helles. He also served with the 8th (Service) Battalion Duke of Cornwall's Light Infantry in the Balkans. But Private Ravenhill's health deteriorated and he was given a medical discharge in 1916 – with a disability pension.

At some stage the family moved from Chipping Norton to the Nechells district of Birmingham, where Ravenhill had been born. On 14 April 1921 the father of eight died unexpectedly at his home, one room in a squalid tenement building that he shared with his wife and five of their children, whose ages ranged from two to fourteen. Ravenhill, aged forty-nine, was given a military funeral. The adjutant of his old regiment, the Royal Scots Fusiliers, based in Ayr, sent a message saying they were unable to be represented because of 'the industrial troubles' [a miners' dispute had won the sympathy of rail workers, among others]. The fusiliers did, however, send a wreath, with the words, 'In memory of a very gallant Scots Fusilier.' There was also a wreath from the 'unemployed ex-servicemen in Birmingham'.

Men of the Royal Warwickshire Regiment carried the coffin to a gun carriage, and the cortege, headed by soldiers with arms reversed, made its way to Witton cemetery, with onlookers lining the streets. The hero of Colenso was buried in a plot marked only '36'. There were no funds for a plaque bearing his name. Local newspapers pointed out that the family were 'practically destitute', and the Lord Mayor of Birmingham, William Cadbury, agreed to pay the funeral costs. Ravenhill's widow Florence also received a government grant of £7 10s. She 'expressed her heartfelt thanks for the many expressions of sympathy' and was grateful that 'my sad case' had become known.

17

A Bootlegging Scandal
Michael O'Leary

Michael O'Leary caught the imagination of the British public after single-handedly storming two German positions and saving many of his comrades from deadly machine-gun fire. His deed even resulted in a recruiting poster, declaring: 'An Irish hero! 1 Irishman defeats 10 Germans.'

O'Leary joined the 1st Battalion Irish Guards in France in late November 1914. The First World War was only a few months old, but the battalion had seen much fighting – Mons and the subsequent retreat, the advance to the Aisne, and the first battle of Ypres, in which it suffered huge casualties defending the area around Klein Zillebeke. The remnants of the battalion were taken from the front line on 18 November, and O'Leary was among reinforcements who joined them as they recovered at Meteren. Rudyard Kipling would write: 'They had been cramped in wet mud till they had almost forgotten the use of their legs: their rifles, clothing, equipment, everything except their morale and the undefeated humour with which they had borne their burden, needed renewal or repair.' In early December King George V paid a visit, telling commanding officers of the 4th (Guards) Brigade: 'I am very proud of my Guards and am full of admiration for their bravery, endurance and fine spirit. You are fighting a brave and determined enemy, but if you go on as you have been doing and show the same fine spirit, there can only be one end, please God, and that is victory. I wish you all good luck.' The 1st Battalion Irish Guards were part of the 2nd Division, which had seen more than

5,700 officers and other ranks killed by the time the first battle of Ypres ended on 22 November.

After a well-deserved rest the Guards Brigade was ordered to relieve Indian and Gurkha troops involved in fighting at Cuinchy, south of the Bethune Canal. The Irish guardsmen were disconcerted to find that the trenches occupied by the shorter Gurkhas were not deep enough, and hurriedly began digging to give themselves cover. Artillery fire and sniping were a daily occurrence, with the nearest Germans only a couple of hundred yards away. The trenches were places of misery, soon filling with water, which did not drain away because of the clay soil. O'Leary quickly distinguished himself, winning a mention in despatches.

On 3 January 1915 men of the King's Royal Rifle Corps relieved them, but after a break of five days they were sent to take over trenches from the Worcestershire Regiment. It was another wet day. The trenches were at least 2 feet deep in water and mud again was a problem – it took six hours to extricate one soldier. The soldiers were soon filthy, and trench foot and rheumatism began taking a toll. An order came that men were not to stand in water 'for more than twelve hours at a time'. On 15 January the 1st Battalion was relieved by the Highland Light Infantry and went to billets at Locon. During this break a second lieutenant gave a bomb-throwing demonstration, killing himself and wounding thirteen others. The officer was buried the next day. Guardsmen did not have much rest. Drill, rifle exercises, marches and kit inspections were carried out 'lest life in the caked filth of the trenches should lead anyone to forget the standard of the Brigade of Guards which under no circumstances allows any excuse'.

At the end of the month the battalion returned to Cuinchy, an area marked by brickworks, trenches and a railway embankment. Early on 1 February a post held by the Coldstream Guards was attacked, and Irish guardsmen were sent to help. Two lieutenants were shot dead, one in the head and the other through the heart. Two other officers were wounded and a sergeant was left in command. Later it was decided to attack German barricades using some fifty Coldstream and thirty Irish guardsmen, including twenty-six-year-old O'Leary, who had been promoted lance corporal. It was here that he won the Victoria Cross, taking out two positions before machine-gun fire could be directed at the attackers. His citation stated:

> When forming one of the storming party which advanced against the enemy's barricades he rushed to the front and himself killed five Germans who were holding the first barricade, after which he attacked a second barricade, about 60 yards further on, which he captured, after killing three of the enemy and making prisoners of two more. Lance Corporal O'Leary thus practically captured the enemy's position by himself, and prevented the rest of the attacking party from being fired upon.

Kipling wrote: 'Eyewitnesses report that he did his work quite leisurely and wandered into the open, visible for any distance around, intent upon killing another German to whom he had taken a dislike.' British casualties that day were ten killed and twenty-seven wounded. There were about thirty German dead, with thirty-two prisoners, 'all of whom, with one exception, wept aloud'. Three days later O'Leary was promoted sergeant, and on 18 February his Victoria Cross was announced.

Reporters were quick to track down O'Leary's parents at their cottage in 'wild mountain country' at Macroom, County Cork. The reaction of O'Leary's mother Margaret: 'Glory be to God. May he protect my brave boy.' Her husband Daniel, a strapping farmer – and a nationalist – was less impressed: 'I am surprised he didn't do more. I often laid out twenty men myself with a stick coming from Macroom fair, and it is a bad trial of Mick that he could kill only eight and he having a rifle and bayonet.'

O'Leary wrote to his parents shortly afterwards:

> I guess you will be glad to hear that I have been promoted full sergeant on the field on account of distinguished conduct on February 1, 1915, when we charged the Huns and routed them in disorder. You bet the Irish Guards are getting back now.
>
> On that date I took some of our men up to a very important position of the Germans and took it from them, capturing their machine gun and killing the gunners, also taking prisoners. The Huns lost terribly. We had only a few casualties. The fighting has

been a lot quieter since, only a few attacks being made, which were repulsed by our rifle fire. You would laugh if you saw us chasing them and mowing them down. Our men would follow them into Berlin if they were left to do so. We haven't properly started yet. Heaven help them when we do! There will be some slaughter.

Later Company Quartermaster Sergeant J. G. Lowry of the Irish Guards gave this account of the attack:

A rain of bullets and shrapnel was kept up for 20 minutes, and No 1 Company [O'Leary's] was then let loose. They went for the enemy at the double. They had about 100 yards to travel, and O'Leary easily outstripped the rest. O'Leary's mark was a machine gun. Before the Germans could manage to slew it round and meet the charging men, O'Leary picked off the whole of the five machine-gun crew, and leaving his mates to come up and capture the gun, he dashed forward to the second barricade, which the Germans were quitting in a hurry, and shot three more. Some of the enemy who couldn't get away quick enough faced our men, but very little bayonet work was needed. The majority did not wait, and we picked off a good lot of them from our trench as they left their holes. O'Leary was extremely modest over what he had done, but his comrades knew that he had probably saved the lives of a whole company.

In May there was a report that O'Leary had been killed in action. But this was denied, with one private saying: 'His chums tell me he has the lives of a cat. A few days ago a shell dropped 4 yards from him and never exploded.' O'Leary confirmed that he was still in the firing line 'doing my bit – came out of the battle with only a few scratches, thank God'.

In June he was on leave in England. The British public were not the only ones impressed with his bravery. The king learned that O'Leary was at Wellington Barracks, where the 1st Battalion had been based at the outbreak of war. The barracks are close to Buckingham Palace, and the king decided it was an ideal opportunity to present O'Leary with his Victoria Cross. A message was sent to the senior officer at the barracks, Colonel Douglas Proby, asking him to pay a visit with the sergeant. They arrived to find the king and Queen Mary, along with their daughter, Princess Mary, sitting in the palace grounds. Shortly afterwards Queen Alexandra and Princess Victoria arrived, and they all watched the king pin the decoration on O'Leary. George V shook hands 'very cordially' with the sergeant and congratulated him on his heroism, wishing him a long life. It was 22 June and probably the most unusual investiture ever held at the palace. O'Leary was the first Irish Guards recipient of the Victoria Cross.

The War Office was keen to use the popular hero to boost recruiting, and he – reluctantly – went to a number of public events. But his appearance on a platform in Hyde Park 'was about as much as his nerves could stand', and he was 'really glad to get back to doing business with the Germans'. One newspaper noted: 'It is to the credit of our war heroes that the braver they are under fire the shyer they seem of popular applause and other marks of appreciation.' Three other Victoria Cross winners – Rifleman William Mariner, Private Henry May and Lance Corporal Joseph Tombs – were so keen to avoid a cheering crowd after a palace investiture in August that they removed their medals and fled in a taxi.

The 1st Battalion Irish Guards spent the rest of the war on the Western Front, taking part in other major encounters, including the Somme, the third battle of Ypres and Cambrai. The regiment lost a total of more than 2,300 officers and other ranks, and won four Victoria Crosses. One of the dead officers was Kipling's eighteen-year-old son John, a casualty of the battle of Loos in September 1915.

O'Leary had not seen out the war with the Irish Guards. In October 1915 he was commissioned as a second lieutenant in the 5th Battalion Connaught Rangers. He was sent on a recruiting drive to Ireland, but at Ballaghaderreen in County Roscommon, birthplace of the nationalist supporter John Blake Dillon, Irish Volunteers booed him. It was pointed out later: 'No one could be found to defend this conduct locally – "attacking" an undoubted war hero was completely unacceptable.' A significant number of Irish Volunteers supported the war effort, but others were involved in the 1916 Easter Rising and the organisation later spawned the IRA. [In 1915 George Bernard Shaw wrote a satirical play partly based on O'Leary titled *O'Flaherty VC*. A soldier called Dennis O'Flaherty, who has won the Victoria Cross, returns to his Irish village to take part in a recruiting campaign. But his Fenian mother did not know that he had been fighting for the British. O'Flaherty actually joined up to escape home life and has no idea why the war is being fought. The mother falls out with his girlfriend, and the soldier longs to get back to the 'peace and quiet' of the trenches, and hopes eventually to have a French wife. The military authorities in Ireland banned wartime performances of the play.]

After his visit to Ireland, O'Leary joined the 5th Battalion in Salonika, Greece, where he received another mention in despatches. The battalion, which had suffered heavy casualties during the Gallipoli campaign, later served in Macedonia and Palestine. O'Leary returned to England in 1918 before the war ended, joining the regiment's 2nd Battalion, stationed at Dover. He left the army, an acting captain, in 1921.

O'Leary was born at Inchigeela, County Cork, on 9 October 1888. At the age of seventeen, after working on his parents' small farm, he joined the Royal Navy and was sent to the training base Vivid at Devonport. Rheumatism in the knees cut short his naval career and he returned to the family farm. However, his rheumatism did not prevent him joining the Irish Guards in 1910, when he signed on for three years' home service. After leaving the army, adventure beckoned and he headed to Canada, signing on with the Royal North-West Mounted Police at Regina, Saskatchewan. Constable O'Leary soon distinguished himself, taking part in a lengthy battle with two gunmen, who were eventually captured. He was presented with a gold ring in recognition of his heroism. After the outbreak of the First World War O'Leary was anxious to re-enlist in the Irish Guards. The Mounties were sympathetic – many Canadians were volunteering to serve overseas – and they gave him a discharge.

In 1919 he married Greta Hegarty from Ballyvourney – 'Town of the Beloved' – in County Cork, close to his parents' home at Macroom. In March 1921 he returned to Canada – without his wife. O'Leary had planned to join the Royal North-West Mounted Police again, but on his arrival in Ottawa he announced he was seeking employment locally: 'I want a job, so if you know of anyone who wants to employ me you may tell him that I am here.' The Canadians were quick to embrace him as the 'first Canadian to win the Victoria Cross in the Great War'. He spent several months giving talks on the war and working for a publisher. Then he joined Ontario's provincial police seeking out bootleggers as prohibition was in force.

Two years later O'Leary's wife joined him, and he changed jobs, becoming a detective sergeant with the Michigan Central Railway. In January 1925 O'Leary was arrested and charged with smuggling aliens into the US from Bridgeburg, a district of Fort Erie, Ontario. Two aliens were found in a freight car by immigration inspectors at Buffalo, New York state. O'Leary insisted he was innocent, a victim of mistaken identity. A report pointed out:

> Canadian railroad men are championing O'Leary's cause. They aver that recently several train crews have been subjected to what they call third-degree methods by immigration inspectors at the Buffalo end of the International Bridge [a railway crossing spanning the Niagara River between Fort Erie and Buffalo]. The railroad men point out that there easily could be an alien in a box car unknown to the train crew. Yet when an alien is found every member of the crew is detained, sometimes for hours, while the captive foreigner is asked to identify some person on the Canadian side who helped in the attempted smuggling.

O'Leary was held for some time in a Buffalo jail awaiting trial, and his treatment angered Canadians. Petitions urging speedy justice were 'signed by virtually the entire population of Bridgeburg and Fort Erie'. On 8 May he was indicted by a federal grand jury, but later that month Rochester's supreme court acquitted him. It emerged that the foreigner who claimed to have given O'Leary a bribe could not speak English. O'Leary returned to his home at Fort Erie, where his family had been helped financially by the local authority. Despite the acquittal, rumours were still circulating and the railway company sacked him.

More trouble lay ahead. He was appointed a police sergeant at Crystal Beach, Fort Erie, but before he officially started the job he carried out a raid on the holiday home of an American under the Ontario Temperance Act. No arrests were made, but it emerged that a large amount of money had exchanged hands. O'Leary was fortunate that he still had friends in the area – a magistrate disposed of the case by ordering an 'indefinite remand'. Like many provinces, Ontario had introduced prohibition during the war, a measure that ended in 1923, although from then on the sale of alcohol was heavily regulated. Prohibition in the United States was in force from 1920 until 1933. During this period Fort Erie became an American 'playground'. It was also the centre of a huge smuggling operation, with boats laden with alcohol, particularly rum, heading across the Niagara River to the US side under cover of darkness.

In 1926 O'Leary became disillusioned with life in Canada, and it seems that the authorities were keen for the tarnished hero to return home. By this time he had four children, and he was loaned money so that his family could sail to Ireland. He had moved to Hamilton, where he worked at a factory and for the local authority. In October the contents of the family home were sold at auction, and the following day his wife and children went to Montreal to board a ship bound for Ireland. Mrs O'Leary was happy to leave. 'The last five years have been awful,' she said.

O'Leary planned to go to the United States to make a living, complaining of the 'hard luck which has dogged him during his residence in Canada since 1921'. He had found his Victoria Cross to be more 'of a curse than a blessing'. At this point Ontario's attorney general, William Price, a war veteran, stepped in after 'representations'. He said: 'It seems a shame that a man who has been honoured by the gift of the Victoria Cross and who has given such wonderful service in his country should be in want in Canada, and as chairman of the soldiers' aid commission I have decided to give him a chance to make a living here.' It is not clear if O'Leary received a job offer. Several bouts of malaria, contracted in Salonika, affected him badly, and he eventually returned to Britain.

Before he left Canada he spoke of the difficulty of remaining an honest police officer:

Unfortunately on the Michigan railway I came into conflict with the bootlegging and smuggling interests, which make it practically impossible for a man to go straight and keep his job. A detective has to wink at a whole lot of things and take bribes to keep his mouth shut or else they are out to get him. In a way I wasn't surprised when that charge of smuggling an alien [aliens] into the States was brought up against me. The bootleggers had told me several times that they would get me if I didn't leave them alone. The man who brought up the case was a close friend of one of the big smugglers, and I suspect it was between them that they tried to trap me.

When I was told that I was under arrest for smuggling an alien I thought they were joking at first. I hadn't smuggled any aliens – I didn't know the first thing about going at it to smuggle them. I asked on what day I was supposed to have smuggled the foreigner from Bridgeburg to Buffalo. As soon as they told me I proved, with the aid of my notebook, in which I had kept a detailed account of every move since I was appointed to the railway police force, that at the time I was supposed to have been smuggling this alien across the river I was actually guarding a carload of merchandise at Welland. When the case was finally brought to court, after a delay of months, I was acquitted. But while the papers were full of the story of the alleged smuggling, only a line or two was given to a mention of the acquittal.

O'Leary also revealed that he had made himself unpopular with some of his arrests – an eighty-three-year-old man who had ignored three warnings about an illegal still, and a prominent campaigner in support of prohibition who was caught making moonshine in his kitchen.

In London, O'Leary was scathing about life as an immigrant: 'Canada is no country for a poor man or an honest man. You've either got to have capital to start with, or be a crook, to succeed over there.' The opportunities for 'graft' were enormous – one could easily become rich but a man who refused bribes was 'framed'. He said: 'I didn't get a square deal in Canada so I left. The difference between the dominion and the old country is the difference between chalk and cheese.' His comments did not go down well with

Canadians. Under the newspaper headline 'Michael O'Leary VC unjust to dominion', it was pointed out that he had been given seven jobs, 'none of which he held for any length of time' and some he left without notice. The city of Hamilton had assisted the family in 'every possible way', with travel expenses and paying off debts. O'Leary, initially welcomed as 'the first Canadian VC', was now referred to as 'the famous Irishman'.

In Britain, the British Legion learned of his problems and gave him a job as a packer at its poppy factory in Richmond, Surrey, and later, with his health improving, he became a commissionaire at the May Fair Hotel, near Park Lane, London, earning 'a scant living holding umbrellas over the heads of painted actresses, crippled old ladies and richly-clad members of the plutocracy'. The hotel did not pay him a wage and he relied entirely on tips, 'but only one person out of ten ever gives me a tip'. A reporter watched him at work:

A crippled old lady, haggard under her rouge, drew up to the door, and O'Leary practically carried her into the hotel, and she gave him six pence. A crotchety old general with a voice like a bull, a face almost devoid of humanity and a skin like purple parchment, came out bellowing for his car, and from him O'Leary got three pence. That's all he got in the hour I was there except for a nice shilling from a blonde French actress with gay laughing eyes.

O'Leary was asked if he felt bitter towards the nation that had left him to earn a living as a doorman. 'Not bitter at all,' he replied. 'No nation ever did bother much about its old soldiers, and why should they bother about me?'

As another world war loomed, he was called up as a reserve officer in June 1939, not with the Irish Guards but as a lieutenant in the Middlesex Regiment, soon to be promoted major and sent to France with the British Expeditionary Force. At fifty-one, his health let him down again and he returned to Britain, diagnosed with diabetes, before the Dunkirk evacuation in 1940. He transferred to the Pioneer Corps and was put in charge of a prisoner of war camp in southern England, receiving a medical discharge in March 1945.

He settled with his family – six sons and a daughter – in north London, and ran a small building business until his retirement in 1954. Two years later he attended the queen's review in Hyde Park, marking the centenary of the Victoria Cross, and was apparently bemused to find a man in a wheelchair claiming to be Michael O'Leary VC. He died in a London hospital on 2 August 1961, aged seventy-two.

Two of his sons served with the Royal Air Force during the Second World War, and both won the Distinguished Flying Cross. Warrant Officer Jeremiah O'Leary was awarded the decoration in April 1944. As an air gunner, he had taken part in an attack on a railway station where a large force of enemy troops had gathered. A convoy was heading towards the station, and in the face of 'considerable' anti-aircraft fire O'Leary raked the defences with machine-gun fire, hitting many vehicles. His 'deadly and unflinching fire' allowed the pilot to complete a successful bombing run. It was noted: 'This air gunner has completed a very large number of sorties and has invariably displayed a fine fighting spirit, great keenness and devotion to duty.' The location of the station attack was not specified, but it may have been somewhere in northern France in the run-up to D-Day. Flying Officer Daniel O'Leary was awarded his DFC in September 1944. In another coincidence, both brothers went on to be promoted squadron leader.

HMS *Arrogant*, left, and HMS *Hecla* in action during the Baltic campaign of 1854. The mysterious William Johnstone and John Bythesea were serving in *Arrogant* when they both won the Victoria Cross for a raid that yielded Russian secrets. Johnstone later killed himself.

Bythesea rose to flag rank but he was court-martialled during his career.

Edward St John Daniel was the only officer to forfeit the Victoria Cross.

Opposite: British soldiers storming a Taku fort in north-east China on 21 August 1860.

Opposite, inset: Thomas Lane, 'a wild Irishman' who enjoyed fighting and mayhem. He found peacetime soldiering a challenge and ended up with a poor disciplinary record.

Above: Teenager Duncan Boyes leading an attack on Japanese forces in September 1864.

Right: Boyes wearing his Victoria Cross. He would be stripped of the honour.

Above: The grave of Rorke's Drift hero Robert Jones, with the headstone facing away from his local church because he had committed the 'sin' of suicide. (*Alamy*)

Below left: Jones was badly wounded during the Zulu attack in January 1879.

*Below righ*t: Michael Murphy was jailed for stealing oats and hay at his barracks.

Above: A defiant Redvers Buller in the rearguard action at Hlobane Mountain in March 1879 that saw him being awarded the Victoria Cross.

Below left: Buller was popular with soldiers but his bluntness made him enemies in high places.

Below right: Henry D'Arcy was twice recommended for the Victoria Cross. After leaving the army he vanished.

Above: James Collis saved sick and wounded soldiers, putting them on his gun and limber, during the disastrous retreat from Maiwand to Kandahar in July 1880.

Below left: Collis was given eighteen months with hard labour at the Old Bailey for bigamy.

Below right: Evelyn Wood joined the army for adventure and rose to the rank of field marshal.

Above: George Ravenhill was one of the soldiers who volunteered to try to save the guns of the Royal Horse Artillery at Colenso, which had become easy targets for the Boers. (*Alamy*)

Below left: After leaving the army Ravenhill, with his family, ended up in their local workhouse.

Below right: Frederick Corbett was found guilty of stealing goods and embezzling money from an officer.

Rushing forward on his own, Michael O'Leary of the Irish Guards took out two German positions before machine-gun fire could be directed at his comrades. Another soldier would later say: 'O'Leary was extremely modest over what he had done, but his comrades knew that he had probably saved the lives of a whole company.'

Right: The *Daily Sketch* gave Mariner front-page prominence but surprisingly described him as nameless, in spite of the fact that King George V had presented the convicted burglar with his named Victoria Cross days earlier.

Below: Gallipoli hell. Men of the 10th Light Horse who survived the slaughter at The Nek, surrounded by unclaimed kitbags of their fallen comrades. Hugo Throssell was one of the officers who showed great bravery. (*Australian War Memorial*)

DAILY SKETCH.

GUARANTEED DAILY NETT SALE MORE THAN 1,000,000 COPIES.

No. 2,326.   LONDON, MONDAY, AUGUST 21, 1916.   [Registered as a Newspaper.]   ONE HALFPENNY.

The V.C.'s Atonement.

UNKNOWN—

Here to the right is the photograph of the V.C. who atoned for his past by laying down his life for his country on the field of battle. Who he was no one knows. The name he bore in the regiment was not his own. But he bore it with honour. Under it he won the greatest distinction a soldier can gain, under it he died with his face to the foe and in the service of his King and country.

PLUCKY ACT.

Miss Winifred Brown, a young pupil-teacher, pluckily rescued a lad named George Payne from drowning in a mill-pond near Harlow, Essex. Divesting herself of hat and skirt, she plunged into the pond and brought him to the bank, after he had pulled her under water.

The nameless and friendless V.C. hero.

—FRIENDLESS

Friends he had none; his identity was lost in his new name. His old name was buried with his past. "They shall know me as a new man," he said. Gloriously he kept his word—and his friends can claim with honour the V.C. that he left unclaimed behind him on the battlefield. Only his bravery, not his past, remains—a noble inscription on a roll wiped clean.

TWO HEROES.

Pte. L. Cooper, 1st East Kent, was publicly presented with the D.C.M. at Woolwich yesterday for carrying a number of wounded men to safety at Hooge.

Corpl. M. Bell, 31st Heavy Battery, R.G.A., at the same time received the Military Service Medal for repairing telephone wires under heavy fire.

Above left: Throssell lost public support in Australia after marrying a fervent communist. (*Australian War Memorial*)

Above right: John Sherwood-Kelly ridiculed 'so-called generals who sit on their arses in offices'. (*Imperial War Museum*)

Below: Sherwood-Kelly, right, heading to his court martial in London in October 1919. He pleaded guilty to three charges. (*PA Images*)

Above: Martin Doyle shaking hands with Queen Mary in the presence of King George V at a Buckingham Palace reception in June 1920, the year he joined the IRA.

Right and below: Gordon Steele served in the Q-ship *Baralong*, which trapped the German submarine *U-27* after masquerading as a neutral US vessel. (*Association of Old Worcesters*)

Above: Lord and Lady
Mountbatten attended a London
reception for Victoria Cross holders
where John Grant slapped her
ladyship 'on the bum' and was
quickly ejected. (*Alamy*)

Left: Grant felt 'nothing but shame'
after the Mountbatten incident in
June 1956. (*National Library of
New Zealand*)

Right: Clive Hulme shot thirty-three German snipers during the Battle of Crete in May 1941. (*National Library of New Zealand*)

Below: John Nettleton led the remarkable low-level raid on Augsburg in southern Germany in 1942. Only five of the twelve Lancaster bombers returned home. (*The National Archives*)

Nettleton was accused of attacking a young woman at an RAF party on New Year's Eve.

Nettleton's accuser was Sheila Mercier, who became a popular TV actress. (*PA Images*)

Above: Bren gun blazing away at the hip, John Kenneally of the Irish Guards made two almost suicidal charges at German troops during a crucial battle of the Tunisian campaign in 1943.

Right: Kenneally joined the Irish Guards after deserting from an artillery regiment. The lad from Birmingham took the identity of an Irishman and was never found out.

Above: An X-craft similar to the one used by James Magennis and Ian Fraser to attack the Japanese cruiser *Takao* at her moorings in Johore Strait, Singapore, in 1945. (*Imperial War Museum*)

Left: Magennis and Fraser. After the war a large sum of money was raised for Magennis in his home city and he later received hate mail when – broke – he sold his Victoria Cross. (*Royal Navy Submarine Museum*)

18

The Burglar
William Mariner

William Mariner was a convicted burglar who had an unusual set of admirers – the police. In 1921 London's police chief, Sir William Horwood, even produced a roll of honour with Mariner's name on it.

As a rifleman in the 2nd Battalion King's Royal Rifle Corps, Mariner had distinguished himself during trench warfare near Cambrin, France, on the night of 22 May 1915. He knocked out a German machine-gun post after crawling 'silently as a cat' through the mud and barbed wire of no man's land in an apparent suicide mission. As one officer explained later: 'The battalion suffered considerably from the activity of a certain machine gun concealed in the German trenches opposite. Its fire was far too accurate to be pleasant. Every few minutes during the night a gust of bullets would come sweeping along the parapet, ripping the top layers of sandbags, and rendering the duties of the sentries even more perilous than usual.'

The thought of silencing the enemy had gnawed away at thirty- two-year-old Mariner. After many hours on duty he knew the location of the machine gun, and had worked out how to reach it. On that night of 22 May a violent thunderstorm provided the opportunity, when both sides thought more of shelter than outright aggression. Mariner went to his platoon sergeant and volunteered for the mission. The sergeant no doubt was just as keen to silence the machine gun, which had caused many casualties, but he must have wondered if the volunteer fully understood the danger he would be facing. Mariner, only 5 feet 3 inches tall but physically strong, was given permission to obtain Mills bombs [grenades] from the store. He crept over the parapet and slithered into the mud, his target many yards away. Another soldier, Jack [John] Laister, went part of the way with him.

Laister gave a dramatic account of the mission:

I had just had my 18th birthday and that night Mariner said to me, 'This is it Chico [Laister's nickname], got your cutters?' He told me he needed two bandoliers of Mills bombs and said, 'I can't drag a box over no man's land.' He shook my hand and told me to crawl up to the German wire with him, cut and then for God's sake get back. Things seemed to be in our favour – it was a pitch- black night although we had to tuck ourselves into the ground when the Very lights went up. We reached the wire and I started to cut, all the time being terrible afraid that if the Germans heard me it would mean certain death for both of us, but they didn't.

Then Mariner took off his tunic and his shirt so they didn't catch on the wire and whispered, 'Now get the bloody hell out of it', and I remember thinking, I'll never see him again. I crawled back as fast as I could but I had only got half way when all hell was let loose. I never saw anything like it – standing on top of the German front-line trench was Mariner. In the light from the Very lights I could see him hurling bomb after bomb into the German trench. Pieces of bodies, limbs, heads were all flying out and up in the air. Again I thought, that's the last I'll see of him because the Germans had opened up with every gun.

A report noted: 'It can well be imagined what a journey that was across the swamp that lay between the trenches, under the pitiless rain, with the ever-increasing risk of discovery as he came nearer the German lines.'

Mariner reached the enemy parapet without being challenged. Slowly he climbed up the slippery bank and when he got to the top he could see the outline of the emplacement, which was 'roofed over so cunningly that its presence could hardly be suspected from outside'. Lying full length on the parapet, he heard men talking and laughing. The emplacement seemed to be full of Germans sheltering from the storm. Mariner took a grenade out of his pocket and tossed it through an opening at the back. In the confined space, the explosion created havoc. Panic-stricken survivors rushed out and fled down an adjoining trench. The night was quiet again 'but for the groans and cries of the wounded'. Surprisingly, Mariner did not start to make his way back. He waited and after about fifteen minutes Germans 'splashed up the trench confident that they would not be disturbed again'. Hearing their return, Mariner crawled round to the other side of the emplacement and when the men had 'settled down once more' he threw in another grenade. There was a stampede to escape – and the bombing continued. With the emplacement wrecked, Mariner slid down the parapet and lay in the mud for an hour as the German line bombarded no man's land. Eventually he crawled back to the British position, only to be nearly bayoneted by a sentry who thought he was a German.

Laister also had reached his trench unscathed, recording: 'My mates grabbed me and one even kissed me, saying, "My God, you got back alive". We sat on our fire-step, keeping our heads down and waiting for a counterattack, and after a while we heard people speaking German, which was strange because they were giving the game away. Then, pushed over the parapet, came two Germans who dropped on to the fire-step and Mariner jumped in after them, carrying part of a German machine-gun.' He was soaking wet and covered with mud from head to foot 'but very happy'. [Mariner did not return with prisoners. Laister was confusing an earlier incident when the hero crossed no man's land, attacked a machine-gun post and brought back two Germans.]

Mariner was immediately recommended for the Victoria Cross. If Laister's account veered towards the dramatic, then Mariner's citation was understated. It gave the barest details, mentioning that he threw only two bombs, though it is known that he had 'filled his pockets with bombs' and was determined to use them. Perhaps Mariner played down his heroics when he was debriefed.

In a letter to his mother, Alice, he told how he 'blew the enemy into a place where they will not be able to take part in another war on earth'. He added: 'The Germans knew I was out there, but they could not see me, and I managed to get back safe after being away an hour and a half. I had, however, a thrilling experience. One of our fellows did not know I had been out with the bombs, and when he saw me coming over the trench he had his bayonet fixed. He would have run it through me if I had not shouted at him. He heard my voice and knew me at once, but said, "It's a good job, Bill, you spoke."'

On 15 May an offensive had been launched at Festubert after a sixty-hour artillery bombardment – which largely failed to damage German defences because many shells were defective. The battle, involving British, Indian and Canadian troops, continued until 25 May. The 2nd Battalion King's Royal Rifle Corps was responsible for holding the front line in the nearby sector of Cuinchy and Cambrin, an area that had already seen heavy fighting. The ruined village of Festubert was eventually captured, marking an advance of up to 600 yards on a limited front. British casualties numbered more than 16,000.

Mariner's Victoria Cross was announced the following month. His mother was quoted as saying: 'Even when he was a little boy he never showed fear. In fact, he was daring from the time he was a baby.' In early August Mariner returned to Britain and shortly afterwards King George V presented him with the decoration at Buckingham Palace. Mariner's mother had travelled from Manchester with his sister and four friends to see him, but they mistakenly went to Windsor and then dashed to London. They arrived in time to see Mariner leaving the palace 'rather flushed and breathless' with the medal pinned to his tunic. Later the rifleman went to his home town of Salford, where he received a hero's welcome. The mayor presented him with a gold watch and an illuminated scroll. But Mariner did not like the adulation, telling one reporter: 'You can tell the people I would much rather do anything there is to do at the front and go through all I have done all over again, than be made a fuss of like this.' He returned to France but was wounded on 24 August and evacuated home. The Secretary of State for War, Lord Kitchener, thought Mariner could help with recruiting. The rifleman spoke – reluctantly – at various rallies, mainly in the Salford area.

In October he appeared at Clerkenwell magistrates' court, London, charged with being absent without leave – two days overdue. Wearing his Victoria Cross, he admitted he had been 'messing about' with a friend but had also done some recruiting.

The magistrate told him: 'Well, take care not to bring that Cross into court again.' Mariner was detained to await an escort.

He went back to France. In May 1916 Rifleman Giles Eyre found himself in Mariner's platoon, and he later wrote of his experiences, with keen observations on 'the battalion hero'. He found Mariner 'tough, brown-faced, reckless, fond of a drop – an old regular of the Kipling type'. Mariner summed up his own philosophy: 'Give me plenty of booze, a woman now and again, a bit of excitement and a chance of making a bit of "tin" over the side, and Bob's yer uncle!' On the night of 30 June 1916, the eve of the Battle of the Somme, B Company of the 2nd Battalion took part in a diversionary attack south of Loos. The assault began with mines being detonated and an artillery barrage, and then groups of men, all volunteers, launched bombing raids on the enemy trenches. Mariner and Eyre were two of the volunteers.

Eyre recorded:

Whistles shrilled out. With inhuman cries and tautened nerves we sprang forward and, cursing, roaring, singing, scrambled forward towards the Boche like a band of fiends. Holes, twisted wire, debris of every kind, seemed to grip and drag at me as I scrambled over the twisted heaps that had been neutral ground. Stumbling and recovering, helmet bobbing up and down, slugs pinging all round me, bewildered and deafened, but determined, I ran forward, tearing through the wreckage of the enemy position like a madman ... I became intoxicated with battle lust, my one thought was to destroy everything that stood in the way.

Mariner ran past him, rifle slung on his back, with a grenade in each hand. The Victoria Cross winner dashed towards a trench, threw the grenades and jumped in, shouting: 'Do them in! Kill the bloody swine!' Several bewildered Germans emerged from a hole and 'we were upon them with bayonet, club and trench knife, and in a few instants were pounding over their bodies'. The carnage continued, although a dozen prisoners were taken and passed back to the British lines under the guard of a 'simple Norfolk yokel', whom Mariner earlier had delighted in frightening with 'bloodcurdling descriptions' of previous raids. Soldiers fought in craters and German artillery plastered the area, 'regardless as to whether it is held by friend or foe'. Machine gun and rifle fire added to the deafening noise.

Mariner's bombing group easily reached its target, setting up a trench block. A general counterattack by the enemy soon ended in retreat, and then Mariner lost 'his remaining senses'. Letting out a roar, he scrambled over the trench block and dashed off in pursuit. Eyre was content to remain in position but he and another soldier felt obliged to follow their comrade. Eyre found him bayoneting a German, but seconds later there was a massive explosion. Stunned, and finding breathing 'a superhuman effort', Eyre managed to get to his feet to discover flesh and blood spattered over his body. In an instant, Mariner had been blown to pieces. There was no body. The battle lasted more than four hours of a day that would end in disaster. Mariner was one of the first of the 20,000 to fall on 1 July 1916. He is commemorated on the Thiepval Memorial, which has more than 72,000 names.

William Mariner was born at Preston, Lancashire, on 29 May 1882, the illegitimate son of Alice Mariner, who later married one John Wignall. After attending a parochial school he moved to Salford and worked as a miner. In 1902 he enlisted in the 2nd Battalion King's Royal Rifle Corps as William Wignall, taking his stepfather's surname. He spent seven years in India, becoming the regimental lightweight wrestling champion. Twice he was court-martialled, once for striking an officer and once for using threatening language. Both convictions led to jail sentences with hard labour. In 1909 he transferred to the reserves and worked as a brick setter in the Manchester area.

On 15 February 1914 William Wignall was arrested and charged with breaking and entering. He had been caught hiding behind a chimney stack on the roof of a Co-op store in Salford. Police discovered that Wignall had removed a number of roof slates to gain entry. On 24 February magistrates sent him for trial, and he was later jailed. But by August Wignall was free again, and within days of the First World War breaking out he re-enlisted in the King's Royal Rifle Corps – under the name Mariner.

In August 1916 the *Daily Sketch* carried a colourful article about Mariner, whom it described as a nameless hero. Even the newspaper was confused about his changes of surname. It stated: 'Behind the death in action of the nameless VC, whose photograph appears on the front page of the *Daily Sketch*, lies one of the romances of the Great War. His past was buried when war broke out, and he enlisted under a name which was not his own. His only enemies became his friends, though they knew his record well, and it can be found at Scotland Yard.'

The report went on:

None felt his death more keenly than the police of this country, who had been his best friends since August 1914. 'We're proud to have known such a man,' said a detective whose duty had been to keep in close touch with all the ex-convict did. Since that time the detective has watched the man's doings, but from different motives, and now we can tell you how and when the hero won his VC and how he came back to a North-country town to be feted by the very people who had seen him in the dock. The police themselves made it their special duty to keep the man, who once showed contempt for law and order, supplied with cigarettes, tobacco and parcels of other good things while he was at the front.

The article appeared to suggest that police in Manchester had tipped off Scotland Yard about Mariner's past. Perhaps his criminal activity had extended beyond the single conviction for breaking and entering.

The *Daily Sketch* article did accurately reflect the fact that police had respect for Mariner – and hundreds of other criminals who volunteered for military service during the war. In 1921 the Commissioner of the Metropolitan Police, Sir William Horwood, a former army officer, issued a roll of honour of known criminals who were killed or died of wounds. The list was not confined to London but covered the country. Mariner was among the 283 names. Two men had been awarded the Distinguished Conduct Medal and three the Military Medal. The roll of honour quoted the tribute given by Pericles to those who fell in the Peloponnesian War: 'Even those who come up short in other ways may redeem themselves by fighting bravely for their country: they may blot out the evil within the good, and benefit the state more by their public services than ever they injured her by their private actions.'

19

A Speech Too Far

Hugo Throssell

Hundreds of people cheered wildly when Captain Hugo Throssell, 'a god-like figure', rose to speak. But within minutes the Gallipoli hero had destroyed his reputation. Years of anguish lay ahead.

On the afternoon of 19 July 1919, Throssell led a victory parade in his home town of Northam, north-east of Perth, Western Australia. Riding a big bay with 'all the natural grace of a born horseman', he wore the uniform of the 10th Light Horse, and on his left breast was the Victoria Cross. Flags decorated the town and bands played. There was a carnival atmosphere. The streets were lined with people, many of them farming families who had come from a wide area. It was a time to rejoice that the First World War had ended. And it was a time to remember the fallen.

That evening Captain Throssell mounted a platform that had been erected in the main street. The crowd sang 'God Save the King' and 'Praise God, From Whom All Blessings Flow'. A clergyman spoke of peace, and the premier of Western Australia, James Mitchell, looked to the future. Then it was the turn of the town's favourite son. Throssell had a speech ready, but it was not what his largely conservative audience wanted to hear. It was neither the time nor the place for a political tirade, but that is what Northam heard. The crowd gasped as he declared himself a socialist and attacked the 'profiteers' of war. The man who had been desperate to join up and fight said: 'I am convinced that only the reorganisation of society on the basis of production for use and for the well-being of the community as a whole can give any assurance of a permanent peace.'

He went on:

> The subject is too big a one to deal with in a few words tonight. But I wanted to say that the only real way to celebrate peace is to do the things which will make for peace. Think, talk to people who are opposing the system of production for profit, study books on the subject, and test what you read by the facts of everyday life.
>
> Don't bother about what the daily newspapers or the people interested in maintaining the system of production for profit may say. You've heard what they've got to say all your lives. Go to the other side! Get their point of view. Then do what is necessary to make your convictions realities, and work for the conditions which will make it impossible for any to make fortunes out of the war.

The speech finally ended, leaving members of the Throssell family stunned and embarrassed. It had been a call for revolution. One newspaper described it as 'a bomb at a peace gathering'. Soldiers returning from the war felt betrayed. But was this really Hugo Throssell speaking? Or was it his wife, Katharine Susannah Prichard, an acclaimed novelist and fervent communist, whom he had married a few months earlier? It is not clear if she attended the event.

Their son Ric, named after Throssell's brother who had died in the war, would later write:

> Katharine encouraged him to make a stand. If he was going to strike a blow for socialism, that would be the time to do it. She helped him to write his speech and heard him try it out. It was a fine statement, she assured him. She was sure that it would make a great impression. He was a natural speaker, easy and relaxed before a crowd. He had the knack of winning people, treating them all as friends – and they would be in Northam, of course. There wouldn't be too many who'd agree with him, he knew that ... All the same Katharine didn't know how hard it was going to be for him to say what he had to. All of the family would be there, and Jimmy Mitchell, the premier, a Northam man and old

friend. They would have the soul-case shocked out of them, if he went ahead with it. He didn't want to hurt them. Katharine reassured him ...

It was not long before military intelligence in Melbourne was alerted to the activities of the Throssells, who attended left-wing meetings. When dockers in Fremantle went on strike, Katharine was quick to offer her support. One official report noted that 'the latest recruit in the ranks of the Social Democrats is Captain Hugo Throssell VC'. Many thought he was under his wife's influence, and the report pointed out that 'he was struck on the head at Gallipoli and further he was a victim of cerebro-spinal meningitis, his mind having perhaps been affected'. In 1920 Katharine helped to form the Western Australian branch of the Communist Party. The authorities would keep a careful watch on the couple for the rest of their lives. And their son Ric, who became a diplomat, would spend much of his life denying that he was a Soviet agent.

Hugo Throssell, known to family and friends as Jim, was born in Northam on 26 October 1884. His father George rose from humble beginnings to become a wealthy businessman and landowner, and at one stage premier of Western Australia. George and his wife Annie had fourteen children, Hugo being the youngest son. At the age of eleven Throssell was sent to a boarding school, Prince Alfred College in Adelaide, where he excelled at sport, especially football, athletics and boxing. Discipline was strict and on one occasion he failed a grammar test. The English master told him to remove his trousers and bend over. He was caned on his bare skin and asked if he now understood the use of a verb. When Throssell replied 'No', the punishment was repeated.

After leaving the school, Throssell declared he had not learnt a 'single solitary thing' that would help him to get a job. He returned to Northam and for some time led a leisurely life, helping out with office work in a family business. Later he took on a tougher task as a stockman. In 1910 George Throssell offered Hugo and his brother Ric 1,000 acres of land at Cowcowing, north-east of Northam, and they jumped at the chance to become farmers. There was a catch – the land was low scrub and needed to be cleared – but the brothers relished the challenge. Over the next four years their efforts were marred by drought and failing crops. After war was declared in 1914 the brothers decided to answer the call to arms. It was 'almost as a reprieve from their unrelenting struggle with the land'. Hugo enlisted days before his thirtieth birthday.

In February 1915 men of the 10th Light Horse sailed from Fremantle, destination Egypt. Not all the soldiers and their horses could be taken in the troopship. Ric left and Hugo stayed behind. Two weeks later Second Lieutenant Hugo Throssell went to war, arriving at a camp near Cairo on 20 March. In May came news that most of the regiment would be joining reinforcements for the Gallipoli campaign. Throssell discovered that he was one of the officers who would be staying behind with some of the other ranks and the horses. He apparently rushed around offering 'big money' to anyone who would do an exchange. There were no takers and he became 'the most disgusted man in Egypt'. His brother sailed for the peninsula.

It was not until July that Throssell and the remaining men were ordered to join the campaign. The horrors of Gallipoli were not confined to bombs and bullets. Diarrhoea and dysentery had taken a heavy toll on the 10th. On 7 August Throssell experienced his first major battle, when Australians were ordered to make what turned out to be a suicidal attack on a narrow bridge of land called The Nek. A bombardment by a destroyer offshore proved to be ineffective and when the 8th Light Horse launched the first wave at dawn Turkish soldiers were back in their trenches waiting. Rifle and machine-gun fire cut down the 8th. A second line, also from the 8th, was ordered to attack but these men, scrambling over the dead and wounded, met the same fate, barely going a few yards.

The futility of the offensive was evident to some officers, but Major John Antill, in overall command, refused to call it off. 'Push on' was the order and the third wave, involving the 10th, went over the top. The slaughter continued, with one officer shouting that it was 'murder'. Throssell was on the right flank of the fourth line and these men charged, although it is not clear if an order was given. They did not get far. As men fell around him, Throssell told the survivors to throw themselves to the ground. They had gone about 10 yards and there they stayed for about ninety minutes until they were ordered to return to their trenches.

One officer would record:

I was expecting a bullet to hit one of my bombs any moment and blow me to glory or somewhere else. I wished those bombs anywhere but around my neck. When the fire eased off a bit I crawled slowly towards our trench. I got within six feet. I made a rush on all fours and tumbled head first into the trench. The trench was in a terrible state – dead and wounded lying everywhere. Some were lying dead half in and half out the trench, some got a yard away, some got more, some were killed trying to get out. About 10 yards away from our trench they were lying in rows and heaps. It was awful.

Throssell's brother Ric, a sergeant, was badly wounded in the chest. The 8th suffered 234 casualties, 154 fatal, and the 10th had 138 casualties, 80 fatal. Both regiments started the attack with around 300 men. There was no respite for the survivors. They were told to stay in their trenches in case the Turks attacked.

After the failure to seize The Nek, senior officers decided on two other targets, Scimitar Hill and Hill 60, known locally as Kaiajik Aghala, a feature that, if captured, would link the Anzac beachhead with Suvla Bay. The Turks had quickly fortified the summit of Hill 60. British and empire troops launched an attack on 21 August but by the following day they had been mostly driven back with high casualties. A renewed attempt on the maze of trenches was made on 27 August, with little success. Only New Zealanders held some trenches near the base of Hill 60.

On 26 August the remnants of the 10th Light Horse had been ordered to leave their position near The Nek. It was welcome news. At last they were being relieved. They expected to go to a rest camp. Some 180 weary men struggled down a slope towards the beach area, 'carrying food, firewood, water cans in addition to rifles and equipment and 300 bombs'. Then they turned inland to a spot known as Table Top, regarded as a relatively safe area. Throssell recalled: 'When we got near Table Top the promised rest disappeared. Bullets were whistling round us and at 9 o'clock in the evening we were ordered to sling off our packs and just take our fighting gear and ammunition. We expected to be right into a charge, but the order was countermanded and we had a long walk to Hill 60 towards Suvla Bay. Wounded men were passing us all the time on their way back from the firing line.'

The 10th spent a bitterly cold night in the open and at about seven o'clock in the morning Turkish artillery spotted them and opened fire. The most senior officer, Lieutenant Colonel Noel Brazier, was among those badly wounded. A new bivouac was found and the men spent the rest of the day digging in. During the afternoon Major General Sir Alexander Godley told the officers he wanted an assault to take a key trench. On 29 August, at 1 a.m., the moonlit attack began and one trench was taken, though it was more of ditch and full of bodies from both sides. All around were scattered dead. Firing was continuous. As a deeper trench was dug and a sandbag barricade erected, bodies were heaved out using arms and legs. The newly killed were treated in the same way. As one trooper put it: 'Poor chaps, they were no use to us after they were killed.' By this time Throssell had shot dead at least five Turks.

The fighting intensified as the enemy launched a counterattack. Bullets and bombs were flying everywhere, and Throssell thought the chances of surviving were 'very remote'. The assault was beaten back only for hundreds of Turks to reappear shortly afterwards. The most serious counterattack came before dawn. The Australians were hopelessly outnumbered, but Throssell continued to urge his men on. The Australians and Turks threw between 3,000 and 4,000 bombs at each other, according to the war diary of the 10th Light Horse. The Turkish bombs were like cricket balls with fuses, and keen cricketer Sid Ferrier bowled back an estimated 500 before they exploded. Ferrier's luck eventually ran out when a bomb with a short fuse 'blew his arm to rags'. Throssell was wounded several times but carried on for hours and only left the action after a direct order. The counterattacks ended with daylight. By 30 August only 70 out of 160 men of the 10th were left alive and fighting on Hill 60. The regiment's original strength had been between 500 and 600.

Throssell was recommended for the Victoria Cross, and part of his citation noted: 'By his personal courage and example he kept up the spirits of his party and was largely instrumental in saving the situation at a critical period.' The attack on Hill 60 was largely inconclusive – the summit was never taken.

Throssell was evacuated to England in a hospital ship – 'heaven, clean bed and fifteen hours' sleep'. When he arrived in Southampton on 12 September he had mostly recovered from his wounds, although he was still suffering from deafness. He was admitted to a hospital in south London. On a day out in the capital he was introduced to Katharine Susannah Prichard at a club in Pall Mall and the attraction was immediate and mutual. Katharine recalled: 'Hugo said afterwards he had fallen in love with me as I walked along the terrace towards him. And I, certainly, was lifted out of my usual aloofness by the gay, irresistible manner of this young soldier.'

Later that month a specialist decided that a nasal condition and not bombing was responsible for Throssell's deafness. But a 'routine' operation left the hero of Hill 60 with bacterial meningitis and fighting for his life. The surgery almost certainly caused brain damage. On 4 December, however, he was well enough to go to Buckingham Palace where King George V presented him with the Victoria Cross. His fame was growing, and in March 1916 he sailed for Australia – and a hero's welcome. 'Thunderous applause' greeted him when he appeared at a civic reception in Perth. And the military authorities were keen to use him to boost recruitment. He may have looked impressive physically, but within he was traumatised. The horrors of Gallipoli and the effects of meningitis were causing mental problems. A medical board in Fremantle recommended three months' leave and further treatment. In May he returned to Northam and the adulation continued. It was the same story the following month when he went to visit his old school in Adelaide. He carried on to Melbourne where he was reunited with Katharine, who came to the conclusion that he had been 'broken by the war'. It would have been easy for Throssell to step back from the conflict, but he decided it was his duty to rejoin the 10th and went out of his way to persuade a medical board. He was declared fit for active service.

When the Gallipoli campaign ended in December 1915, the regiment – its depleted remnants – went to Egypt, where a rebuilding exercise was carried out. Another harsh campaign was on the way, shaped by oppressive heat, constant dust, disease and water shortages. There was one major consolation for Throssell – he was reunited with his brother Ric, who had been promoted lieutenant. The Turks were driven from Sinai and the 10th were part of the force that advanced into Palestine. In the second battle of Gaza Throssell was wounded again. His brother was killed. Throssell's remaining war service would either see him fighting or spending time in hospital. Stomach cramps were down to tapeworms, one 9 feet long. He took part in a victory parade in Jerusalem in December 1917, but malaria, which sometimes reduced him to 'shuddering helplessness', kept him out of action for many months. A weakened Throssell returned to Australia before the end of the war.

In Melbourne he was soon back with Katharine, who found 'a tall, masterful figure in uniform', despite his health problems and mental scars. The couple were married on 28 January 1919 and set up home at Greenmount, a 40-acre farm in the hills near Perth. They both had roles to play. Perhaps reluctantly, Throssell would continue, in public, to be the war hero. Katharine had no qualms about her role of political activist. She had been reading the works of Marx and Engels, and was embracing the revolution in Russia. And then came that speech at Northam on 19 July 1919.

Throssell's father had left him well off but he tended to be extravagant, and after leaving the army he needed to earn a living. His share of the farm he ran with his brother was mortgaged. He decided that property speculation was the answer, and he borrowed more money to buy up blocks of land near his new home, believing that they would make ideal sites for holiday and weekend retreats. According to Katharine, the land deals involved Throssell in 'reckless expenditures'. Another financial responsibility came in May 1922 in the form of a son, named Ric after Throssell's brother. The baby was wrapped in a gown displaying a hammer and sickle. Throssell had an army pension and also received a salary as a member of a settlement board for discharged soldiers. In late 1925 he was told that his work for the board was being severely curtailed.

After the Wall Street Crash of 1929, which led to widespread hardship in Western Australia, he was asked to resign his post at the board. The speech at Northam had not been forgotten, and many veterans regarded the communist activities of Katharine, supported by her husband, as treason. Throssell's real estate business collapsed, he lost more money speculating on wheat futures, and shares in an oil-prospecting company turned out to be worthless. All the time his health was deteriorating. Then the answer to his financial woes appeared, or so he thought – a gold find 300 miles from Perth. One man did make a fortune after discovering a lump of solid gold weighing 78lb, but it was not Throssell, who eventually returned home with even greater money worries. Although Katharine was a successful novelist, her royalty cheques were small. A friend managed to get Throssell a temporary job as an inspector of fertilisers.

In May 1933 Katharine, who was under increasing scrutiny by the authorities, sailed for London, and from there she went to the Soviet Union, planning a 30,000-mile journey across her utopia, the 'greatest event of my life'. She would write about the wonderful life under communism, the collective farms, the opportunities for women to become engineers, the attraction of Siberia. Her heavily blinkered view of the regime would see her unaware – or ignoring – its contempt for millions of citizens who were dying of starvation. And Stalin's Great Purge lay ahead.

Throssell had encouraged his wife's trip, realising its importance to her. He also realised that they needed a break from each other because of strains in their relationship, caused by his poor health and financial troubles. He hoped that by the time of her return towards the end of the year he would have sorted out the finances. Soon after Katherine set off from Greenmount, Throssell came up with yet another idea that he thought would be a money-spinner – a 'dude' ranch. He would stage a rodeo with lots of attractions on his property. 'Dude' ranches, where city and town dwellers could pretend to be cowboys, had taken off in America. The people of Perth would surely jump at the chance of doing something similar. He also thought it would help to sell off some of the land he had bought. Of course, he needed to borrow a lot more money to put on the show, planned for Sunday 30 July. The bank insisted that he put his property up as security, something he promised his wife he would not do.

A massive amount of work went ahead, but good fortune was not on Throssell's side. A horse crushed one of his feet, officialdom told him that buildings he had erected did not have planning permission, he was sacked as an inspector of fertilisers – and, worse, on the morning of 30 July he learned that he could not charge for admission to the 'Lazy H Ranch' because it was a Sunday and against the law. Any money collected would have to go to charity. Throssell was ruined before the first visitor arrived. Ironically, some 2,000 people turned up, with a local newspaper describing the event as 'an outstanding success'. Another show was staged but Throssell's problems were growing. It seemed that the authorities, increasingly, were putting obstacles in his way. His wife's communist propaganda was not helping.

In letters to Katharine he gave no hint of his latest failure, suggesting all was well at Greenmount. Their son recently had been staying with friends, and Throssell arranged to meet Ric in Perth one Saturday in early November for a cinema trip. To pay for this Throssell pawned his Victoria Cross for 10s. On the morning of Sunday, 19 November 1933, he sat in a deckchair on the veranda at Greenmount, put his legs up on the railing, and raised his army pistol to his right temple. He died shortly afterwards. He was forty-nine. It was reported that a note found near the body said, 'I can't sleep and I feel my old war head. It's gone "phut" and that's no good for anyone concerned.'

In a note with his will, Throssell pointed out that he had never recovered from 'my 1914–18 experiences' and thought his wife should get 'the usual war pension'. Katharine, whose journalist father had committed suicide, finally ended her visit to the Soviet Union, arriving back in Fremantle on Boxing Day, more than a month after the funeral. Remaining at Greenmount for most of her life, she enhanced her reputation as a novelist and continued to promote communism, rejecting any criticism of the Soviet Union, even when Stalin agreed to a non-aggression pact with Hitler in 1939. She died in October 1969, aged eighty-five. The Soviet flag covered her coffin.

After army service during the Second World War, Ric Throssell was allowed to pursue a career as a diplomat, despite misgivings about his mother's links with communism. Surprisingly, he was even given a posting to Moscow. In 1954 a Soviet defector, Vladimir Petrov, named him as a spy. A royal commission cleared Ric but suspicions remained for the rest of his life. Over the years the Australian Security Intelligence Organisation (ASIO) built up a large file on the Throssells and their son.

In 1984 Ric Throssell aroused controversy by announcing that he was giving his father's Victoria Cross to a nuclear disarmament group to raise funds. The move angered ex-servicemen. The Returned Services League successfully offered AU$38,000 to stop the medal going to auction, and it was presented to the Australian War Memorial. Ric's wife Dodie died on 20 April 1999 after a long illness, and he killed himself later that day.

The town of Northam took a long time to forgive Hugo Throssell. It was not until 1999 that a memorial appeared, a bronze plaque at the spot where he had made that speech. Reporting the tribute, one newspaper produced the headline 'Outcast ANZAC Honoured'.

20

Churchill's Outspoken Critic
John Sherwood-Kelly

There is no doubt that Lieutenant Colonel John Sherwood-Kelly was an inspiring figure on the battlefield. According to some of the men who served under him during the First World War, he won the Victoria Cross not once but half a dozen times. His fighting qualities, however, were matched by an explosive temper, and he made an enemy of a man he could never defeat: Winston Churchill.

'Bomb Kelly', as he became known, served in a remarkable number of campaigns, from the Matabeleland rebellion of 1896 to north Russia in 1919. When he left the British Army in disgrace, he tried to join the French Foreign Legion.

Sherwood-Kelly's Irish grandfather, James Kelly, reputedly took part in the Charge of the Light Brigade, though there were two riders of that name, Troop Sergeant Major [later Captain] James Kelly of the 4th Light Dragoons and Private James Kelly of the 11th Hussars. Sherwood-Kelly's father, John, left Ireland in the 1860s to start a new life in Cape Colony, South Africa. There the lawyer took a young bride, Emily Didcott, who went on to give him ten children. Sherwood-Kelly and a twin brother, Hurbert, were born on 13 January 1880. At one point the family moved to the rugged interior of Transkei. John Kelly had joined a local militia unit, and one day he happened to be near the Transkei coastline when a report came in that an Italian vessel was breaking up on rocks during a storm. He helped to rescue the crew and later received the Royal Humane Society's silver award.

At the age of twelve, Sherwood-Kelly, known to family and friends as Jack, suffered a devastating loss. His much-loved mother was killed when a horse bolted, overturning her cart. The following year Hurbert died in a riding accident, and from that time on Sherwood-Kelly found it increasingly difficult to control his temper and behaviour. His father's marriage to the family housekeeper less than two years after the death of Emily probably did not help. The troubled teenager shone at sport but that did not prevent his expulsion from school in 1895. He was then sent to a leading boarding school, where he excelled at boxing and riding, happily joining the cadet force, but poor discipline saw him being expelled again. Returning to the family home at Lady Frere – and an unsympathetic father – was not an attractive proposition. The solution, he decided, lay in the Matabeleland rebellion, on the borders of Transkei. He joined the Cape Mounted Police, aged sixteen.

The young warrior went on patrols but it is unclear whether he saw much action. His 'nasty temper' continued to be a problem, and by February 1899 his superiors decided they had had enough of him. His despairing father found him a job in the Cape's native department, but another escape plan quickly materialised in the shape of the Second Boer War. In September 1899 the Imperial Light Horse Regiment was raised. Thousands volunteered but only some 500 were chosen, including Sherwood-Kelly. The regiment quickly gained a formidable reputation, and one of its admirers was a young war correspondent, Winston Churchill, who rode with the men on a number of occasions. The Light Horse took part in the key actions of Elandslaagte, Ladysmith, Colenso and Spion Kop. Sherwood-Kelly showed qualities of leadership and he was promoted sergeant in the field. He was among those chosen for a flying column that helped to break the siege of Mafeking in May 1900. Later he transferred to Kitchener's Fighting Scouts as a lieutenant, but after a few months he resigned his commission following an argument with a senior officer. The Light Horse won a total of four Victoria Crosses during the war, which ended on 31 May 1902.

Sherwood-Kelly was still not keen to return home, and another opportunity for military service presented itself – an expedition to Somaliland to quell the so-called Mad Mullah,

Muhammed Abdullah Hassan, and his Dervishes. Britain was keen to protect its interests in the region in the face of nationalist aggression. A large number of colonial units were sent, including the Burgher Corps, which twenty-two-year-old Sherwood-Kelly joined as a sergeant. Once again he was used as a mounted infantryman, travelling long distances. The British forces suffered early reverses, but the Dervish leader was defeated at Jidbdalli and Illig, and the campaign ended in May 1904. Sherwood-Kelly returned to Transkei, demoted to private after criticising his commanding officer.

He took a job as a trader and also recruited native labour for work in the Cape's mines. It was not long before he was back in uniform, helping to put down a Zulu rebellion in Natal. Native chiefs had objected to white settlers taking over farmland and disturbing the traditional way of life. East Coast fever produced another challenge, but the tipping point was the introduction of a poll tax by the colonial authorities. Military operations were ordered after the killing of two police officers, and several chiefs were rounded up. Soon afterwards another chief, Bambata, led an attack on a police column and besieged several towns. More forces were sent, and Bambata was killed and beheaded – apparently to confirm identification – in one engagement. The natives were finally defeated at Izinsimba on 8 July 1906. It had been an unequal struggle – Zulus armed mostly with assegais and knobkerries facing soldiers with machine guns and cannon. Up to 4,000 natives were killed, some fighting in support of the colonial authorities. An interesting aspect of the revolt was the participation of Mahatma Gandhi, who backed the fight against the Zulus and served as a sergeant major in an Indian stretcher-bearer unit.

The next six years were largely uneventful for Sherwood-Kelly. He went back to recruiting native labour and married a wealthy and much older widow, Emily Snodgrass, against his father's wishes. The marriage did not last. By 1913 the free spirit that was Sherwood-Kelly had found another outlet for his aggression in the growing unrest in Ireland. With his younger brother Edward, he headed to Belfast to join the Ulster Volunteers in support of the Unionist cause. It was soon evident that a greater conflict was unfolding in Europe, and after a short time the brothers travelled to London.

In August 1914 they enlisted in the 2nd King Edward's Horse. Within days Private John Sherwood-Kelly, tall and stocky and charming – when it suited him – was promoted lieutenant. He transferred to the Norfolk Regiment and was swiftly given the rank of acting major because of his previous military experience. To his frustration he remained in Norfolk helping to train soldiers, but in 1915 he managed to join another regiment, the 1st Battalion King's Own Scottish Borderers, which was fighting in the Gallipoli campaign. The official battalion history would record: 'The new major was a Herculean giant of Irish-South African origin with a quite remarkable disregard for danger.'

During August and September he saw fierce fighting, acquiring the nickname Bomb Kelly after using a catapult technique, as the battalion history explained:

> Major 'Bomb' Kelly would reach for a pile of former tins of beef which were now packed with explosive and shell casings and a rough fuse through the base, light the fuse, the troops around him stood back, he stood up and holding a long stick in his left hand with a leather strap in his right would launch the home-made bomb across the dead ground towards the Turks. Occasionally if he got his timing wrong, the tin would shoot off behind him or to his side and men scrambled for their lives as it went off – but it didn't half keep you on your toes. Often, when the tin hit the mark, out would jump Turkish soldiers to be shot by the KOSBs and up would go a cheer as the tin exploded. Much like a deadly game of cricket ... The major knew no fear and laughed and cheered if we got one right into their holes.

On 15 October the commanding officer was killed in an explosion, and days later Sherwood-Kelly was gassed, which would permanently affect his breathing. Remarkably, the following month he was given command of the battalion with the rank of acting lieutenant colonel. True, there was a shortage of suitable officers, but his outstanding bravery and leadership qualities were difficult to ignore. By the time the campaign ended in January 1916 he had been recommended for the Distinguished Service Order and his tunic would display three wound stripes.

Sherwood-Kelly returned to England and during a break from the war he married a wealthy divorcee, Nellie Crawford, who lived in Kensington, London. The couple had met after he joined up, introduced by her brother, an officer in the 2nd King Edward's Horse. The dashing and charming South African soon found himself at ease in his future wife's social circle. Days after the wedding in April 1916 he went to France, attached to yet another regiment, the 1st Battalion Royal Inniskilling Fusiliers. On 4 June he was shot and badly wounded in fighting that would lead to the great Somme offensive. He was not expected to survive, but after hospital treatment he returned to London in his wife's care. When he was well enough he sailed for a three-month spell in South Africa, where he helped in a recruiting drive, patriotism that saw him made a Companion of the Order of St Michael and St George (CMG). By March 1917 he insisted he was fit again for active service and returned to northern France and the 1st Inniskillings. A gas attack put him back in hospital but he recovered to become the battalion's commanding officer.

Sherwood-Kelly won the Victoria Cross at the battle of Cambrai on 20 November 1917, a British attack noted for the large-scale use of tanks. As his battalion advanced, he saw that troops on his right were being held up by heavy rifle fire at a canal crossing. He raced across open ground and under the cover of a tank's guns led the men over the canal. Reaching higher ground under intense machine gun and rifle fire, he reconnoitred the position and then ordered his company commanders to cross the canal with their troops.

A report said:

Colonel Kelly, as coolly as though he were taking part in a field-day at home, allotted each company the frontage for which it would be responsible, and gave the order to advance. The battalion had hardly gone forward a quarter of a mile when its left flank was held up by a thick belt of wire. Colonel Kelly, who was as usual with the leading wave, ordered the companies on the right to halt and open covering fire, and himself dashed across to the post of danger on the left. Calling on a Lewis Gun team to follow him, he forced his way through the wire. He brought the gun into action on the far side, and thus enabled the whole battalion to cross the obstacle.

With their gallant colonel at their head, the battalion now advanced upon a line of gun-pits, from which the enemy was keeping up a continuous and destructive fire. When close enough, he gave the order to charge, and was himself amongst the first half dozen to reach the pits. After a short and fierce hand-to-hand struggle, the forty-six Germans who survived surrendered, and five machine guns were also captured.

As the Inniskillings reinforced their position, Sherwood-Kelly walked up and down the battalion front encouraging tired men and 'inspiring them to fresh efforts'. All the time he was under heavy fire, 'but he seemed to be absolutely careless of his own safety in his regard for the safety of his own men. He showed such contempt for the German fire that he never attempted to take cover, and frequently picked up rifles to fire at the enemy.'

The London Gazette recorded: 'The great gallantry displayed by this officer throughout the day inspired the greatest confidence in his men, and it was mainly due to his example and devotion to duty that his battalion was enabled to capture and hold their objective.'

By early December Sherwood-Kelly was no longer in command of the battalion, which had moved to rear lines for a well-earned rest. He had been gassed again and was in hospital. On 12 January 1918 he was well enough to go to Buckingham Palace, where King George V presented him with the Victoria Cross. A medical board decided that he should not go back to the front and he was given six months' leave to visit South Africa. It would prove to be a controversial trip.

He took part in another recruiting campaign on behalf of the South African authorities, but refused to account for his expenses. He also upset the English community by appearing to identify with the nationalist cause. James Hertzog, a former Boer general and a future prime minister of the Union of South Africa, was a friend. At one recruiting rally Sherwood-Kelly made 'some injudicious remarks', and was summoned to see the British military commander, Brigadier H. Martyn, in Cape Town. The brigadier, who had not been consulted about the recruiting role, told the War Office: 'He assured me that he had not meant politics by any remark he had made, and after considerable conversation I was quite satisfied that his remarks were made in the excitement of the moment and that his educational attainments in my opinion did not suit him to making speeches, as he made statements which he considers harmless and not political which in a country like South Africa are at once seized on by the opposite political parties and turned to their advantage.' But he added: 'No more loyal or gallant officer in my opinion is serving in HM Army.' Brigadier Martyn decided that his troublesome visitor should return to England and found him a passage on the troopship *City of Karachi*, which sailed in June.

The troops were placed under the command of Sherwood-Kelly. He soon fell out with their South African officers, who complained of bullying. He had reportedly referred to 'damned South Africans' – an irony given his nationality – and described them as an 'undisciplined rabble'. Relations deteriorated so much that when the ship reached Sierra Leone the commander of British troops in West Africa, Major General Charles Thompson, felt obliged to hold an inquiry, noting that the South Africans were 'suffering from a deep sense of wrong'. Sherwood-Kelly denied calling them 'damned South Africans'. General Thompson thought it 'unthinkable' that any officer would use such an expression but if it had been spoken in the heat of the moment then Sherwood-Kelly would be the first to recognise the fact and apologise. The lieutenant colonel 'acquiesced readily'. The general told the War Office: 'I was fully under the impression that the matter was settled, that all parties were satisfied and that no further trouble would arise.'

He was being too optimistic, because a Major King made an official complaint after the *City of Karachi* reached England. Statements repeating the allegation of bullying were given to the South African high commissioner in London, who contacted his country's minister of defence. The result was a request for a War Office investigation. Sherwood-Kelly, who was back in France commanding the Norfolk's 12th Battalion, pointed out that during the voyage he was forced to reprimand a lieutenant for 'inviting men into his cabin', and he had repeatedly remonstrated with Major King about 'slackness on board ship'. He denied referring to 'damned South Africans'. The Army Council concluded that

Sherwood-Kelly should have shown 'a little more tact' in dealing with the South African officers. The high commissioner was told that it was unfortunate that command of the troops aboard the ship had been given to the lieutenant colonel as he did not have 'those qualities necessary for the preservation of discipline without causing resentment among his subordinates'.

When the war ended in November 1918, there was no doubt that Sherwood-Kelly had shown outstanding bravery. He was wounded and gassed several times, and his health would pay a price for the rest of his life. But if he had any thoughts of enjoying the peace, they soon disappeared. With the ink on the Armistice barely dry, a new campaign emerged and Sherwood-Kelly, far from being war weary, stepped forward. The focus was north Russia.

The Russian Revolution of 1917, which saw the downfall of Tsar Nicholas II, shook royalty and political circles in Britain. Russia had been fighting Germany on the Eastern Front, incurring huge losses. Britain sent large quantities of war material to its ally, and munitions were held in the ports of Archangel and Murmansk, guarded by British troops to stop them falling into the hands of Bolsheviks. As civil war engulfed Russia, it was decided to send an expeditionary force to extricate the men, who found themselves caught up in fighting between the Bolsheviks and White Russians. On the surface the expeditionary force appeared to be a limited operation – bring the soldiers home. But Secretary State for War Winston Churchill had another agenda, fearing the spread of communism and the threat to Baltic states. The defensive operation morphed into an offensive struggle and, for the first time, Sherwood-Kelly would object to sending his soldiers into battle. Despite the horrors and carnage of the First World War there were plenty of volunteers for the mission, including six other officers who had won the Victoria Cross. Sherwood-Kelly was given command of the 2nd Battalion Hampshire Regiment, which arrived at Archangel in May 1919, and the following month he began leading patrols into the interior.

It soon became apparent to him that the British force, totalling around 15,000, was too small to adopt an offensive role against the Bolsheviks in such a vast country. The turning point came during a planned attack on the villages of Troitsa and Topsa. The Hampshires were detailed to support a Russian regiment, which did not advance on time, and at the last minute Sherwood-Kelly withdrew his men without firing a shot, fearing they would be outflanked. The British commander, Major General Edmund Ironside, decided that Sherwood-Kelly had disobeyed orders. In July Sherwood-Kelly refused to carry out another attack, complaining that it was pointless and his men would be killed for nothing.

He had been at odds with senior officers since arriving in Russia, as Ironside pointed out after reprimanding him for gross insubordination in a case involving Brigadier George Grogan, a Victoria Cross winner: 'The officer was very contrite and I decided to give him one more chance and I clearly explained this to him. Since this time Lieutenant Colonel Kelly has served under General Turner who has reported to me that Lieutenant Colonel Kelly has been far from satisfactory. Lieutenant Colonel Kelly is a very hot-headed and quarrelsome man and has had rows with practically everyone with whom he has come into contact.'

Grogan had listed eight specific complaints, including: 'Continual questioning of all orders or instructions issued him by the brigade, many of which he treated with open contempt before junior officers.' A captain involved in the operation at Troitsa and Topsa revealed that Sherwood-Kelly had ridiculed another brigadier and his staff in front of junior officers and other ranks, with the remarks drawing 'frequent laughter from the men'. There was also criticism of 'so-called generals who sit on their arses in offices', making 'us poor, bloody fools do such idiotic stunts as these'. Another officer quoted Sherwood-Kelly as saying: 'It is all very well for those damn people who sit on their ruddy backsides and run the show to tell us the Russians are going to fight, but I know they are not and we shall have to do the whole thing.'

There is, however, another view of Sherwood-Kelly's decision not to engage the enemy – he had lost his nerve. That was the opinion of Lieutenant Colonel Charles Hudson, a Victoria Cross winner. Hudson came to the conclusion that Sherwood-Kelly was 'a very burnt-out case'. During a tour of defences he apparently shook with fear even at the sound of distant explosions. And General Lord Rawlinson, who took over from Ironside, noted: 'It may be that his frequent outbreaks of irritability in this country are an indication that he has not recovered from the breakdown of his health in France.'

Sherwood-Kelly sealed his fate by writing letters home containing details of military movements, knowing that a censor would intercept them. In a letter to a woman friend in Somerset, he complained that many Russians were going over to the Bolshevik side, 'murdering or capturing all the British officers with them'. He told another friend in London that newspapers should publish 'the true state of affairs and cease advertising Ironside, who is weak and not fit for the job'. In August 1919 Sherwood-Kelly was relieved of his command and sent back to Britain.

He was still angry when he arrived in London and decided to expose what he saw as the fiasco of the Russian intervention, accepting that it would almost certainly end his army career. A letter from him appeared on the front page of the *Daily Express* under several headlines, including 'ARCHANGEL SCANDAL EXPOSED', 'DUPLICITY OF CHURCHILL POLICY IN RUSSIA' and 'THE PUBLIC HUMBUGGED'.

Sherwood-Kelly wrote: 'I volunteered for service with the North Russian Relief Force in the sincere belief that relief was urgently needed in order to make possible the withdrawal of low-category troops in the last stages of exhaustion, due to fierce fighting amid the rigours of an Arctic winter. The wide advertisement of this relief expedition led myself and many others to believe that affairs in north Russia were about to be wound up in an efficient and decisive manner.'

He went on:

Immediately on arrival at Archangel, however, towards the end of May, I at once received the impression that the policy of the authorities was not what it was stated to be. This impression hardened as time went on, and during the months of June and July I was reluctantly driven to the following conclusions – that the troops of the relief force, which we were told had been sent out for defensive purposes, were being used for offensive purposes, on a large scale and far in the interior, in furtherance of some ambitious plan of campaign the nature of which we were not allowed to know. My personal experience of those operations was that they were not even well conducted, and that they were not calculated to benefit in a military or any other sense a sound and practical British policy in Russia. They only entailed useless loss and suffering on troops that had already made incalculable sacrifices in the Great War.

There was also criticism of the disloyalty of Russian troops, who were often more of a danger to British soldiers than the Bolsheviks, and the waste of taxpayers' money, 'poured out like water'. Sherwood-Kelly's parting shot: 'I became convinced that my duty to my country lay not in helping to forward a mistaken policy, but in exposing it to the British public.'

The *Express* was quick to attack Churchill and called for an immediate investigation: 'It is possible now to give all the facts about the Archangel expedition. They constitute a public scandal of the first importance; they suggest double-dealing on the part of the government, as represented by Mr Churchill, and they shatter to bits a number of bubble military reputations artificially created out of the misleading information on which the country has been fed.'

A week later Sherwood-Kelly fired another salvo from the front page of the *Express* after a personal attack by Churchill. He complained that the minister had suggested he was sent home from Russia 'because I have done something of a disgraceful nature'. Churchill used the words, 'For a serious offence under the Army Act.' The officer pointed out that this could be twisted to mean anything, and he felt compelled to reply, giving a detailed account of his time in Russia and quoting various correspondence with senior officers, including a message from Brigadier Grogan congratulating him on the 'very gallant way' he had led a patrol.

The first *Express* article caused consternation at the War Office, with one leading figure writing: 'He is not normal, and suffers from an ungovernable temper. I should have liked to have seen him tried two or three years ago for an assault on a waiter in a hotel, and I should still like to see him tried now, were it not that we should be attacked in the press for giving him different treatment from that accorded Sir F. Maurice.' In 1918 Major General Sir Frederick Maurice had been placed on retired pay, without any deductions, after criticising Prime Minister David Lloyd George in a letter to

The Times. General Sir John [later Field Marshal Lord] French was also cited as a precedent. He had survived after tipping off the press in 1915 about a shortage of high-explosive shells for the campaign in France.

If Sherwood-Kelly refused to go quietly, the War Office thought there were four options to end his army career: court-martial him, charge him with misconduct under a royal warrant, request his resignation, or force him to leave under demobilisation. The War Office recommendation was dismissal because of misconduct.

The decision was taken out of the hands of the War Office by Churchill, who was incensed at the second letter to the *Express* and insisted that Sherwood-Kelly should be court-martialled, something the officer wanted anyway. On 13 October Sherwood-Kelly was under open arrest at Wellington barracks, near Buckingham Palace, and later that month he faced a court martial. It was over quickly. There were three charges, all involving contact with the *Express*, and he pleaded guilty to them. He was sentenced to be severely reprimanded. Shortly afterwards the army ended his career by using the excuse of demobilisation. The *Express* had declared that the fighting in north Russia was 'not worth the bones of a single grenadier', and the campaign, under Rawlinson, soon ended.

Not surprisingly, Sherwood-Kelly found it difficult to adjust to civilian life. His relationship with his wife Nellie was far from smooth. He had been involved with other women, and he spent some time living at the fashionable Hotel Rubens in Buckingham Palace Road. During a national train strike he bizarrely volunteered as a railway stableman at Blackfriars. Over the next few years he would make several attempts to re-enlist in the army, even writing to Churchill for help. The War Office did not hesitate to turn him down. One official observed: 'He is the sort of person who is unlikely to find congenial employment until there is another war.'

In 1923, with his wife's support, he tried his hand at politics, standing as the Conservative parliamentary candidate for Clay Cross, Derbyshire, a Labour stronghold. He lost and stood there the following year, increasing his share of the vote but still losing. At one public meeting a heckler called him a liar and refused to withdraw the remark. Sherwood-Kelly stepped down from the platform and 'gave the man a thrashing amid the applause of the audience'.

In August 1925, at the age of forty-five, he tried to join the French Foreign Legion for operations in Morocco. The military attaché at the French embassy in London took the request seriously and wrote to General Sir John Burnett-Stuart at the War Office asking if there were any objections. The War Office did not object – but pointed out that Sherwood-Kelly had been court-martialled for contacting the press, which put an end to the application. Later Sherwood-Kelly went to Bolivia to help with the building of roads and railways. In 1930 he travelled to Tanganyika [now Tanzania], apparently to hunt big game, but contracted malaria and returned to England. On 18 August 1931 he died in a Kensington nursing home, aged fifty-one. He was buried with military honours at Brookwood cemetery in Surrey. His wife did not attend.

21

Her Ladyship Is Not Amused

John Grant

John Grant stumbled towards the reception for Victoria Cross holders in London. He had endured a tiring journey from New Zealand. But he was clearly drunk.

Lord and Lady Mountbatten were hosting the gathering. Lieutenant General the Lord Freyberg, a former governor general of New Zealand who had won the Victoria Cross during the Battle of the Somme, was also present. Grant went up to Lady Mountbatten and shouted, 'How yer goin', Edwina?' He then slapped her on 'the bum'. After a handshake with a surprised Lord Mountbatten he went to the bar, threw down some money and yelled, 'My shout, lads!' He promptly fell over a table. According to one report, a horrified Freyberg had sixty-six-year-old Grant 'discreetly removed from the function'. Another report suggested he was 'frogmarched' out. Lady Mountbatten, a wealthy socialite, was no stranger to scandalous behaviour, though it is certain she had never before experienced an approach so lacking in subtlety. The occasion, in June 1956, was to mark the centenary of the Victoria Cross. There was also a review of holders by the queen in Hyde Park.

In 2012 Corinne Grant reflected on the behaviour of her great-uncle, who was known as Jack:

I love this story because it makes my uncle human. At the time, however, it caused him nothing but shame. No one wanted a war hero who wasn't faultless. Jack never came to terms with the adulation. Trying to live up to what other people wanted him to be turned him into someone he wasn't and he did things that were completely out of character. War changes people but so do the expectations of a demanding public. He lived in a lonely world and died a lonely man. We shouldn't deify our war heroes. We should respect and honour them, but we should remember that they are made of flesh and blood just like the rest of us. To deny them that denies them their humanity and, in the case of my uncle, destroys them ... If Jack was alive today, I am pretty sure he'd tell you he wished he'd never won a VC.

Four years earlier a great-nephew, Mike Merrick, had been quoted as saying, 'Some relatives take the dim view that he was an alcoholic to be avoided. Others were really quite fond of him. But the general consensus now is that he was suffering from post-traumatic stress and maybe that goes some way towards explaining his behaviour.'

John Grant was born at Hawera, a town on New Zealand's North Island, on 26 August 1889. His father George died when he was a youngster and after basic schooling he took a job in the building trade. In June 1915 Grant enlisted as a private in the New Zealand Expeditionary Force, soon afterwards sailing to Egypt and joining the 1st Battalion Wellington Regiment, which was seriously understrength after being mauled at Gallipoli. The arrivals were not immediately welcomed, as a regimental history observed:

During the strenuous days of training in Egypt there was a certain amount of acrimony between new soldiers and those of Gallipoli fame. While for the time it may have caused personal distress, yet it seemed to have the effect of instilling into both sections a spirit of enthusiasm, bringing with it a determination to show that the newcomers were as good soldiers as the old hands, while the old hands took care to prevent the newcomers showing any superiority in drill and efficiency.

The regiment, with two battalions, formed part of the New Zealand Division. In April 1916 the men sailed for Marseille, southern France, and then headed north to the Western Front. The following month the 1st Battalion went to the town of Armentieres. Its first task was to defend a salient known as The Mushroom, which jutted into no man's land close to the German front line. On 1 June the men had their first experience of intensive shelling. There was sometimes humour on the battlefield. One day the Germans stuck up a large board saying the British fleet had been destroyed at the Battle of Jutland. The board was shelled. The enemy launched a major attack on The Mushroom on 8 July. The battalion's casualties were two officers and twenty-one other ranks killed and nearly 100 wounded. But a greater challenge lay ahead for both battalions and the rest of the New Zealand Division: the Somme.

> No division ever better earned the gratitude of its commander or, indeed, of the nation than did the New Zealand Division in that famous battle. Engaged continuously from 15 September to 3 October, under the worst possible weather conditions, faced by a great mass of artillery and machine guns, the division to a man fought with the steadiness of regular troops and with a spirit intrepid and indomitable. With one or two trifling exceptions where parties failed to gain their objectives, the division carried out the tasks allotted to it.

The division continued to serve with distinction, particularly during the battles of Messines and Passchendaele. By the time of the Hundred Days' Offensive in August 1918 it was one of the strongest divisions, with more than 12,000 men. In this last great campaign of the First World War the Allies began driving the Germans eastwards. On 21 August the British Third Army, which included the New Zealanders, attacked on a wide front north of Amiens. The enemy retreated towards the key town of Bapaume. On 25 August, after capturing Grevillers, Loupart Wood and Biefvillers, the New Zealanders reached Bapaume. There was a steady flow of prisoners, who were often relieved of their possessions, as one account noted:

> The 'ratting' of prisoners was a very interesting process. Some men were too proud to plunder, and stood aloof from the whole business; others, out of a thirst for knowledge, or a desire for souvenirs, displayed a deep interest in all that was Fritz's, from his jewellery [watches were prized] to the photos of the 'frauleins'

he carried in his pocket book. Fritz was usually quite amiable, and showed a very proper spirit of resignation. Usually the search was conducted in a perfectly friendly spirit, and the unfortunate was consoled for the loss of his girl's photo, or of his Iron Cross, with cigarettes and tobacco.

Bapaume was taken after several days of fierce fighting, and the advance continued east through the nearby villages of Fremicourt and Bancourt, which had been occupied by the Allies in March 1917 but lost during the enemy offensive of spring 1918. It was near Bancourt that Grant won the Victoria Cross on 1 September. After being driven from the village the Germans took up positions along a ridge 800 yards away, defending it stubbornly. On the open slope leading to the top men went down 'in scores'. Enemy counterattacks were fought off. Grant, a sergeant, led a platoon with the near-suicidal aim of silencing a line of five machine-gun posts that were proving 'a serious obstacle'.

Despite withering fire, the platoon advanced and when they were 20 yards away Grant rushed forward, closely followed by a lance corporal, and attacked the centre post – 'how the German bullets missed them will ever remain a mystery'. The machine gunners were silenced and Grant raced to another post, with the same result. The remaining posts were quickly cleared by the platoon. Grant's citation recorded: 'Throughout the whole operation on this and the two previous days Sergeant Grant displayed coolness, determination and valour of the highest order, and set a splendid example to all.' The lance corporal was awarded the Distinguished Conduct Medal.

Another remarkable Victoria Cross winner was Sergeant Reginald Judson of the 1st Battalion Auckland Regiment. In the space of a month he was awarded three gallantry decorations: the Distinguished Conduct Medal for bravery near Hebuterne and at Rossignol Wood on 24 and 25 July 1918; the Military Medal for action near Puisieux-au-Mont on 16 August; and the Victoria Cross for taking out several machine-gun posts south-west of Bapaume on 26 August.

Grant was sent to Britain for officer training soon after his Victoria Cross action and in February 1919 he was commissioned second lieutenant, returning to New Zealand in October and receiving a hero's welcome. A newspaper reported: 'Lieutenant Grant will be remembered in Auckland as a prominent member of both the Waitemata Swimming Club and the Grafton senior football team in 1907 and 1908. He competed in New Zealand swimming championships and the important swimming event with Brigadier General Freyburg and Malcolm Champion, and it is worthy of note that both Brigadier General Freyburg and Lieutenant Grant have won the coveted VC.' The paths of Grant and Freyburg did, of course, cross again in less than happy circumstances at the reception for Victoria Cross holders in London in 1956.

Grant was discharged in January 1920 and took up work as a carpenter, also joining his country's territorial force. In October 1924 he married Elizabeth Merriman, but three years later he left his wife and two children, a son and a daughter. At about the same time he was declared bankrupt. His commitment to the territorial force also wavered, and in 1929 he was discharged 'apparently indifferent regards training'.

The Great Depression of the 1930s saw many New Zealanders unemployed. In the early years there was little welfare support and riots broke out in Dunedin, Auckland and Wellington. The government's response was to pass public safety laws and to send jobless men to remote labour camps. In 1935 a newspaper reported the 'surprise discovery' of a Victoria Cross holder at Paeroa camp. An army officer was asked to investigate, and Colonel John Duigan did Grant no favours:

> I am given to understand that one J. G. Grant VC is working at a relief camp at Paeroa race course ... As far as I can find out, Grant has on several occasions been provided with permanent employment, but is alleged to be unable to hold it, owing to his erratic habits. It appears that he is extremely unreliable, and it is to this factor alone that he owes his present position.

In June 1915, shortly before his enlistment, Grant had become a freemason. He died at the Roskill Masonic Village, Auckland, on 25 November 1970, aged eighty-one.

22

The IRA Terrorist
Martin Doyle

At Buckingham Palace on 8 May 1919, King George V pinned the Victoria Cross to the chest of Company Sergeant Major Martin Doyle of the Royal Munster Fusiliers. Little did the king know that Doyle would soon be engaged in another war – this time against the Crown, as a member of a terrorist organisation, the IRA.

Doyle, who also won the Military Medal, returned to his native – and divided – Ireland as a hero of the First World War. It was not long before he joined the republican cause, swept up by years of bitterness and fervour. Perhaps life in the trenches in France, reading letters from home, had helped to shape his mind. He would, however, remain a contradiction to the end. As the years passed, both sides to some extent found him an embarrassment. Was he a British Army hero or a nationalist hero? He would be buried in Dublin, the heart of the republic, but with a headstone depicting the regimental badge of the long-disbanded Royal Munster Fusiliers and giving his British gallantry decorations, VC and MM, and old rank, with no indication of his double life.

Doyle was born at Gusserane, County Wexford, on 25 October 1894, the son of Larry and Bridget Doyle. His father worked on the land. The family later moved to the nearby town of New Ross, which has its roots in the fourth century. In 1649 Oliver Cromwell seized the town, and the 1798 rebellion saw one of the fiercest battles there, when British forces defeated rebels with the loss of more 2,000 lives and the destruction of many homes. Stories relating to local history were no doubt passed from generation to generation. After a primary school education Martin Doyle became a farm worker, but by the time he was fifteen he decided he did not wish to continue in his father's footsteps. He went to Kilkenny and joined the Royal Irish Regiment, claiming to be seventeen. He took to soldiering and following a brief spell of home service he sailed for India. Improving his education and sport were two of his interests, and he won the regiment's lightweight boxing championship.

After the First World War broke out the regiment returned home, going to France in December 1914. Doyle transferred to the 2nd Battalion Royal Dublin Fusiliers, which was understrength after seeing action in the battles of Le Cateau, the Marne, the Aisne and Messines. The battalion took heavy casualties the following year at the second battle of Ypres, a series of clashes between 22 April and 24 May. The fighting at St Julien, which raged for eleven days, was particularly brutal, with the Germans launching gas attacks against soldiers who had only handkerchiefs soaked in urine for protection. The fusiliers received such a battering that they did not take part in another major battle until the launch of the Somme offensive on 1 July 1916, a day that ended with nearly 60,000 British casualties. That year saw Doyle promoted sergeant.

In March 1918 he transferred to the 1st Battalion Royal Munster Fusiliers, which had been involved in fighting at Gallipoli, the Somme, Messines, Passchendaele and Cambrai. The Western Front had been relatively quiet during the January and February, but it was known that the Germans were preparing a major offensive, determined on a breakthrough before American forces made a difference. The British line, with reduced and exhausted divisions, stretched 125 miles, and there was no indication where the Germans would strike.

Before dawn on 21 March the answer came. The enemy, with reinforcements from their Russian and Italian campaigns, launched a massive bombardment on a 54-mile front, from the Sensee to the Oise. Germans advanced under clouds of gas with tanks, pushing back many defenders. The 1st Battalion held positions around the village of St Emilie and it was not until late afternoon that they came under attack. The enemy failed to get further than wire entanglements, leaving many dead, but fresh attempts were made at half hourly intervals until about 9 p.m., when they retreated, apparently exhausted. Early the next day German artillery pounded the positions, and troops under the cover of thick fog crept forward, cutting gaps in the wire, but all attacks were repulsed. Then it was noticed that the battalion's right flank was completely exposed and the fusiliers were ordered to fall back.

On the morning of the 21st the battalion had twenty-four officers and 950 other ranks; by nightfall on the 22nd the numbers were seven officers and 450 other ranks. The next day the battalion was ordered to cover the withdrawal of the 39th Division. It would be the signal for a general retreat. Within days the British were being forced back across the old Somme battlefields, losing territory that had taken months to secure. On 24 March Doyle showed his courage when he led a group of volunteers in a bayonet charge across no man's land to silence a machine-gun post in a barn. When he reached the objective he discovered he was alone but he carried on, bayoneting the gunners and seizing their weapon. Later he was captured and badly treated. He escaped during a counterattack by his unit. Doyle's bravery that day was recognised by the award of the Military Medal. The battalion was engaged in fierce fighting until 29 March, taking many more casualties.

The 1st Battalion was so depleted that it merged with the regiment's 2nd Battalion in April. It would enjoy a peaceful few months, even taking part in the divisional sports and horse-riding show at St Leger-les-Authie on 21 July, winning a cup and a day off trench duties. The war, of course, was still being fought, and three days later saw a turning point, with a German retreat to the Vesle. On 21 August the Allies began their great push from the North Sea to Verdun, which would lead ultimately to victory.

The 1st Battalion was soon back fighting, this time near Riencourt. At 5 a.m. on 2 September the battalion took part in an assault on a series of trenches, advancing as gas shells burst among the men. It was the day that Doyle won his Victoria Cross. The acting sergeant major took command of a company after all its officers had been killed or wounded. Seeing that some men were surrounded, he led a party to help them, showing 'skill and leadership'. Doyle killed several of the enemy as they worked their way along the trenches, successfully extricating the trapped soldiers. Then, under heavy fire, he carried a wounded officer to safety. Later he went to the aid of men in a blazing tank. When a machine gun opened up at close range, preventing the rescue of the wounded, he charged and silenced it, taking three prisoners. He also carried another wounded soldier to safety despite intense fire. During a counterattack on his position, 'he showed great power of command, driving back the enemy and capturing many prisoners'. The commander of XVII Corps, General Sir Charles Fergusson, was so impressed with the battalion's actions that he paid the soldiers a visit to congratulate them. The fighting had cost the battalion more than 300 casualties.

There was little respite for the fusiliers, and by 30 September the battalion was down to only ten officers and 150 other ranks. That day saw the loss of the commanding officer, Lieutenant Colonel Robert Kane, who had 'so long and so brilliantly' led the battalion. He had been hit in the head by machine-gun fire. The war would last only a few more weeks.

In March 1919 Doyle returned to his home town of New Ross, where he received a hero's welcome. His parents were in a large crowd at the railway station. A local newspaper reported:

> The meeting between the young hero and his aged parents was very touching. Going straight to his mother and father he embraced them. He was escorted to his home in Mary Street amidst a scene of great enthusiasm. As they approached the Royal Hotel a trumpeter standing on the steps sounded a stirring bugle call which evoked ringing cheers. There was a profusion of decorations in the town along with scrolls bearing words of welcome to the New Ross hero.

That May saw his visit to Buckingham Palace, where the king presented him with the Military Medal as well as the Victoria Cross. Doyle apparently had the opportunity of gaining a commission but he decided to leave the army and was demobilised in July. He went back to Ireland and a few months later married one Charlotte Kennedy, who would produce three daughters. Doyle was again at the palace on 26 June 1920 for a garden party in honour of 324 recipients of the Victoria Cross. He was pictured shaking hands with Queen Mary. At some point he had joined the old comrades' association of the Munsters and was a member of the regimental party that took part in the unveiling of the Cenotaph in Whitehall on 11 November, the second anniversary of the Armistice. It was during 1920 that he also joined the IRA.

Ireland had witnessed centuries of conflict – the battle of the Boyne in 1690, the 1798 rebellion, the Fenian revolt in 1867. By the beginning of the twentieth century the Catholic majority was exerting pressure for home rule, much to the concern of many Protestants who wished to remain in the ascendancy and keep Ireland's links with Britain. In January 1913 the unionist politician Sir Edward Carson founded the Ulster Volunteer Force (UVF) to oppose home rule – by force if necessary. In November the pro-home rule National Volunteers was formed, only to split and give birth to the Irish Volunteers, forerunner of the IRA. The First World War largely changed the focus of Irish politics, although the Easter Rising in Dublin in 1916 was a sharp reminder that a major problem remained. Irishmen had responded well to the call to fight for king and country. In 1914 some 22,000 were serving in the army but by 1918 more than 200,000 had fought in the war. The UVF, with more than 80,000 members, formed the 36th (Ulster) Division and went on to have a distinguished record.

As peace descended on Europe, so conflict arose again in Ireland. In December 1918 Sinn Fein won a landslide victory in the Irish general election, and the IRA was straining to wage a war of independence. An attack on 21 January 1919 signalled the start of another conflict that would become increasingly vicious. Nine IRA men ambushed two council workmen and two Royal Irish Constabulary (RIC) constables who were taking a consignment of gelignite and detonators in a cart from military barracks in Tipperary town to Soloheadbeg Quarry. The 'village bobbies', both Catholics, were shot dead. The IRA later announced that it had a 'moral and legal' duty to kill police and soldiers. The pattern of the 21 January attack would be repeated many times, with large groups of terrorists targeting inferior numbers of police in rural areas. Some of the attacks had an element of farce. One raid on a police post was called off mid-battle when the terrorist bringing a supply of home-made grenades failed to turn up because he had fallen off his bicycle. The IRA regarded itself as a proper army, with brigades, battalions and companies, and ranks such as commandant, captain and lieutenant. It had around 70,000 members but in reality only some 3,000 were active. Many of its leaders lacked military training, including Michael Collins, who at one time had been a post office worker, later taking up accountancy.

Doyle retained his links with the British Army, getting a civilian job at barracks in Ennis, County Clare. He was recruited as an intelligence officer for the IRA's Mid-Clare Brigade and began passing on information about army movements, leading a double life as a Victoria Cross hero happy to attend a Buckingham Palace reunion and a member of a terrorist organisation that wanted to kill British soldiers. Michael Collins was aware that Doyle had been recruited as a spy. Up to 400 infantry, several hundred mounted troops and about fifty police were stationed in Ennis.

Doyle was not the only ex-soldier in the town helping the IRA. After demobilisation Patrick Mulcahy returned to his job at the local post office and quickly offered his services. He obtained keys to military and police ciphers and translated messages. He would later boast that the messages were usually in the hands of the Mid-Clare Brigade commander, Frank Barrett, before they reached the intended destination. 'Many a message ordering the arrest of a volunteer was intercepted and the volunteer warned before the local district inspector was aware of the contents of the cipher wire,' Mulcahy recalled. 'On two occasions I got such warning through to General Brennan [Michael Brennan, then commanding the East-Clare Brigade] enabling him to get away before the raiding party arrived at his billet.'

On 22 September 1920, fifty IRA men ambushed a police lorry near Rineen, killing six officers. An army convoy turned up shortly afterwards and several soldiers were wounded. The terrorists had neglected to cut phone lines and a priority message was sent to Ennis for reinforcements. 'I was able to delay the delivery of the message for nearly an hour and the volunteers just got clear before the arrival of the reinforcements,' said Mulcahy. During 1919 and 1920 the police and military kept in touch with all outposts hourly by phone. 'A favourite annoyance operation by volunteers was to cut the telephone wire. This always resulted in intensive enemy activity. In order not to dislocate civilian communication,

I prepared telegraph pole diagrams and, by marking the wires to be cut, ensured that only police and military wires were interfered with.' Mulcahy, who also intercepted official letters, added: 'Hardly a day passed that some information was not procured either from cipher messages or telephone conversations. I was assisted greatly by the stupidity of the RIC and military who discussed the most secret plans over the telephone. The RIC were especially at fault in this respect. The military erred only in times of stress when nerves were not too good.'

Mulcahy, who served in the Royal Engineers during the First World War, had telling observations on Irish soldiers when they were demobilised. At a barracks in Wales he went on parade with 500 men to be addressed by the camp's commanding officer:

> He wished us good luck and hoped we would get work when we returned home. He told us that Ireland was in a very disturbed state and that we should be careful to avoid contact with Sinn Fein – pronounced by him as Sin Fin. He attempted to air his views on Sinn Fein but an almost instantaneous outburst of 'mind your own fucking business' brought his speech to an abrupt conclusion. A shout of 'Come on, boys. Out of this fucking camp' was the signal for the men on parade to march off in a more or less disorganised way to the railway station. Prominent songs on the way were 'A Nation Once Again', 'Wrap The Green Flag Round Me, Boys' and 'Tipperary'. Some local military police attempted to stop the row but to no avail. The men's attitude at the time was one of resentment at any adverse criticism by an Englishman of the people at home.

Doyle and Mulcahy would have been in contact with another ex-British Army soldier, Paddy 'Con' McMahon, who was the IRA chief in Ennis. On 16 April 1921 McMahon led an attack on a loyalist pub in Ennis that killed a sergeant of the Royal Scots. One of the attackers, Peter O'Loughlin, recalled: 'At about 10 p.m. a party of eight or nine men under Paddy Con McMahon, all armed with revolvers, called at O'Shaughnessy's pub. The door was shut at the time but was opened at Paddy Con's knock. He hurled a Mills grenade into the bar and the rest of us fired into the place with our revolvers.' The woman who ran the pub was wounded, along with another civilian and a police constable. McMahon was also linked to the murder of a former police sergeant, John Gunn, in Ennis on 23 April 1922 after the war of independence had officially ended. Gunn may have threatened to expose local IRA members who had been spies for the British.

Drinking in bars remained a hazardous business for soldiers and police despite the truce. Scores were still being settled. David Finlay, a Scottish provost sergeant, had acquired a fearsome reputation for beatings during interrogation of prisoners in Ennis. On one occasion he took IRA member William Shanahan to a toilet and shot him in the head. Thomas McDonagh, an IRA transport officer, was among those beaten by Finlay. After serving a prison sentence McDonagh returned to Ennis. 'I chanced to be in the Queen's Hotel one day when Finlay came in,' he said. 'He was in civilian clothes and I am sure that I would scarcely have recognised him were it not for the fact that he approached me and, wagging his finger, said, "I know you." I learned that he was a regular visitor to the hotel bar. I passed this information on and that night, when Finlay left the hotel, he was met by some of our boys in Ennis who took him down a lane and administered such a dose of his own medicine that he died from its effects the following day.' McDonagh later joined the police, rising to the rank of chief superintendent.

Obtaining weapons was a problem for the Irish Volunteers and later the IRA. In the early days republicans bought shotguns from farmers and gamekeepers who had 'no great love' for their landlords. But these weapons had limited value. For a time soldiers on leave were allowed to take their rifles and equipment home. Some of these guns were handed over or sold, others seized. It was not unusual for a soldier to lose his weapon after being bought a few drinks in a pub. A significant number of weapons disappeared after a yeomanry regiment, the South Irish Horse, was stationed near Ennis. The regiment was soon given another posting. Army Service Corps driver George Roberts, originally from Devon, who survived an IRA ambush, admitted giving guns to terrorists. Roberts had married a local girl.

The IRA also tried to obtain arms from soldiers in England. Edward Lynch, a captain in the Mid-Clare Brigade and well known to Michael Collins, was sent to London to buy weapons. He was having a drink with a contact in a West End pub when two soldiers in uniform, a sergeant and a corporal from the Irish Guards, walked in and the four began chatting. The soldiers were plied with drinks and Sergeant Michael Roche expressed so much sympathy for the republican cause that he 'would have given us Chelsea barracks if we were in a position to take it'. Roche was attached to the Welsh Guards at the barracks as a machine-gun instructor, and he agreed to steal weapons from the armoury. He was warned 'bluntly of the consequences which would follow any double crossing on his part'.

Two nights later Lynch and two other IRA men, along with Roche, took a taxi to the barracks where they were waved through, parking outside the armoury. The sergeant invited the three Irishmen and the taxi driver to the sergeants' mess, introducing them as Welshmen who were about to head off to a regimental dance. Remarkably, the ruse worked, no doubt because of drink and limited conversation. Roche disappeared and shortly afterwards the group left in the taxi, which had ten rifles and two machine guns hidden under overcoats. The weapons were discovered missing the next day but Roche was not suspected.

A few days later, 'after having to apply a great deal of persuasion', Roche agreed to raid the Irish Guards barracks in Windsor. Lynch noted that 'his consent was given subject to his wife's approval of his conduct which also included his desertion from the British Army to throw in his lot with the IRA in Ireland. This meant a big sacrifice on his part. He had upwards of twelve years' service, was in possession of the Distinguished Conduct Medal, and with his wife and two children enjoyed comfortable quarters in Windsor barracks. The approval of his wife was forthcoming.' The three IRA men and Roche drove from London in a van in thick fog, finding no sentries at the Windsor barracks. Roche scaled a wall but the raid was almost jeopardised by a patrolling policeman who approached one of the IRA men. Instead of asking why he was loitering outside the barracks, the officer wished him 'Goodnight'. The van eventually drove off with about forty rifles and six machine guns.

Roche was not so lucky this time. The disappearance of the arms and the sergeant quickly led to a Special Branch alert and he was picked up trying to board the Irish boat train at Euston, a rather obvious escape route. He was grilled at Scotland Yard and with the prospect of a lengthy prison sentence turned king's evidence. Lynch, however, had luck on his side. He was also spotted at Euston and questioned but allowed to go. A search would have uncovered an automatic pistol and secret IRA documents. Lynch returned to Dublin but his two IRA companions were also arrested. All the arms were recovered from a railway goods depot in west London.

The IRA had a significant number of ex-soldiers serving in its units in Ireland. One former soldier, William Corrie, who joined the Dublin Brigade, observed: 'During my service with the IRA I met hundreds of ex-servicemen.' The RIC reported that in Belfast 'many ex-soldiers with good war records have become IRA criminals'. Seamus McKenna, an IRA intelligence officer, revealed that the Belfast leadership valued the experience of former soldiers over raw recruits with stronger republican credentials. Such support was not confined to Ireland. IRA companies in London, Liverpool, Sheffield and Nottingham were said to have recruited large numbers of ex-soldiers.

But former British Army soldiers were also drawn to the other side. The Royal Irish Constabulary was under pressure soon after the war of independence broke out and it was decided to create two other forces to help, the Special Reserve and the Auxiliary Division. Thousands of ex-soldiers were recruited. The Special Reserve was created so quickly that members appeared in a mixture of uniforms, gaining the nickname Black and Tans. They were seen as foreigners but some of the recruits were Irish, including dozens from Clare. The Auxiliaries were mostly former officers and numbered about 2,200. They held a remarkable 632 gallantry awards, including two Victoria Cross winners: George Onions, who had been on duty during the Easter Rising, and James Leach. The battle-hardened Black and Tans and the Auxies, as they became known, were more than a match for the IRA when it came to committing atrocities.

At some stage Martin Doyle was under suspicion in Ennis and he suddenly left his job at the barracks, joining the IRA at Tralee, County Kerry. It is not clear if he remained an intelligence officer or began taking part in attacks. The town saw much violence during the war of independence. In November 1920 Black and

Tans besieged Tralee for a week after the IRA murdered two police officers. A reign of terror saw homes and businesses burned down, three civilians shot dead and food supplies cut off.

The British prime minister, David Lloyd George, was among those who wanted an end to the war and a solution to the Irish question. A ceasefire was announced on 11 July 1921, and months of negotiations followed. The Irish negotiators included Sinn Fein founder Arthur Griffith and Michael Collins. On 6 December a treaty was signed. Among the key provisions: Ireland would become a self-governing dominion of the British Empire; King George V would be the head of state; and Northern Ireland would have the option of withdrawing from the Irish Free State. The Dail backed the treaty but the IRA leadership was split. The treaty also signalled the disappearance of famous regiments, including the three in which Doyle served, the Royal Irish Regiment, the Royal Dublin Fusiliers and the Royal Munster Fusiliers.

The new state formed a National Army, and most of the recruits were IRA men who supported the treaty. Doyle was keen to resume military life and he enlisted in February 1922, confirming only that he had been with the IRA in Ennis and Tralee, and giving no details of his terrorist activities. Another recruit was Patrick Mulcahy, the post office worker in Ennis who had passed on so much information about British Army and police movements. In 1955 he became the Irish army's chief of staff. Mulcahy's brother Richard – another post office worker! – had been appointed the IRA's chief of staff in 1919 and he served as minister of defence in the new government.

With great irony, the British government began supplying arms and equipment in large quantities to the former terrorists in the National Army. There was an even greater irony when IRA men opposed to the treaty decided to fight their old comrades. On 28 June 1922 National Army soldiers opened fire on 180 IRA men who had stormed the Four Courts in Dublin. It was start of a civil war, which would see many deaths. Six days earlier in London, Field Marshal Sir Henry Wilson, Westminster MP for the Ulster seat of North Down, had been assassinated by two IRA men. One of the killers, Joseph O'Sullivan, served in the Royal Munster Fusiliers during the First World War. Michael Collins may have ordered the murder. On 22 August Collins died in an ambush by anti-treaty IRA men in County Cork. He had predicted that the treaty would be his death warrant. The civil war ended with the defeat of the rebels in May 1923. The National Army executed dozens of IRA men.

Doyle served with the army in Waterford, Kilkenny and Tipperary. He was wounded in the left arm in Limerick, which was seized from the IRA in fighting between 11 and 19 July 1922. Eight soldiers and up to thirty IRA men were killed. Hundreds of rebels were captured. Doyle remained with the army until 1937, rising to company sergeant major, his British Army rank. He got a job as a security guard at the Guinness brewery in Dublin, but his life as a civilian was cut short. A survivor of three wars, he contracted polio and died in hospital on 20 November 1940, aged forty-six. Doyle chose to be buried at Grangegorman, the British military cemetery in Dublin, wearing his Royal Munster Fusiliers uniform.

23

The *Lusitania* Avenged

Gordon Steele

When author Alan Coles interviewed Gordon Steele shortly before his death at the age of eighty-nine, the Victoria Cross holder revealed that he had endured many 'terrifying nightmares' over what has become known as the Baralong Incident.

Steele was serving as a twenty-three-year-old sub-lieutenant in a Q-ship, the *Baralong*, when she sank a German submarine in controversial circumstances in August 1915. There were no survivors from *U-27*, and several weeks later American newspapers began condemning the action with headlines such as 'British Slaughter Submarine's Crew'.

The *Baralong* was a 4,200-ton cargo ship that had been requisitioned by the Royal Navy as a supply vessel the previous year. It was decided she would make a promising 'special service ship', armed with hidden 12-pounder guns. The aim was to trap U-boats that were taking a heavy toll of merchant shipping off Britain's shores. Her commanding officer was Lieutenant Commander Godfrey Herbert, a flamboyant career officer keen to distinguish himself. The First World War, so far, had been too quiet for him. He wanted to see action and to be decorated like some of his contemporaries. Herbert and Steele, a Royal Naval Reserve officer, had served in another Q-ship, the *Antwerp*, a former railway steamer, which failed to destroy any submarines during three months of masquerading in the North Sea and the English Channel. Herbert came to the conclusion that this 'old tub' was unsuitable and persuaded the Admiralty he needed a bigger and faster Q-ship.

He took command of the *Baralong* at Portland, Dorset, in March 1915. The ship's original master, Lieutenant George Swinney, a Royal Naval Reserve officer, stayed on. The ship's company of around sixty was made up of Royal Navy and merchant seamen and Royal Marines, all volunteers. Herbert had been impressed by Steele's efficiency in the *Antwerp* and asked for his transfer to the *Baralong*. To a large extent he was a maverick in his role as a Q-ship commander, little concerned with ranks and discipline. Herbert, who adopted the pseudonym William McBride, wanted his men, who wore civilian clothes, to appear as casual as possible, so that any U-boat captain who surfaced to use his main gun rather than a precious torpedo would be taken in. Sailors were even encouraged to smoke or spit when on duty. Action stations did not see them rushing to their posts. It was not unusual for merchant navy captains to take their wives on voyages, and in another ploy Herbert wanted a crewman to appear on deck dressed as a woman, but it was a deception too far and no one volunteered. The three 12-pounders would always be manned during daylight hours. Two of the guns were hidden behind fake lifeboat lockers and the third was concealed in what appeared to be a sheep pen.

The *Baralong* began her secret mission in April, with orders to sail in the Channel no further east than Folkestone and to the western limit of the Isles of Scilly, 'but if submarines are operating off Queenstown [southern Ireland], you are at liberty to extend your cruise to that part'. Herbert was told to report directly to the Admiralty. By 22 June he was a frustrated Q-ship captain, finding no quarry and pointing out: 'This makes nearly 18,000 miles that I have hunted.' His gloom deepened the following month when he learned that another Q-ship, the *Prince Charles*, a former collier weighing in at a mere 373 tons, had sunk *U-36* in a classic deception.

According to one of the *Baralong*'s gunners, George Hempenstall, the crew never knew where they were going because Herbert refused to allow anyone else to see the charts. Swinney, who remained the nominal skipper, and the merchant seamen resented this secrecy. Hempenstall also revealed that the ship used flags of various nationalities and suitable name boards, 'depending on where we were operating'. Herbert even had the funnel painted different colours to fool the enemy – along with his initials, GH.

In New Orleans on the night of 31 July, the crew of the British freighter *Nicosian* descended on the city's bars and brothels for the last time. The next day they sailed for Liverpool, knowing that as they neared their destination they would be entering a war zone and U-boat alley. The 6,400-ton ship's cargo included cotton, tinned meat, timber – and 600 mules for the British Army in France. To look after the animals forty-eight muleteers had been hired, forty-six of whom were American. It was an unpleasant job in stifling conditions, and the captain, Charles Manning, knew that the Americans would have the added discomfort of an unfriendly crew, who were mostly from Liverpool. Manning had the muleteers searched for weapons when they came aboard, which brought immediate protests.

The captain was well aware of the U-boat menace. A sister ship, the *Armenian*, also carrying mules, had been sunk off Cornwall in June, with the loss of twenty-nine lives. On the afternoon of 19 August, some 70 miles south of Queenstown, Manning's worst fears were realised. *U-27* was spotted on the surface 2 miles away and closing. A shot went over the *Nicosian*, which had no chance of escaping. A shaken Manning ran from the bridge to the wireless room and shouted to the operator to send a distress call, forgetting to give the ship's position. The captain headed back to the bridge as a messenger from the wireless room searched for the navigating officer. The vital call went out before the ship's aerial was shot away. Manning gave the order for the engines to stop, and the crew and muleteers took to the lifeboats. As they pulled away *U-27* opened fire again. The *Nicosian* took a number of hits but remained afloat.

To Lieutenant Commander Herbert it seemed that it was going to be yet another frustrating day. On the morning of 19 August, the *Barlong*, cruising off the Scillies, picked up an SOS from the White Star liner *Arabic*, which had spotted the British freighter *Dunsley* in the distance being shelled by a U-boat. The 15,800-ton *Arabic*, sailing from Liverpool to New York with 186 passengers on board, did not have long to live either. Less than half an hour later a torpedo hit the zig-zagging liner and she soon disappeared, stern first, but not before sending out another distress call, which reached the *Baralong*. Eighteen of the *Arabic*'s passengers and twenty-one crew died. The *Baralong* was only 25 miles away and Herbert ordered full speed to the scene, hoping once again to lure the enemy. It proved to be another failure. Unknown to Herbert, the *Arabic* had given the wrong position and the Q-ship was 30 miles from the spot where she sank. The *Dunsley* and the *Arabic* had been attacked by *U-24*.

Germany had agreed not to sink passenger liners, and the attack on the *Arabic* would soon add to the international outcry over the torpedoing of Cunard's *Lusitania* off the south coast of Ireland in May 1915. The *Lusitania* was carrying more than 1,900 passengers and crew, and 1,198 lost their lives, including 128 Americans.

After the alerts over the *Dunsley* and the *Arabic*, a dejected Herbert ordered the *Baralong*, about 100 miles south of Queenstown, to head eastwards towards the Scillies. That afternoon there was another SOS: 'Being chased by enemy submarine.' The signal was strong, and when Herbert scanned the horizon with his binoculars he spotted a cargo ship. Shortly afterwards there was another message: 'Captured by enemy submarine.' The *Baralong* closed on the vessel. It was not long before a U-boat was seen near the *Nicosian*'s stern.

On the bridge of *U-27* Kapitanleutnant Bernhard Wegener was also busy looking through his binoculars. The United States flag was flying from the masthead and stern of the approaching vessel. Her name was clearly visible, *Ulysses S Grant*, and she hoisted the international signal VIC-QRA, meaning 'Save life'. Convinced that this was a neutral vessel coming to the aid of survivors, Wegener took his boat along the port side of the *Nicosian* to continue the shelling, but this manoeuvre cut off his view of the *Ulysses S Grant*.

In his official report of the clash with *U-27*, written on 20 August, Herbert said only that he approached the submarine 'flying neutral colours'. He continued:

The moment she was out of sight behind *Nicosian* I struck the neutral colours and hoisted the White Ensign, and trained two guns just in front of that vessel's bow ready for the next appearance of the submarine, which I knew would be at close range. In a few seconds she appeared 600 yards off and Sub-Lieutenant Steele, in charge of the guns and their disguise, carried out his duties admirably; and I consider it largely due to his smartness that we received no shot from the enemy, and I respectfully submit his name for consideration.

The Marines kept up an incessant rifle fire from the start, and accounted for several of the gun crew before it was possible for them to retaliate. Thirty-four 12-pounder shells were fired mostly taking effect, the second and third being hits on the water line under the conning tower; she heeled over about 20 degrees towards us, and the crew could be seen making every effort to save themselves by jumping overboard. She disappeared in little over a minute, and shortly afterwards two large volumes of air escaped to the surface indicating that she had submerged for the last time.

The *Nicosian*'s boats were now called alongside, and whilst clearing the boats I observed about a dozen Germans who had swum from their boat swarming up ropes and the pilot ladder which had been left hanging down from *Nicosian*. Fearing they might scuttle or set fire to the ship with her valuable cargo of mules and fodder, I ordered them to be shot away. The majority were prevented from getting on board but six succeeded.

The *Baralong* went alongside the *Nicosian* and a party of marines under Corporal Fred Collins was put on board. Herbert warned Collins to watch for 'snipers' as rifles and ammunition had been left in the *Nicosian*'s charthouse. The Germans did not survive, as Herbert explained: 'A thorough search was made which resulted in six of the enemy being found, but they succumbed to the injuries they had received from Lyddite shell shortly afterwards, and were buried at sea.'

Despite the hits, the *Nicosian* did not sink and the *Baralong* took her in tow, heading for Avonmouth on the Severn Estuary. Herbert ended his report on the sinking of *U-27* with the sentence: 'The enclosed cap ribbon is all that I could pick up.' He asked the *Nicosian*'s captain to warn his crew – and the muleteers – not to reveal details of the attack when they went on shore leave, particularly the use of the Stars and Stripes. Captain Manning, who was under the impression that he was dealing with 'Captain McBride', replied that he had done 'all in my powers to impress upon the crew and muleteers the necessity of silence. It is not possible for me to express in words the gratitude and admiration felt by all on board this vessel to you, your officers and men for the magnificent way in which the whole affair was carried out.' At Avonmouth the muleteers were warned by police not to talk about the *Baralong*'s actions.

The Admiralty noted the 'skill and discretion' Herbert had shown in sinking *U-27*, and within days he was awarded the Distinguished Service Order and marked for early promotion. The Distinguished Service Cross went to Lieutenant Swinney and Corporal Collins received the Distinguished Service Medal. Steele was mentioned in despatches and given the privilege of transferring from the reserve to the Royal Navy, soon being promoted lieutenant.

By 1 October most of the muleteers were back in the bars of New Orleans after another unpleasant voyage in the *Nicosian*. *The New York Times* had already picked up on rumours of a possible atrocity by a British ship flying the US flag, and in New Orleans German agents keen to exploit the propaganda value were busy trying to get sworn statements from muleteers who had witnessed the attack. The result was a major story in the *New York World* on 7 October, with the headline 'Affidavits State How British Slew 11 German Sailors'. The newspaper wrongly described the *Baralong* as His Majesty's ship – she remained a merchant vessel – and gave the name of the master as Captain William McBride. Combining the sworn statements of four of the muleteers, there was this account after the *Baralong* unleashed its devastating broadside on *U-27*:

> Eleven of the German sailors, including the captain, dived into the water and swam towards the *Nicosian*. Five of them were successful in reaching the rope ladder and clambered aboard. The other six swam around to the tail lines used for the lifeboats, which had been lowered, and grasped the ropes. They were in plain sight. In the meantime all of our boats went alongside the *Baralong* and went up their ladder to the decks. The captain of the *Baralong* went around shaking hands and seemed to be highly elated over the outcome of the encounter, as he claimed they had been cruising around for two months looking for submarines. He then ordered his men to line up alongside the rail.

They started firing and all of the six men [in the water] were killed in cold blood. There was a remark made that five men had been seen going up the side of the *Nicosian* and the captain ordered his ship over to the *Nicosian*. When she reached there she was made fast and the British marines, accompanied by some of the officers of the *Nicosian*, started after the five Germans. Captain McBride, when ordering the marines out in charge of a petty officer, gave the command: 'Get them all – take no prisoners.'

The ship's carpenter was one of the first to board the *Nicosian* and he was off in the lead with the marines and the chief engineer following. Some of the marines rushed to the engine-room hatch, while the carpenter and the remainder went down the hatch to the fire rooms. One of the German sailors was shot in the engine-room hatch as he was going down the ladder by the marines. The carpenter and the marines, who had gone down the fire-room hatch, got away below before encountering any of the Germans. The carpenter was the first to strike the Germans. He levelled his revolver at one of them and ordered him to throw up his hands and told him to come towards him. As the German sailor approached the carpenter, he shot him in cold blood. He then reported to Captain Manning, shouting, 'I got one of them', and described the shooting, subsequently telling the story to everyone on the ship.

The chief engineer claims to have shot one of the remaining three and the marines got the rest. The marines, to make sure that a good job was done, shot each of the dead Germans through the head.

The death of Wegener, the U-boat captain, was also detailed:

The German captain was hiding in the bow of the ship, and about this time he rushed to the side of the ship and dived overboard. A shout went up, 'There's one of them!' The marines and Captain Manning went over to the bow. The German captain was swimming toward the *Baralong*. The marines opened fire. The captain looked up at the *Baralong* and threw up his hands in token of surrender. He was hit in the mouth, as blood was seen streaming from his chin. He clenched his teeth and waited for the end. One of the shots in the next volley hit him in the neck and he rolled over on his back dead, floated a while and sank.

There was 'great rejoicing' among the marines as they returned to the *Baralong*. Similar accounts appeared in other US newspapers, and later that month the *Chicago American* carried a series of articles by one of the muleteers, Jim Curran, who gave this account after all the Germans had been shot:

At 6pm Manning ordered the crew to bring up the bodies of the Germans through the fire-room hatch and engine-room hatch. One from the engine-room hatch was the body of a young fellow, not more than a boy. I saw more than a dozen bullet marks in his body and one hole in the forehead. The body was put down at the door of my cabin. The others were given even less ceremony. The donkey-engine chain was let down into the engine-room ash waste. One by one the bodies were hoisted up. They were three young men. Chains were fastened about their necks and they were dragged along the deck. Each body was torn by bullets. Each had a bright red spot on the same part of the forehead.

The crew stripped the garments and left the naked, bloodied bodies. One of the crew kicked the face of a dead man and cursed. The others followed his example before throwing the bodies in the sea. There was a roar from the English crew as the bodies went over. Then there was a trumpet call from the *Baralong* as the last one went over, where the American flag hung in shame. The howl from the *Baralong* that rose when the last maimed body of the German sailors was tossed into the sea was followed by a drunken song. The British marines and their officers were celebrating the red day and they kept at it all night.

The *Baralong* was towing the *Nicosian*, which was in a sinking condition. There were twenty-seven of the American lads on board the *Baralong*. The American flag was still hanging over the sides of the British ship. As the German bodies floated out and sank a great punch bowl was set out on deck. Men and officers dipped their cups into the bowl, which was filled time after time. There was whisky all over the ship and all hands got drunk. They went around boasting to each other of what they had done and argued as to who had killed the most Germans.

By late October alarm bells were ringing at the Admiralty. The Germans were still busy protesting at the killing of *U-27*'s crew to counter the outcry over the sinking of the *Lusitania* and the *Arabic*, whose dead included two Americans, and US Secretary of State Robert Lansing had made an official complaint to the British embassy in Washington. But on the same day as the *Baralong* attack the German navy had committed another atrocity. The British submarine *E-13* ran aground near the Danish island of Saltholm. Two German destroyers attacked the submarine with torpedoes, shells and machine-gun fire, setting her on fire. *E-13* was abandoned but the Germans continued firing at sailors in the water. Fifteen of *E-13*'s crew did not survive.

The First Lord of the Admiralty, Arthur Balfour, had a statement prepared in case the matter was raised in the House of Commons: 'In Mr Balfour's view the point to be emphasised is that whatever happened on board the *Nicosian* was done in "hot blood", without authority, in fair fight against an armed enemy in possession of the ship; and should be contrasted with the deliberate shooting of the defenceless crew of *E-13*, stranded in a neutral's territorial waters, under definite orders from officers commanding German destroyers.'

The Admiralty was also keen to point out that the Royal Navy had saved around 1,300 lives from the crews of enemy ships sunk up until May 1915 'while no British lives had been saved by Germans in similar circumstances'. Germany, however, kept up its protests, and on 10 November Herbert was summoned to see Balfour, who then changed his mind about seeing him. Herbert instead faced the First Sea Lord, Admiral Sir Henry Jackson, who showed some sympathy. The Q-ship hunter was asked to go through the allegations in the *Chicago American*, many of which he refuted, including the killing of Wegener, the captain of *U-27* – 'nothing seen of this and not believed'. He ended up making a statement, stressing: 'The recapture of the *Nicosian* by an armed party was a perfectly legitimate act of war, and the party put on board to do this could not afford to take risks, especially with people who it was thought had a few hours previously just sunk the defenceless *Arabic*.' Lieutenant Swinney, Sub-Lieutenant Steele and Corporal Collins were never questioned. In the end, Balfour decided that some of Herbert's actions were justified and blamed the U-boat captain who sank the *Arabic* for triggering *U-27*'s deaths.

The Germans refused to let the matter drop, and in January 1916 *The Times* reported on a *Baralong* debate in the Reichstag, which 'produced language of extraordinary violence'. A prominent politician, Count Kuno von Westarp, condemned 'cowardly murder'. A British diplomatic note was dismissed as 'full of insolence and arrogance'. Britain was willing to agree to an independent inquiry into the *Baralong* attack – but only if the Germans agreed to investigations involving the *Arabic*, *E-13* and the merchant ship *Ruel*, sunk by a U-boat, which also opened fire on survivors in lifeboats. Germany did not take up the offer.

There was a remarkable sequel to the destruction of *U-27*. Herbert had not returned to the *Baralong*; Lieutenant Commander Andrew Wilmot-Smith replaced him. On 24 September 1915, little more than a month after *U-27*'s destruction, *U-41*, operating off the Isles of Scilly, sank the British merchant ship *Urbino*. From early May to that date *U-41* had sunk a notable twenty-eight ships, including several vessels from the United States, Russia and Norway. As survivors, many of them with wounds, pulled away in lifeboats from the 6,650-ton *Urbino*, sailors on the deck of the submarine jeered. Not long afterwards the submarine's captain spotted another ship approaching, which was flying ... the Stars and Stripes. The *Baralong* sent *U-41* to the bottom. There were only two survivors, who later complained that crewmen of the *Baralong* jeered at them as they floundered in the water and the ship tried to run them down. The *Baralong* did rescue the pair and headed for Falmouth, Cornwall, where intelligence officers boarded her with sealed orders. The Q-ship was to be renamed *Wyandra*. Wilmot-Smith was duly awarded the Distinguished Service Order. But *U-41*'s destruction by the *Baralong* still flying the American flag further incensed the Germans.

Gordon Steele was born in Exeter, Devon, on 1 November 1891, the son of a Royal Navy captain, Henry Steele, and Selina May, daughter of a major general in the Royal Marine Light Infantry.

After attending a college in Ramsgate, Kent, Steele went to the Thames training ship HMS *Worcester*, proving to be an exceptional student. In 1909 he joined the P&O liner *Palma* as a cadet, also enlisting in the Royal Naval Reserve. After war broke out he served in the battleship HMS *Prince George* and the submarines *D-8* and *E-22* before joining Q-ships. In April 1916 he went to the battleship HMS *Royal Oak*, which took part in the Battle of Jutland. He also served in the battleship *Iron Duke*.

Britain's conflict with the Bolsheviks in Russia in 1919 saw Steele taking part in a daring raid. In the early hours of 18 August, he was in a fast coastal motor boat speeding towards warships moored in Kronstadt harbour, at the entrance to the channel leading to Petrograd [St Petersburg]. Eight torpedo-carrying CMBs, each with three-man crews, had set off from a base 30 miles away and they swept into the harbour, catching the defences by surprise. Searchlights and guns eventually opened up, and a destroyer sank three of the boats.

Machine-gun fire raked CMB *88*, under the command of Lieutenant Archibald Dayrell-Reed, and Steele and an engine room artificer instinctively ducked for cover. Steele would recall:

When I looked up I noticed the splashes, although falling everywhere in the harbour, were not close to us. I turned round and was just going to say to Reed 'Where on earth are you going to?' – as we were heading for a hospital ship – when I noticed that although still standing up and grasping the wheel, his head was resting on the conning tower in a pool of blood. I instantly took hold of him and lowered him down in the cockpit. I put the helm hard over and tried to get on our proper course again, behind [CMB] *31*.

We were quite close to the battleship *Andrei Pervozvanni* now and I knew in a few more seconds it would be too late. I throttled the engines as far back as I could and was just going to fire a torpedo when *31* turned right round to go out of the harbour – she went across our bows and I was nearly going to fire, hoping the torpedo would go under her, but then thought better of it. Directly she had passed I pulled the lever to fire the starboard torpedo.

The target was hit and a second torpedo struck the battleship *Petropavlosk*. Steele skilfully manoeuvred *88* out of the harbour under heavy fire. Another boat torpedoed a submarine depot ship. Lieutenant Dayrell-Reed had been shot in the head. Steele wrote: 'Reed nearly recovered consciousness once and tried to speak. We all shook hands with him in turn. I think he knew that *88* had played her part and died happily in consequence. We soon lost sight of Kronstadt – and the most welcome sight of all, a British destroyer waiting for us at the edge of the minefield, which unlike us they can't go over.'

Soon other warships appeared and Steele headed for the cruiser HMS *Delhi*. Just before reaching the ship, *88*'s engines 'gave out completely'. Steele and Commander Claude Congreve, who led the raid in CMB *31*, which also torpedoed the *Andrei Pervozvanni*, were both awarded the Victoria Cross.

In 1923 Steele was promoted lieutenant commander and over the next six years he held various appointments, including service as a commander on the China Station. His career in the navy continued to look promising, but in 1929 he decided to take up the appointment of captain-superintendent of his old training ship, *Worcester*, guiding the careers of young sailors, a post he held until his retirement in 1957. His final rank was honorary captain, Royal Naval Reserve.

Unlike his VC action, Steele never wrote about the *Baralong*. He was, however, interviewed by author E. Keble Chatterton for a book that appeared in 1931, *Gallant Gentlemen*. Steele revealed how the callous behaviour of U-boat crews had affected those on board the *Baralong*, particularly the sinking of the *Lusitania*. He was quoted as saying:

This unspeakable outrage inflamed the minds of the *Baralong*'s crew – it was just the culminating point of a long series of minor violations of war, and inhuman practices. Small colliers torpedoed in a gale of wind, without any attempt at rescue; a sailing ship under full sail; destitute lifeboats left hundreds of miles from land – all these had been witnessed by the *Baralong*'s people. It just required the sight of those silent figures of drowned children from the *Lusitania*, as they were laid out on the front at Queenstown in a temporary mortuary to rouse the deepest hatred in the *Baralong*'s crew, composed as they were of a mixed collection – naval, mercantile and marine ratings – who had never hated before. A meeting was held, in which the captain of a second small decoy ship was present, and it was agreed to avenge the *Lusitania* by giving no quarter to German submarine crews.

But Steele made no mention of Germans being shot in the water after the *Baralong* opened fire, apart from the U-boat captain who had tried to escape after boarding the *Nicosian*. Of the Germans who remained on board the *Nicosian*, he said: 'Our boarding party, with cries of '*Lusitania*!' shot four remaining Germans at fairly long range. The ship was unlit below, and it was not possible to ascertain whether these men were armed or not at the time, for they were discovered in dark passages and the engine room. Anyhow they were pirates, and were treated as such. Only two hours earlier before they had sunk an unarmed outward bound steamer, forty-four women, children and men being drowned. They had taken no part in rescue work, but had steamed callously among the survivors, and only by most splendid seamanship was the *Arabic*'s death toll so small.' It is strange that, so many years after the war, Steele appeared not to know another U-boat, *U-24*, had sunk the *Arabic*.

He was scathing about those muleteers who had returned to the United States after being rescued by the *Baralong* and 'fell easy victims to the dollars of the anti-British press, who invented the most astounding tales of the action'.

In 1980, shortly before his death, Steele admitted to author Alan Coles that some of the men from *U-27* had been murdered:

At that time we regarded all German submariners as murderers. We believed U-boat crews were pirates and meted out punishment to them as they had done to their innocent victims. It was revenge for the sunken *Arabic* and the *Lusitania*. Herbert just wanted to give the Germans some of their own medicine. He definitely told the marines to take no prisoners. But my feelings have changed since then. I've thought about the shootings hundreds of times over the years and have shed bitter tears and had terrifying nightmares. But that is because the killings have been taken out of context of other horrifying events of the war. At the time I justified the murders because of the *Lusitania* and *Arabic* tragedies. We had a passionate desire for retribution.

Over the years Steele turned increasingly to religion, becoming a lay reader in the diocese of Canterbury. He wanted to be ordained but the Church told him he was 'too old'. In 1973 he had a book published about his faith, *To Me God Is Real*. In a chapter titled 'Thoughts That Disturb', he wrote: 'The psychologist and clergyman know all about them and help those who come their way, but it needs Saint Paul to say, "In the Name of Jesus you are made whole". In which state every disability of body and mind, including disturbing thoughts, is cured.'

When Coles interviewed Steele he was living in a care home in Devon. He never married and seldom had visitors. He died on 4 January 1981.

24

A War Criminal?
Clive Hulme

Sergeant Clive Hulme showed such bravery during the Battle of Crete in May 1941 that the story of his exploits was 'on everyone's lips'. In 2006 – twenty-four years after his death – academics branded him a war criminal.

Alfred Clive Hulme, usually known by his second name, was working as a farm labourer in Nelson on New Zealand's South Island when the Second World War broke out. He was a tough, stocky man who had been a keen amateur wrestler in his youth. In January 1940, aged twenty-nine and married, he enlisted in the 23rd (Canterbury-Otago) Battalion, a wartime creation which became part of the Second New Zealand Expeditionary Force under the command of Major General Bernard Freyberg, a Victoria Cross winner who would go on to hold the fate of Crete in his hands.

Many of the 23rd recruits were miners and farm workers, and most were 'freedom-loving New Zealanders who believed that they themselves were the best judges of what they should do and how and when they should do it'. There was also 'a good percentage of ratbags' who kept going absent without leave, according to one officer. But training and pride made a huge difference, and in the end only a few men failed to make the grade. In May 1940 the 23rd Battalion sailed in some comfort in the luxury liner *Andes* for Egypt. The ship called at the Australian port of Fremantle, where soldiers were allowed ashore. The *Andes* left with an additional passenger: a live kangaroo. Later the liner was diverted to Britain. Hulme, a forceful character, was promoted sergeant during the voyage.

223

On 20 June the New Zealanders arrived at a camp in Aldershot. Further training followed. Secretary for War Anthony Eden paid a visit, declaring: 'They are a magnificent body of men and are looking exceedingly fit. We are delighted to have them here.' King George VI was another visitor. Major General Freyberg's idea of a fitness test was a 100-mile route march. Prime Minister Winston Churchill carried out an inspection in September, telling the men: 'I am sure you will crown the name of New Zealand with new honours, with a lustre which will not fade as the years pass by.' They were given the task of defending an area of Kent in case of an attack by airborne troops.

In January 1941 the 23rd sailed for Egypt, arriving two months later to find 'sand, sand and more sand'. Many men were missing the Kent countryside and local girls, but orders soon came to go to Greece. They were given a warm welcome when they arrived at the port of Piraeus. Nearly 60,000 British, New Zealand and Australian troops had been sent to help the Greeks defend their country. In late March the 23rd were ordered to take up defensive positions on the Olympus–Aliakmon line. To the south-east was Mount Olympus, 'the home of the gods'. It was immediately apparent that defence of a narrow ridge nearly 4 miles long would be difficult, but the soldiers dug in, clearing scrub to improve fields of fire. In the rear, with the help of engineers, work began on roads for supply trucks. Anti-personnel mines were needed for some of the approaches, and they duly arrived – without fuses.

Early on 6 April Germany invaded Yugoslavia and Greece. With overwhelming air power, German troops supported by armour quickly routed the Yugoslav army and crashed through north-east Greece. Two days later the 23rd could see fires in Salonika. Some New Zealand units, in danger of being outflanked, were told to fall back. On 16 April German infantry began probing the defences of the 23rd and there were several exchanges. But it was not long before the battalion joined a general withdrawal.

The battalion's official history noted:

The march to Kokkinoplos will always be remembered by those who took part in it as the toughest they ever endured. The troops were tired before they started – tired with standing-to on three consecutive nights and with slopping about in the mud and rain; they were heavily laden with their arms and ammunition, their greatcoats and large packs, many of which were to be discarded during the withdrawal; the gradients were steep and the road, as far as it went, had been churned into a sea of mud; the night was so dark that it was nearly impossible to see the man in front; the only consolation was that there was no enemy interference during the march. The distance was approximately eight miles but the going made it appear more like twenty-eight to the dog-tired troops.

At Kokkinoplos the men were in action but the Germans suffered the greater casualties. Major General Freyberg ordered a further withdrawal south. On 19 April the 23rd took up positions on the Thermopylae line, scene of an epic battle between the Spartans and the Persians in 480 BC. However, there would be no epic battle for the New Zealanders; on 22 April it emerged that the Greeks were ready to surrender. It was time to evacuate Greece.

The 23rd headed for the coast, where the Royal Navy was waiting to take the men to the strategically important island of Crete. Vehicles and heavy weapons were dumped. Early on 25 April the warships sailed. 'We were greeted with the most wonderful kindness and the most wonderful cups of cocoa,' said one soldier. That afternoon the 23rd arrived in Suda Bay on the island's north coast. The battalion had not been involved in any major fighting, but it showed its worth. Casualties were nine men killed and eight wounded, with around thirty taken prisoner. The 23rd was in Greece for less than a month, and the controversial decision to send such an inadequate force to defend the country would be debated for a long time to come.

After disembarking at Suda the battalion marched some 5 miles to a camp west of the town. Two days later Major General Freyberg was given command of 'Creforce' – 15,000 British, 7,750 New Zealand and 6,500 Australian troops. Many of these soldiers had been forced to leave their weapons in Greece. There were also 10,000 Greek soldiers who mostly lacked training. Freyberg told the Commander-in-Chief, Middle East, that his force was unlikely to cope with the expected airborne attack: 'Unless the number of fighter aircraft is greatly increased and naval forces are made available to deal with a seaborne attack I cannot hope to hold out with land forces alone, which, as a result of the campaign in Greece, are now devoid of any artillery, have insufficient tools for digging, very little transport, and inadequate war reserves of equipment and ammunition.' Supplying the force was a problem because ports on the north coast were being heavily bombed.

The New Zealanders, with some Greeks, were given the task of defending the Maleme sector, which included a key airfield. The 22nd Battalion was sent to the airfield, and the 23rd Battalion took up positions among olive trees about a mile away, with orders to be ready to launch a counterattack if paratroopers landed. The weather was good and for a few days it was a relaxing time, as one private wrote in his diary: 'All we do is eat oranges and swim.'

It was the calm before the storm. From 13 May the Luftwaffe launched a series of bombing and machine-gun attacks on Maleme and other targets. The invasion came on 20 May. Shortly after dawn a large force of bombers and fighters attacked the airfield. Stukas dived with their terrifying screams. There was no opposition in the air. The small number of RAF planes at Maleme had been sent to Egypt. Huge numbers of gliders and Junkers troop-carriers appeared after the blitz, 'and the sky seemed to fill suddenly with opening black, white, brown and green blossoms'. Many paratroopers were shot in the air, others as they crashed into olive trees or struggled on the ground to release their chutes. The historian Antony Beevor described the chaos:

New Zealand officers told their men to aim at the boots of the paratroopers since their descent was deceptively rapid. This seems to have worked well to judge by the number who jerked, dangled limply, then crumpled on hitting the ground. They were covered by their own parachutes as by instant shrouds ... For most parachutists, the idea of jumping from the air and then floating down to attack their enemy gave a sensation of invincibility. To find themselves so vulnerable instead was the most disorientating shock of all. That the defenders should shoot at them when helpless struck many of them as an outrageous violation of the rules of war.

Few Germans survived the drop around Maleme. Those who did landed in unoccupied territory, and the 23rd sent out a patrol to stalk them. Twenty-nine were killed for the loss of two men, and an officer observed: 'Before long every man in the platoon was wearing a Luger and a pair of Zeiss binoculars.' There were other mopping-up operations. Estimates of the number of enemy killed in the area varied from 200 to 600. Battalion casualties were seven killed and thirty wounded.

Hulme was a provost sergeant with the Field Punishment Centre at Platanias. Prisoners were offered a pardon if they took up rifles against the attackers, which they did with great enthusiasm. There were frequent cries of 'Got the bastard', and within an hour sixty former inmates had killed 110 of the enemy. One officer reported that later Hulme 'got cracking very aggressively. He stood in full view of any German and fired bursts into any suspected places.' The sergeant also went out on stalking missions to eliminate snipers in an area he regarded as 'all his own country'. From one dead paratrooper he acquired a Mauser sniper rifle with telescopic sights and a camouflage smock and a hat, 'which could be worn either rolled up like a balaclava or down in a hood, with eye slits, over the face'. Before the battalion withdrew from Maleme, Hulme killed other Germans and torched two planes that had landed. He was waging a one-man war.

One problem was communications between the 22nd and the 23rd. Telephone wires had been cut and signalling failed. Significantly, it later emerged that Germans had been trying to pass themselves off as New Zealand soldiers. And officers of the 23rd wrongly assumed that the airfield defenders were having the same success. In fact, the 22nd needed a counterattack by the 23rd but that message never got through. Earlier bombing and machine-gunning had taken a toll on the 22nd positions, and Germans who landed unopposed west of the Tavronitis riverbed cut off its headquarters. The next day, despite fierce fighting, more paratroopers were able to land on or near the airfield. Mountain troops arrived as reinforcements. The enemy was also threatening other sectors, especially Retimo, Heraklion and Canea.

On 23 May the 23rd took part in a brigade withdrawal. Two days later, after reconnaissance work by a group that included Hulme, the battalion headed for Galatas, a key village near the coast. Other units were ordered to hold the Galatas line. As men of the 23rd moved towards the village, they met machine-gun fire. Under cover of darkness and aided by two light tanks, they attacked, letting out 'the most blood curdling of shouts and battle cries', which startled the enemy, as well as some of the New Zealanders, one of whom recalled: 'The howling and shouting sounded like the baying of dogs, it made my flesh creep.' House-to-house fighting ensued. Hulme and a private cleared one strongpoint. The battalion's history recorded: 'Bayonets, rifle butts, pistols and bare hands were all used in what was the closest fighting in which the 23rd ever engaged.' The battalion suffered serious casualties but the Germans lost up to 200 men. There was much indignation early on 26 May when the 23rd was ordered to leave Galatas and withdraw to a new line. One position would be known as 42nd Street. Withdrawal would become a familiar word. Hulme learned that his brother, Corporal Harold 'Blondie' Hulme of the 19th Battalion, had been killed. Incensed, he stayed behind as troops pulled out and shot dead three Germans in a patrol.

The official history of the 23rd also records this act:

During a conference of senior officers, including Australian and British, at 5 Brigade Headquarters behind 42nd Street, German snipers sent bullets whistling over. Hulme volunteered to deal with the trouble. He climbed the hillside from which the Germans were firing, came out above four Germans, and shot the leader. He was wearing his camouflage suit at the time and, when the Germans looked round to see where the shooting was coming from, Hulme also looked round, giving the impression he was one of them. When the two men looked down again, he quickly picked off two of them and then shot the fourth as he moved up towards him. A fifth he shot as he came round the side of the hill towards him. Most of these proceedings were watched by Major [Bert] Thomason through his binoculars.

Near Stilos the battalion came under attack and men raced to occupy a ridge and return fire. Hulme led the way and was seen sitting side-saddle on a stone wall, firing at the enemy on lower slopes. He also hurled grenades. He was stalking yet another sniper when he received a serious shoulder wound. His example 'did much to maintain the morale of men whose reserves of nervous and physical energy were nearly exhausted'.

By 30 May, after long marches in the hills in high temperatures, it was clear that evacuation from southern Crete was the only option. The next morning the battalion assembled at the coastal village of Sfakia and that night it once again boarded Royal Navy ships. Eleven days earlier the battalion had numbered 571. On 31 May its strength was 230.

Hulme was awarded the Victoria Cross for his actions in Crete, when he 'exhibited most outstanding and inspiring qualities of leadership, initiative, skill, endurance and most conspicuous gallantry and devotion to duty'. The citation pointed out that he had stalked and shot thirty-three snipers. Major General Freyberg wrote to him: 'It is a just reward and I hope that you live long to enjoy the satisfaction that your great deeds in Crete have been acknowledged.'

The hero returned to New Zealand in July 1941, and the following February he was declared medically unfit because of his shoulder wound. Later he was able to join the country's home defence force, reaching the rank of warrant officer. Recalling the fighting at Maleme, he admitted that seeing 'all the dead Huns was more of a thrill to me than half a dozen VCs'. Of the death of a young artillery officer he had dodged bullets with, he paid the tribute: 'He died what he was, a fighting soldier, and in this war no greater honour or compliment can be paid by any man. My brother went out the same way, went on walking till a machine gun tore him to pieces and if my time comes that's how I would wish to go too.' On another occasion he revealed that the wrestling skills he acquired in his early years saved his life. Grappling with a German who produced a pistol, he twisted the soldier's wrist so violently that he shot himself.

After the war Hulme ran a transport business at Pongakawa, near Te Puke in the Bay of Plenty region. He was also involved in water divining and oil prospecting. In 1968 he rescued the driver of a truck that had overturned in a water-filled ditch. Often outspoken, at a London reunion of Victoria Cross holders he expressed 'shock and horror' that so many heroes were on the dole.

Clive Hulme died at his home in 1982, aged seventy-one. He had a son, Denis, and a daughter, Anita. 'Denny' Hulme had learnt to drive a truck by the time he was six after sitting on his father's lap. He went on to become the 1967 Formula One world champion, dying of a heart attack in 1992, aged fifty-six.

In 2006 a book on New Zealand winners of the Victoria Cross was published. Written by two of the country's academics, Glyn Harper and Colin Richardson, *In the Face of the Enemy* detailed Clive Hulme's service in Crete and pointed to the fact that he had worn a German camouflage smock when he stalked enemy snipers. The authors wrote:

> Such a ruse, however, was against the rules of war at the time, being defined as a 'perfidious act'. Any soldiers perpetrating such a ruse, if caught, risked summary execution. Many German soldiers were shot in late 1944 and early 1945 for just such an offence. Regardless of this risk, Hulme continued using this ruse in his campaign against the German snipers.

The criticism aroused controversy, but other academics supported the view that Hulme had been involved in a war crime. Bill Hodge, Associate Professor of Law at Auckland University, was quoted as saying that killing soldiers while wearing their uniform was 'prima facie a war crime'. Peter Wills, deputy director of the Centre for Peace Studies at Auckland University, declared that Hulme had been involved in 'unsanctioned murder' and that the New Zealand government should apologise to the families of the soldiers he killed.

The claim shocked Hulme's daughter Anita, whose mother Rona had died several years earlier. 'It's awful what they have done,' she said. 'It's so upsetting. When war is on, war is on – and you do what you have to do.' She added that she was called 'out of the blue' by one of the authors and asked if she had known that her father wore a German uniform during the Battle of Crete. When she said she did know, the caller asked: 'Is he still a hero in your eyes?' She replied: 'Yes.'

25

'He Raped Me'
John Nettleton

In 1994 actress Sheila Mercier, known to millions of television viewers at the time, had her autobiography published. It was a typical show business tale apart from one claim. She revealed that a Royal Air Force pilot had raped her – a twenty-year-old 'unworldly virgin' – at a wartime party. She became pregnant and gave birth to a daughter. The pilot later won the Victoria Cross. Mercier did not name the man but a newspaper soon identified him.

John Nettleton was born at Nongoma, a town in Zululand, South Africa, on 28 June 1917, the son of a civil engineer, also named John. When he was six, the family moved to Cape Town. At an early age it was decided that he would follow a family tradition and join the Royal Navy, but he failed the Dartmouth entrance examination. Instead, he became a merchant navy cadet in the training ship *General Botha*, the former cruiser HMS *Thames*. He qualified as a third officer and went to sea for eighteen months. In 1935 he returned to Cape Town with second thoughts about a naval life and decided to train as a civil engineer, no doubt influenced by his father. In 1938, during a visit to Britain, it occurred to him that the RAF might offer more excitement than civil engineering, and he volunteered for basic pilot training. He showed promise and was given a short service commission. There were several postings, and in November 1939, shortly after war broke out, twenty-two-year-old Pilot Officer Nettleton was sent to Cottesmore, Rutland, where Hampden bombers were based. He served as an instructor and promotion was rapid. By the time he was posted to 44

(Rhodesia) Squadron at Waddington, Lincolnshire, in July 1941 he was an acting squadron leader. Still flying Hampdens, he took part in raids over Europe and was mentioned in despatches.

In late 1941, 44 Squadron was given a far superior bomber, the Lancaster. It flew its first mission with Lancasters on 3 March 1942, a mine-laying operation – known as 'gardening' – in the Heligoland Bight. The Lancaster could carry four times as many mines – 'vegetables' – as the Hampden. Later there was a successful raid on the steel centre of Essen in the Ruhr. Early the following month the squadron, along with 97 (Straits Settlements) Squadron, based at nearby Woodhall Spa and also recently equipped with Lancasters, was told to practise low-level formation flying. The distances grew and it soon became apparent to the crews that a long-range mission in daylight was more than a possibility. The training involved a total of sixteen Lancasters. The final practice, with a round trip of more than 1,200 miles and a bombing run on Inverness, was on 14 April.

Air Marshal Arthur Harris, appointed chief of Bomber Command in February, had decided it was time for an audacious raid on Germany. His target was the MAN factory at Augsburg, in the south, which produced diesel engines for U-boats. The twelve Lancasters chosen for the mission, with four in reserve, would have to fly some 600 miles over enemy territory at low level in daylight – and back again, if they survived.

Wing Commander Rod Rodley, one of 97's pilots, recalled:

When the curtain drew back at the briefing there was a roar of laughter instead of a gasp of horror. No one believed that the air force would be so stupid as to send 12 of its newest four-engined bombers all that distance inside Germany in daylight. We sat back and waited calmly for someone to say, "Now the real target is this". Unfortunately it was the real target, a factory near Munich that was a major manufacturer of diesel engines for submarines.

After the briefing Rodley, then a flying officer, went to the station's armoury. He knew that the only armour in the plane was behind the pilot's seat, which would be no protection from ground fire at low level. Rodley was too late. Other pilots had come to the same conclusion. All the armour plate had been snapped up. He decided to improvise by sitting on his steel helmet for the entire mission.

The briefing for Operation Margin was on 17 April. Waddington and Woodall Spa would each send six Lancasters and the plan was for a rendezvous over Grantham. But the two groups failed to meet up. There was, of course, radio silence. The 44 Squadron bombers, led by Nettleton, headed for northern France, with 97's planes, under the command of Squadron Leader John Sherwood DFC and Bar, some distance behind. As a diversion, Boston bombers were sent to attack targets in Cherbourg and the Pas-de-Calais. Fighters also carried out sweeps.

Nettleton's planes crossed the French coast in the late afternoon. The planned route should have taken them away from Luftwaffe bases but they were several miles off course, probably because of a fault in his master gyrocompass. Their luck ran out when a pilot from the crack second group of Jagdgeschwader 2 spotted them as he returned to his base at Beaumont-le-Roger after a sortie. It was not long before up to thirty Messerschmitt Bf 109s and Focke-Wulf 190s were in pursuit. The six Lancasters closed formation and hugged the ground, 'leaving rippling wakes of flattened grass behind'. But the bombers' gun turrets were no match for the firepower of the fighters. T-Tommy was the first Lancaster to be attacked and the pilot managed to crash land after seeing V-Victor shot down, a fate also suffered by P-Peter. Nettleton's right-hand wingman, Sergeant George Rhodes in H-Howe, was trying to evade the attackers with all his guns jammed.

Former bomber pilot Jack Currie would record:

The death throes of H-Howe were terrible to see. At first, it put on speed, as though the throttles of the burning Merlins had been opened wide, and then it climbed, rearing like a frightened animal, and veered to port, until it hung directly over Nettleton and Garwell [Flying Officer John Garwell in A-Apple]. They did not know if Rhodes was flying the aircraft or if it was flying itself, and that was never to be known, but whatever or whoever held the stick ran out of flying speed. Lift could fight with weight no more, nor thrust contend with drag. H-Howe hovered, stalled and fell, the nose descending like a headman's axe. In B-Baker [Nettleton's plane] and A-Apple, they flinched and held their breath. Some watched the flaming monster plunge towards them, others shut their eyes. To those who watched, it seemed to try to grasp them, as a drowning man might snatch at anything afloat. Then it was past, by inches, and struck the ground, and crumpled on itself, and disappeared in a kaleidoscope of flames and sparks and smoke.

In fifteen minutes Nettleton had lost four bombers and twenty-one of his men were dead. B-Baker and A-Apple were also hit but they pressed on. The enemy, low on fuel and ammunition, broke off the attack. Only one fighter had been hit and it landed in a field. Sherwood's Lancasters were not spotted and had an uneventful journey over France. After crossing the German border Nettleton headed for the northern end of Lake Constance. Then he swung east towards Munich before turning for the approach to Augsburg.

The last thing the Bavarian city expected on 17 April was an air raid. The war seemed a long way off. In the centre, thousands were enjoying Augsburg's annual folk festival, with bands playing and dancing in the streets. Then came the roar of the Merlins as Nettleton's two low-flying bombers headed north-west for the sprawling MAN plant, easily identified by its tall chimneys. There was little fighter cover in the area but anti-aircraft batteries covering the factory had been alerted. Flak defences soon engaged the planes. The bomb doors of B-Baker opened as Nettleton lined up the main assembly shed. The load of four 1,000lb bombs with delayed fuses fell away and the bomber banked. A-Apple was hit as it made its run in, and Garwell heard the dreaded words, 'Skipper, we're on fire.' The pilot carried on. Then came, 'Bombs gone.' Garwell knew his plane was doomed and looked for somewhere to crash land. Struggling with the controls, he managed to put the bomber down in a field. It slid for some 50 yards, breaking in two. But Garwell and three members of his crew emerged alive. They were taken prisoner.

As Nettleton headed for home, retracing his route, Sherwood's six bombers made their approach to the factory in line astern. The defences were waiting for them. Flak even blasted rooftops. Sherwood's K-King was hit but 'glowing like a blow torch' dropped its bombs before crashing. The pilot was the sole survivor, thrown clear of the cabin still strapped to his seat. Another Lancaster was a ball of fire and exploded after dropping its bombs. The remaining planes delivered their payloads and eventually returned home. Twelve Lancasters had set out from Waddington and Woodhall Spa and only five came back. Of the eighty-five men, forty-nine were missing.

News of the raid was reported briefly the following day, and on 20 April Nettleton gave this account: 'As soon as the French coast came into sight I took my formation down to a height of 25 to 30ft, and we flew the whole of the rest of the way to Augsburg at that height. Soon after we crossed the coast enemy fighters appeared in fairly big numbers. A fierce running fight developed. We kept in the tightest possible formation so as to support each other by combined fire. Fighter after fighter attacked us from astern. The fight lasted 15 minutes or so, and aircraft were lost by ourselves and the Germans.

We swept across France and skirted the border of Switzerland into Germany. We charged straight at Augsburg. Our target was not simply the works but certain vital shops in the works. We had studied their exact appearance from photographs, and we saw them just where they should be. Low-angle flak began to come up at us thick and fast. We were so low that the Germans were even shooting into their own buildings. They had quantities of quick-firing guns. All our aircraft had holes made in them.

The big sheds which were our target rose up exactly ahead of me. My bomb aimer let go. Our bombs, of course, had delay action fuses. We roared on past the town. Then I had the painful experience of seeing one of my formation catching fire. The aircraft was ablaze, hit all over by flak. It turned out of the formation and I was thankful to see it make a perfect forced landing. At that moment all our bombs went up. I had turned and could see the target well. Debris and dust were flying up in the air. Then I set course for home.

Prime Minister Winston Churchill praised the operation: 'We must plainly regard the attack of the Lancasters on the U-boat engine factory at Augsburg as an outstanding achievement of the Royal Air Force. Undeterred by heavy losses at the outset, the bombers pierced in broad daylight into the heart of Germany and struck a vital point with deadly precision.'

The Times enthused:

Nothing like the brilliant attack on Augsburg has ever been dared by the enemy ... All who went and all who sent them out must have known that so bold a stroke could only be delivered at a heavy cost in lives; and in fact less than half the force returned. But the prize to be attained had been carefully assessed and judged worth the sacrifice; at point blank range the factory, working for the U-boat fleet, can scarcely have been missed. Once more the enemy has been taken in the rear; and another campaign, this time against allied shipping in the Atlantic, will be weakened throughout its course as the result of these gallant airmen's work.

The Daily Telegraph commented: 'In the wonderful daylight attack by RAF bombers on Augsburg, hedge-hopping 600 miles across enemy territory, our Air Force achieved a masterpiece of skill and daring to which there is nothing comparable in the record of the Luftwaffe.'

On 27 April Nettleton appeared at a press conference but he had been told what to say in a briefing note: 'You may ask – and the families of those splendid chaps whom we left behind may ask – was it worth the loss involved? My answer to that is absolutely. Naturally it isn't easy to be 100 per cent certain where your bombs go when they are fitted with delay-action fuses, especially when your aircraft is flying at 200 feet and covering 100 yards a second. But we were able to see the bombs as we turned after the attack and we were all pretty confident we had hit the target. Today I am delighted to be able to tell you that we have now got a report which shows that the MAN factory was heavily damaged.'

It was certainly a propaganda victory, but did the raid curb the U-boat menace? Later analysis showed that of the 2,700 machine tools only eight were destroyed and sixteen badly damaged. Five of 558 cranes were destroyed and six badly damaged. Five of the seventeen bombs that hit the factory failed to explode. Four bombs had struck a nearby textile works. A total of twelve people, including two women, were killed.

The attack left the Minister of Economic Warfare, Lord Selborne, seething. He wrote to Churchill pointing out that the MAN factory was a low-priority target because the Germans had other plants capable of producing diesel engines for U-boats. Even the complete destruction of the MAN factory would not have significantly hit overall production.

Selborne complained: 'What disturbs me is that such a target should have been given priority over all the targets which have been so often recommended by this Ministry and which I believe are accepted by the Air Staff as being of the highest priority.' Some of the high-priority targets were near Augsburg. The minister added: 'On the operational side the raid seems to have been brilliantly conceived and carried out. But the planning which directed it seems to bear no relation to the intelligence on which it should have been based.'

As a result of Selborne's complaint, Air Marshal Harris was told to carry out a check on the economic importance of any target selected for special operations. In another message to Churchill, the minister pointed out: 'While there can be no question of the authority of Bomber Command and the Air Staff to measure the tactical results of their weapons, I feel that in estimating the probable effects of damage on production, this Ministry has something useful to say.'

Nettleton and Sherwood were both put forward for the Victoria Cross on 19 April. Nettleton 'showed in this action the finest qualities of skilled airmanship, leadership, courage and determination'. Of Sherwood, who was listed as missing, the recommendation noted: 'While bombing the target his aircraft was hit by anti-aircraft guns and caught fire. Squadron Leader Sherwood continued to lead his section away from the target with one wing well alight and until such time as the aircraft became uncontrollable. By extreme devotion to duty, Squadron Leader Sherwood ensured the success of the operation with which he was charged, and continued his daring leadership to the end.' Both awards were 'strongly recommended' by Harris. But someone at the Air Ministry decided that Sherwood did not deserve the Victoria Cross and scribbled on the recommendation: 'To be recd for DSO if found to be alive.' The pilot, taken prisoner, survived the war. A number of other decorations were awarded. Nettleton received his Victoria Cross from George VI at Buckingham Palace on 1 November.

At the age of twenty, Sheila Mercier – then Sheila Rix – was an aspiring actress. She had been to drama school and was touring with a theatre company. Years later she would be known to television viewers as Annie Sugden in the long-running soap opera *Emmerdale*. In December 1939 she returned to her family's comfortable home in the seaside resort of Hornsea on the east Yorkshire coast for Christmas celebrations. She was still there on New Year's Eve when a family friend at a nearby RAF base phoned to say that a group of officers on their way to another station were throwing a party that night. Would Sheila and her sister Nora like to come? They had been to the base before and their parents said yes.

The girls arrived to find a lot of young men getting 'very merry'. Mercier was given a drink called a green goddess, and was soon chatting to 'a rather good-looking' South African pilot. After about ten minutes the pilot suggested they go upstairs to persuade his cousin, who had gone to bed, to join the party. The cousin declined the invitation, saying he was too tired. The pilot then suggested that they go to his room to 'stoke the fire'. In her autobiography, *Annie's Song*, Mercier told how the pilot suddenly attacked her. She also gave an account to the *Daily Mail*.

It was then, as I stood at the door, that he dragged me inside. There in his room he seized me, threw me onto the bed and raped me. I screamed and fought and kicked. I was so naïve I had only the most tenuous idea of what was happening, but I was convinced I had fought him off. Trembling with terror, I dashed out of his room, found Nora and went home. I told nobody what had happened. I knew I had been subjected to a horrifying assault but I did not imagine I could possibly be pregnant.

And even when I started to be sick each night, I failed to make the connection. In response, my mother called the doctor. He asked if I had misbehaved. I answered no. I did not believe I had. I was too frightened of my parents' reaction to broach the subject of the assault with them. Neither did I dare tell the doctor. He diagnosed catarrh on the stomach. However, the terrible truth soon began to dawn as my stomach started to swell.

Mercier left the family home, saying she was going to London for theatre work. She stayed with a cousin, and confided in her. The cousin insisted on telling the parents and they travelled down for the 'inevitable confrontation'. Mercier, sister of the comic actor Brian Rix, who became Lord Rix of Whitehall, told the *Mail*:

> I still cannot put into words how distressed they were, but their anguish was for themselves, not me – for the shame an illegitimate pregnancy would bring on their comfortable middle-class lives, for the awful stigma of being the subject of village gossip in a close-knit community of which they were hitherto unblemished members.
>
> They left telling me I'd have to fend for myself from then on. It was the cruellest desertion ... For the next few months I was in a permanent state of shock. I wandered from one set of digs to new lodgings and finally to a flat in Nottingham. I was friendless, desolate and completely ignorant of what was to come.

Her parents would not allow sister Nora or brother Brian to visit her 'in case they were tainted by my shame'. But her father was determined to track down the pilot and with the help of a friend at the Air Ministry he did so. In her autobiography, Mercier told of a bizarre encounter: 'It says something for the man's character that he at least admitted his crime and came post-haste to the flat. I asked him if he knew he had actually had sex with me and he said yes, he did. So I asked him why he had not told me.'

The pilot quickly proposed marriage. She recoiled at the idea but then thought that despite the 'ghastly mess he had landed me in, he really was a nice young man'. She said yes. Her parents said no. Mercier was desperate to keep the baby and thought marriage was the only answer. When the baby was born, Mercier named her Karen. Her parents insisted on adoption, and the girl was given to a 'solid, respectable family'. For a few years Mercier was allowed to write letters but then she was told to stop because the adoptive mother 'wanted to feel that the child was truly her own'. She recalled: 'I do not really know how I coped. I felt my heart would break and every time I saw a baby in a pram I wept. I longed for my child.'

Some five weeks after the Augsburg raid in April 1942 John Nettleton went to a cocktail party in London, where he met a twenty-one-year-old WAAF officer, Betty Havelock. Within four days he had proposed marriage, and a church ceremony took place in

Lincoln in July. At some stage during the war Mercier, surprisingly, joined the WAAFs and went on to be commissioned. She met Nettleton's wife after being posted to her base. The encounter with the pilot at the New Year's Eve party was never mentioned.

After his marriage Nettleton was sent on a goodwill tour of the United States. Returning to Britain, he refused to be grounded or become an instructor, and continued operational flying. On 12 July 1943 Nettleton, now a wing commander and the leader of 44 Squadron, took off from Dunholme Lodge, near Lincoln, with Turin the target. Fourteen Lancasters were involved and his was the only one not to return. His fate remains a mystery. His bomber may have been shot down by fighters over the Bay of Biscay or hit by flak after straying too close to Brest. In February 1944 Betty Nettleton gave birth to a son, who was named John. Four days later Wing Commander John Nettleton was officially presumed dead. That month the RAF returned to Augsburg with a vengeance. Nearly 600 aircraft destroyed large parts of the city, killing an estimated 730 people and injuring more than 1,300.

In 1951 Sheila married an actor, Peter Mercier, and three years later they had a son, Nigel. In 1969 she received a letter from her long-lost daughter, a mother with three girls. 'I was absolutely wild with joy and phoned her immediately. The rapport was instant. We talked and talked. We couldn't wait to meet and we did so at Brian's house. I told her how she had come to be. She was horrified for me. I explained that we had never brought charges against the man who raped me because he had been a pilot fighting for his country.'

It was the *Mail on Sunday* that named John Nettleton. It quoted his son, a businessman, as saying: 'I haven't decided what I am going to do about the book. Attacking people who are alive and defenceless is sick, but one step more sick is to attack people who are dead. This happened before I was born and the whole thing strikes me as odd. It would be so out of character.'

In 2017 Sheila Mercier was believed to be living in Spain, aged ninety-eight.

26

The Phoney Irishman
John Kenneally

Lance Corporal John Kenneally thought he might have won the Military Medal for bravery after two remarkable charges at the enemy, his Bren gun blazing away at the hip. But when awards for a decisive battle in the Tunisian campaign of 1943 were announced, he was 'slightly miffed' to find that his name was not among them. There was the small consolation of promotion to sergeant. Several months later he happened to be listening to the radio and a news item shocked him. It was announced that he would receive the Victoria Cross.

Unknown to him, many men in his regiment, the Irish Guards, had been interviewed about his deeds, but the entire process was kept secret. Kenneally was the last to know. He would soon be a celebrated hero. There was a problem, however: his past.

Kenneally was born on 15 March 1921, the illegitimate son of eighteen-year-old Gertrude Robinson. He was called Leslie. Gertrude came from a middle-class family in Blackpool, and the social stigma of pregnancy saw her parents sending her to friends in Birmingham, with a warning 'not to darken our doors again'. She changed her surname to Jackson and her son became Leslie Jackson. Gertrude got a job as a dance hostess at a city ballroom, and Kenneally – Leslie Jackson – later discovered that she was actually 'a fairly high-class whore'. He was sent to a private school. A succession of 'uncles' visited their home, and Kenneally thought how lucky he was to have so many as they 'gave me coppers to buy sweets and keep me out of the way'. But other children were deterred from visiting. 'I was rather a lonely boy,' he recalled.

His school closed after the headmistress jumped to her death from the roof of the four-storey building. He went instead to a tough primary, and because he appeared 'posh', lacking a strong Brummie accent, he had a hard time at first but developed a natural resilience 'which bore me in good stead in later life'. With his mother out most nights or going away with her latest lover, he became 'rather wild and undisciplined', often skipping school. Petty theft and collecting illegal bets for a bookmaker were two of his activities. When he did attend school, he was often caned. It led to a showdown with his mother, a school inspector and the headmaster. With his mother's promise of a new bicycle, he was persuaded to work harder. He won a place at a grammar school, where he shone at athletics and swimming, and had 'great fun' in the Cadets, also joining the Scouts.

As she got older, Gertrude's finances suffered. She had several jobs and she and her son moved frequently from rented accommodation, usually when money was owed. At the age of seventeen Kenneally left school and got a job as an office boy at an engineering firm, which he 'absolutely hated'. His 'wildness' ensured his early departure, and he went to work at a petrol station. In January 1939, with war looming, Kenneally, under his real name of Leslie Jackson, enlisted in a Territorial Army unit of the Royal Artillery, starting 'a love affair with the British Army'. When war was declared in the September he became a regular soldier. But he took a dislike to officers who had attained their rank through wealth and privilege. 'Being young and at times foolish I began to develop a raised eyebrow type of insolence ... I suffered for it and it took me a long time to learn that you can't buck the army.'

Kenneally expected to see action in France after training, but to his dismay he was transferred to the Honourable Artillery Company (HAC) based in London. Given a spell of leave, he met up with a friend in Birmingham and returned to barracks nine days late. A court martial sentenced him to one month's detention. He was sent to the nearest detention centre, which happened to be at Wellington Barracks close to Buckingham Palace, where he encountered 'the magic of the Irish Guards'. He was most impressed when a drill sergeant shouted down his gunner escort for being slovenly.

The going was tough but the month passed quickly. Soon after rejoining the HAC he asked for a transfer to the Irish Guards, which was refused. He was sent to a light anti-aircraft battery helping to protect an RAF base near Waltham Abbey, Essex, where he witnessed some of the dramas of the Battle of Britain. A posting back to London prompted a second request to join the Irish Guards, which was also turned down. He became a driver making deliveries to gun sites scattered around the capital, and was 'bored to tears'.

One day in February 1941, at a café in Cricklewood, he met a group of labourers from southern Ireland. There was an invitation to an Irish dance and 'for the first time in my life I got drunk'. Towards the end of the evening the inevitable fight broke out, and Kenneally 'punched and kicked with the best of them. My adrenalin was running high through the drink I had taken, and I did not feel any of the blows I was receiving. I felt great and was enjoying my first fracas.' Local and military police turned up and Kenneally fled with some of his new friends. But he had not escaped unscathed – swollen lips, a black eye and various bruises, along with a torn uniform and a missing cap, would take some explaining if he returned to his unit. He knew he faced a severe punishment. The labourers were heading to well-paid jobs in Glasgow and, impressed by his fighting ability, suggested he join them. All he needed was a different identity card. Another labourer happened to be returning to Ireland and handed over his card. The name on the card was John Patrick Kenneally. So Leslie Jackson deserted and took the identity of John Patrick Kenneally.

After a few weeks working hard in Glasgow, and with plenty of money in their pockets, the Irishmen decided to return home. They tried to persuade Kenneally to take the trip with them but he was still determined to join the Irish Guards. He ended up going to a recruiting office in Manchester, where he produced his new identity card, took an educational test that would not have challenged 'a boy of 12', passed the medical, gave the oath of loyalty – and he was in the Irish Guards. He was 'quite elated', but 'deep down I was ashamed of myself for deserting the Royal Artillery'.

Kenneally went to the Guards Depot at Caterham, Surrey, for basic training. There was little time to reflect on the fact that he was still a deserter. The constant drills and physical training were so gruelling that 'it was not unusual to go to bed at 6.30pm absolutely shattered'. One sergeant was suspicious, asking if he had previous experience of military training. 'The army cadets' was his quick response. He was required to learn the regiment's history, including the names and ranks of those who had won the Victoria Cross. What remains a mystery is how he was able to keep up the pretence of being an Irishman.

After passing out Kenneally went to another barracks for further training, where the emphasis was on weapons and learning to kill 'in a hundred different ways, nothing was too low or too dirty'. He impressed his superiors and was promoted lance corporal. On leave, a trip to Dublin born of curiosity no doubt helped him to cement his Irish identity, but a long overdue visit to his mother and a meeting with his future wife led to swift demotion after returning to barracks three days late. His spirits lifted shortly afterwards when he was posted to the 1st Battalion, 'the cream of the regiment'. But it was an even tougher regime. He was again promoted lance corporal and married his new love, Elsie Francis, before sailing with the battalion in the P&O troopship *Strathmore* for North Africa in February 1943. Enemy attacks in the Mediterranean were frequent, but the ship escaped unscathed. The greatest challenge was the size of the hammocks, made for men who were 5 feet 8 inches tall at most. The guardsmen were usually at least 6 feet tall. They disembarked at Algiers and a few days later boarded another ship for Bone, along the coast, to take part in the Tunisian campaign. German aircraft attacked the vessel, and Kenneally, one of the Bren gunners, got 'the adrenalin pumping' by emptying three magazines.

At Bone they drilled in preparation for 17 March, St Patrick's Day. The British commander, General Sir Harold Alexander, commissioned in the Irish Guards, had shamrock flown in for the all-important ceremony. The next day the battalion went to the Medjerda Valley – 'immediately renamed Happy Valley by the lads' – and took up positions facing a long ridge, which concealed a German stronghold. The slopes of the ridge were covered by heavy machine guns, and much of the area was mined. One night No. 2 Company – 103 officers and other ranks – carried out a probing attack. Only five wounded guardsmen returned. Later the ridge was captured but it needed a full battalion of the 78th Division supported by tanks. The Germans took up new positions, heavily reinforced, on a line of hills near Medjez. The prize of Tunis lay beyond. Tanks could not be used this time because of the steep and rocky terrain, and the task of clearing the enemy was given to the 1st Irish Guards, along with the 5th Grenadier Guards and the 1st Scots Guards.

On the night of 23 April, the men moved out and an early objective was taken. Then they dug in. The main German position was a massive feature called Djebel Bou Azoukaz, known simply as the Bou. Days later twenty-two-year-old Kenneally was given a reconnaissance mission to check on a possible enemy counterattack. He was pleased because 'I hated skulking in the slit trenches. I felt claustrophobic in them and did not enjoy having time to think and brood.' He crawled forward with a radio operator. In front was a steep valley, with slopes leading up to the Bou. The men took cover in an abandoned gun pit when German artillery opened up, later noticing that their heavy radio had been silenced, 'with a lump of 88mm shell sticking out of it'. When the firing ceased Kenneally scanned the area with his binoculars. There was a house about 600 yards away. A German army cook emerged and began stirring a large pot. Kenneally put his Bren on single shot and aimed at the man's white apron. He was on target and the radio operator, looking through the glasses, observed, 'There goes their fucking stew.' The pair darted away 'giggling like schoolboys'.

An attack on part of the Bou by the Guards brigade was planned for dusk on 27 April but it was brought forward to the afternoon, to the disbelief of Kenneally, who thought the general giving the order should be shot. It meant crossing rocky land and cornfields for about a mile in daylight, in full view of the enemy and in sapping heat. The attackers, as expected, took heavy casualties. 'It seemed that all the artillery in the German army was having a go,' Kenneally recalled. 'I was dazed and shocked: the noise was devastating; the hot blasts from explosions were scorching my face; patches of corn were burning fiercely; stones and earth thrown up by shell bursts were rattling down on my steel helmet; machine gun bursts were scything down the corn like a reaper and down with the corn went officers and men alike. It was a bloody massacre.' Eventually they reached the slopes of the Bou in fading light. Halfway to the ridge they were ordered to fix bayonets. The Germans retreated.

The ridge of the Bou stretched for about 1,500 yards between two points, which were numbered 212 and 214. The next day, 28 April, saw repeated attacks by the enemy, which were repulsed by a diminishing band of defenders. Kenneally was busy with his Bren, moving among the rocks looking for targets. As he crept along he heard German voices and took cover behind two large boulders. In a gulley was a large group of the enemy. Most of them were squatting around an officer. 'Some were lying down taking a breather and they were bunched up like cattle,' Kenneally observed. 'What an opportunity. I crawled back to the boulders and quickly took off all my equipment – speed was to be the essence of this operation. I put a new magazine on the Bren gun and one in each pocket.' Taking a deep breath, he ran forward, firing from the hip and achieving complete surprise. 'I hose-piped them from the top of the gully. They were bowled over like ninepins and were diving in all directions. I had time to flip on another magazine and gave them that too. Enough was enough, and I fled back to the boulders and safety.' The remaining Germans scattered and began firing at each other. Hearing the shooting, some of the men from Kenneally's No. 1 Company swooped down 'screaming like banshees and were picking them off left, right and centre'.

Kenneally collected his equipment and went off for a cognac. Later that day he helped to attack Germans setting up a machine-gun position, and forced the retreat of three tanks using land mines he had recovered from a wrecked carrier. On the morning of 30 April, he spotted another large group of Germans in the same gulley where he had sown such devastation. 'It was almost a re-run,' he noted. He was with a sergeant from the Reconnaissance Corps armed with a Sten gun and they charged down, each emptying a magazine. Then they sprinted back as men from No. 1 Company fired and tossed grenades. Some of the Germans returned fire and the sergeant was wounded fatally. As Kenneally reached the top of the ridge 'a great blow' to his right leg sent him flying. Despite the bullet wound he hobbled around and carried on fighting. A guardsman tried to take his Bren and was told to 'piss off'. Kenneally felt that the gun had 'served me well and was going to serve me more'. The Germans eventually retreated – with Kenneally in pursuit. The enemy never returned, and 700 Germans lay dead around the Bou. Only eighty men of the 1st Battalion Irish Guards survived.

General Alexander sent a message: 'Heartiest congratulations to you and all ranks of the battalion for your magnificent fight, which has not only added fresh laurels to the illustrious name of the regiment, but has also been of the utmost importance to our whole battle.'

The award of the Victoria Cross to Kenneally was announced on 17 August 1943. The citation noted his remarkable charges at the enemy and said:

> The magnificent gallantry of this NCO on these two occasions, under heavy fire, his unfailing vigilance, and remarkable accuracy were responsible for saving many valuable lives during the days and nights in the forward positions. His actions also played a considerable part in holding these positions and this influenced the whole course of the battle. His rapid appreciation of the situation, his initiative and his extraordinary gallantry in attacking single-handed a massed body of the enemy and breaking up an attack on two occasions, was an achievement that can seldom have been equalled. His courage in fighting all day when wounded was an inspiration to all ranks.

Tunis had been captured in the May, signalling the end of the German and Italian occupation of North Africa. More than 230,000 prisoners were taken, including most of the Afrika Korps. After the battle of the Bou Kenneally was sent to a hospital in Algiers to have the bullet removed from his leg. Later, when making his way to Tunis to join his battalion, he wondered if he was about to be unmasked as a deserter. He encountered a gunner who recognised him from his time in the artillery and was puzzled by the Irish Guards shoulder flashes. 'I transferred,' said Kenneally. His battalion was so depleted that it was given the job of guarding some of the prisoners.

In December a strengthened battalion crossed the Mediterranean and disembarked at Taranto, southern Italy, where a bar of chocolate secured a copious amount of red wine and five cigarettes 'bought a woman'. The following month saw the unopposed Anzio landings, and like many of the soldiers on the beachhead Kenneally expected a bold advance to Rome. But dithering by the American commander, Major General John Lucas, allowed the Germans to build up their forces and inflict heavy casualties. There were days and nights of close-quarter fighting similar to the struggles on the Bou. In one impressive episode Kenneally took out a sniper after stalking him and then emptying a whole magazine of his Bren at a tree, a thud on the ground confirming the kill. He took the sniper's watch, 'which served me for many years'. Later he was wounded again and ended up in a hospital in Naples. His battalion, once more badly mauled, sailed for Britain in April. He recorded: 'The 1st Battalion never fought again as a single unit.'

General Alexander had presented Kenneally with the ribbon of the Victoria Cross at a parade in August 1943, and on 24 May 1944 he went to Buckingham Palace to receive the medal from King George VI. Even Prime Minister Winston Churchill paid tribute to the 'Irish hero'. The authorities still believed he was John Patrick Kenneally and not the deserter Leslie Jackson. The day before he went to the palace a lieutenant colonel had pointed out to him that he was about to become 'a living legend of the Irish Guards' and his behaviour needed to be exemplary. It was at this point that Kenneally wondered if it was time to reveal the truth. But he decided his identity was irrelevant. 'I was an Irish Guardsman. They had seen fit to give me the medal; I had not asked for it. I was just as proud and honoured to be a member of the regiment as he was; and anyway, if I told the old bugger all this I might give him a heart attack.'

Soon afterwards the regiment's 2nd and 3rd Battalions took part in the invasion of Normandy. Kenneally, with other veterans of the North Africa and Italy campaigns, toasted them in the sergeants' mess at Chelsea Barracks, thankful for once that they were not part of the action. Towards the end of the war Kenneally was posted to Germany and then the peace brought its own problems. On one occasion he narrowly escaped a court martial after stealing an ambulance for a night out with friends, which ended in a drunken fight with locals and an angry bar owner claiming a huge amount in compensation for his wrecked premises. With a wife he had barely seen and the addition of a son, he was under pressure to leave the army. He thought of joining the police but, much to his wife's annoyance, he signed on for a more challenging role – five years with the 1st Guards Parachute Battalion. He admitted: 'I was glad to leave the fleshpots of Germany; I had been drinking far too much and I was unfit. Still the Paras would put that right for me, and how.'

He went to barracks at Colchester where the instructors 'took a fiendish delight in turning these cocky guardsmen into exhausted wrecks'. Those who survived graduated to an RAF base for full parachute training, which led to a series of jumps. Kenneally passed out with his wings and red beret. In 1947 he appeared in court accused of taking and driving away a car without the owner's consent and having no insurance. He was fined. A posting to Palestine, where Jews and Arabs were in armed conflict, added to his wife's displeasure and while he was there she gave birth to a second son. One of his tasks was the defence of a kibbutz in northern Galilee. His leadership was responsible for beating off a major night attack. The defenders tried to persuade him to join the new Israeli army. A lot of money was offered, and Kenneally – half Jewish – was tempted, but he could not desert a second time. He remembered he was 'a living legend' of the Irish Guards. 'I still had that devil-may-care attitude, but to cast a slur on the regiment – no, not even a rogue like me.' He returned to Britain and received an ultimatum from his wife. Reluctantly, he purchased his discharge but was annoyed to find that his conduct had been rated very good rather than exemplary – 'it would not have cost them anything'. He left Pirbright Camp in Surrey in July 1948 wearing civilian clothes and feeling 'like a defrocked priest'.

He returned to the Midlands and opened a car showroom in Solihull. His marriage to Elsie ended in 1955 and he married a divorcee, Elizabeth Evelyn, who had a son. They had four more children. His business later failed and for a time he worked as a security guard.

In 1969 he gave a revealing interview to the *Sunday Express* in which he admitted his false identity and claimed that his father was a wealthy industrialist, Neville Blond, then seventy-one. Blond denied the claim. Kenneally told the newspaper: 'My mother – she was only about eighteen when I was born – was a Christian. Mr Blond is a Jew. As a child I can vaguely remember him coming to visit us in a black Bentley. My first firm recollection is when I passed into grammar school. He came and told me how pleased he was and rigged me out with clothes. But after that he went off and things were very hard. One winter I had to go to school in gym shoes.' When he was twelve his mother obtained a court order against Blond, who was made to pay 20s a week in child maintenance.

Of his enlistment in the Irish Guards, Kenneally said:

I dreamed up a complete Irish background and gave a false address in Tipperary as that of my parents. I have never seen or heard of the real Kenneally again. When I won the VC I was scared stiff. It was the worst thing that could have happened to me. It made me a public figure and I thought, 'Now I'm bound to get caught.' But I never was. For all I know the Royal Artillery are still after me as a deserter. I've met the Queen and Prince Philip several times and George VI too. Every time I thought, 'What a hoot. If only they knew!'

After I got the medal I went to my father's London office in Millbank. He was a civil servant then. He said how proud of me he was, gave me £10 and said he would set me up in business after the war. He asked after my mother. When I left the army I went back to see him. But he showed me the door. That's what really hurts. I would have been loyal to him if he had been loyal to me. But can you blame me for being bitter? There are my half brothers [Anthony Blond, a prominent publisher, and Peter Blond, a successful businessman] with everything they could wish for. I hear Anthony had a party where wine flowed from a fountain. And here am I buying a house on a mortgage and in dead trouble if I can't sell thirty cars in a week.

Neville Blond, who had been an officer in the Royal Horse Guards during the First World War, was quoted as saying: 'Kenneally is not my son, and it is untrue that I kitted him out for grammar school.

I have seen him only once, when he won the Victoria Cross. He had written and told me about himself. I gave him a tenner because I thought it was very brave of him. I have never supported him apart from the paternity order his mother brought against me. I do not remember if I contested paternity at the time. When you're a young fellow you do these things. I was only one of his mother's many friends. But I happened at the time to have a bob or two, which meant, "go for that fellow".'

In 1992 Kenneally had an autobiography published. *Kenneally VC*, later retitled *The Honour and the Shame*, was reviewed by Anthony Blond in the *Sunday Express*. Blond, to his credit, had not accepted his father's denial: 'The author and I are half-brothers. We share a father, Neville Blond.' He revealed: 'My mother did not know of Kenneally's existence until he called at the house in 1939 to tell his father he was going to join the army. She recognised him immediately – it is one of God's little jokes that bastards are the spitting image of their dads – and gave him £25, saying "that enough?" and told him to keep in touch.' Blond ended his review: 'I salute you brother. I hope all *Sunday Express* readers will get this marvellous book. Sergeant Kenneally VC deserves to be rich.'

In retirement Kenneally lived at Lower Rochford, Worcestershire. On St Patrick's Day 1998, in the absence of the Queen Mother, he was given the honour of distributing shamrock to the Irish Guards at Wellington Barracks, where he had once spent a month in detention as a gunner who would desert his regiment. He died some two years later, on 27 September 2000, aged seventy-nine.

27

The Wild Submariner
James Magennis

It was not the first time that Leading Seaman James Magennis VC had been charged with drunkenness. He stood before the captain's table, cap in hand, as officers told of his unacceptable behaviour. Unlike one sailor, he had not urinated in the skipper's cabin. But the punishment was severe. He was demoted, deprived of his good conduct stripe and given twenty-one days in the 'rattle' – the Royal Navy's detention quarters in Portsmouth, a throwback to Victorian times. And when he emerged, probably not too chastened, he was forced to leave the Submarine Service.

The year was 1947, and some of the excesses of wartime were no longer being tolerated. In the war years, when a submarine returned safely from patrol, sailors often celebrated to excess, surprised that they were still alive. There was a staggering casualty rate of 38 per cent. Only Bomber Command of the Royal Air Force had a worse rate. Magennis had been in the 'rattle' before, and the peacetime Submarine Service was not to his liking. Senior officers wanted a return to pre-1939 days and exclusiveness, when submariners were volunteers and selected. The war had led to many men being drafted, and Magennis was one of those.

As former submariner George Fleming observed: 'Wartime over, the petty trivialities of a peacetime navy returned. The naval routine of spit and polish merchants were back in power again and worse still they were even creeping into the Submarine Service. They train men to blow up warships, to risk their lives for their country. When it is all over they want them to behave like Sunday school boys, without understanding the mental pain and anguish some of them have been through.'

Reserve officers also found the same prejudice, as Lieutenant Ian Fraser, who won the Victoria Cross in the same action as Magennis, discovered to his disappointment. He was keen to obtain a regular commission after the war, but gave up trying after meeting too many obstacles. The service did, of course, need to slim down at the end of hostilities, but perhaps there was too much enthusiasm for shedding the 'extras'. Magennis also encountered resentment because of his prestigious award. He was the only junior rating in the Submarine Service to win the Victoria Cross. Nearly all the awards in the two world wars had gone to submarine commanders.

In September 1947, after detention, Magennis was transferred to general service, a move that further demoralised him. He was sent to Devonport and the cruiser HMS *Orion*, which had joined the reserve fleet. John Daly, a petty officer stoker on board the cruiser HMS *Cumberland*, recalled: 'Like many other Irishmen he got into trouble with his superior officers and the powers-that-be. Unwanted in submarines, he was discharged back into general service. He was detached to my department, the engine room, to do small electrical repairs. He was very much a loner and like many at that time wanted to get out of the service.' His remaining time would be spent in reserve ships, and Magennis left the navy in 1949 after fourteen years' service. He returned to his native Belfast with his wife Edna, whom he married in 1946, and took a civilian job at a naval air station.

James Magennis was born in west Belfast on 27 October 1919. His surname was actually McGinnes, but it somehow became Magennis when he joined the navy and he stuck with it. He was known as Jim to family and friends. His father, William, a musician and part-time mill packer, and his mother, Mary, were Roman Catholics, and sectarianism and religious bigotry would always be unpleasant features of life in the city. The family, which grew to five children, struggled to survive, not helped by the fact that William McGinnes, a Scot, disappeared. Magennis's mother took sewing jobs, often working at home to the early hours. At one stage she was forced to put four of her children into temporary care at a local orphanage. A daughter, Peggy, died from a blood disorder when she was fifteen. Measles, whooping cough, diphtheria, chicken pox and tuberculosis were common threats to the young.

At the age of fourteen, Magennis left school and found a job cleaning bottles in a wine store. He also sold ice cream in a fish and chip shop until he was sacked for giving generous portions. The following year he tried to join the army but was turned down, a recruiting officer telling him his education was too poor. The navy took him on, and he headed off for the tough regime of the Ganges training base at Shotley, Suffolk.

One of the punishments on base involved going around the parade ground at the double carrying a cannon ball, which became even more challenging in cold weather. A cannon ball dropped on a foot could end a naval career. Caning was common, with a physical training instructor holding a boy down over a gym horse as the punishment was administered. During his nine months at Ganges Magennis ended up in the 'rattle' several times for offences that included smoking.

On 6 March 1936 Boy Seaman Magennis joined his first warship, the battleship HMS *Royal Sovereign*, at Portsmouth. After three weeks at sea he transferred to the cruiser HMS *Dauntless* at Gibraltar. Bad behaviour during a run ashore at Malta led to six 'cuts' of the cane. In October 1937 he was promoted ordinary seaman and other drafts followed before war broke out. He was an able seaman when he went to the destroyer HMS *Kandahar* in October 1939. *Kandahar* witnessed Lord Mountbatten's HMS *Kelly* being torpedoed in the North Sea in May 1940, with the loss of twenty-seven lives. Years later Magennis admitted: 'It was the sight of the dead and dying that struck real fear in me for the first time in my life. It made me sick. It paralysed me.' *Kelly* was saved, but the following year she sank in the Mediterranean during an air attack, with much loss of life.

In June 1940 *Kandahar* helped to sink the Italian submarine *Torricelli* in the Red Sea. Magennis showed his bravery by diving in to rescue of some of the Italians. Some time later, after a night in Mombasa, he missed the last liberty boat and decided to swim to his ship half a mile offshore. He turned up at another ship and was taken to *Kandahar*. The next morning he appeared before the first lieutenant's table charged with entering his ship improperly dressed. He lost a day's leave. The destroyer saw plenty of action in the Battle of Crete in 1941, when the Royal Navy paid a high price in men and ships. Magennis once again showed his courage by helping to rescue sailors in the water. In the December *Kandahar*'s luck in the Mediterranean ran out. She struck a mine, suffering heavy casualties, and was scuttled. Magennis, one of the survivors, was sent to Devonport. After a spell of leave in Belfast he returned to the base for his next draft. If he was expecting another destroyer or cruiser, he was in for a surprise. He was about to become a submariner.

On 3 December 1942 he reported for training at Dolphin, the submarine base at Gosport, across the water from Portsmouth, and after a few weeks was sent to the depot ship HMS *Cyclops* at Rothesay on the Isle of Bute. He experienced his first dive in *H50*, a boat built during the First World War. His sleeping area was a torpedo rack. Although he was 'pressed', he soon took to the role of a submariner. He volunteered for special service in new midget submarines called X-craft. At 5 feet 4 inches tall, he was the ideal size for the cramped craft.

In September 1943, six X-craft, towed by conventional submarines, set off from their Scottish base for the 1,000-mile journey to northern Norway to attack the German warships *Tirpitz*, *Scharnhorst* and *Lutzow*. Magennis was one of the three-man passage crew in *X7*. Nearing the target, another crew took over for the attack, and Magennis and the two others with whom he had shared an uncomfortable and often frightening eight days boarded the submarine *Thrasher* for the return trip. In the end, only *Tirpitz* was attacked, by *X6* and *X7*. The battleship was badly damaged. All six X-craft were lost and nine of their crews died. Lieutenant Donald Cameron of *X6* and Lieutenant Basil Place of *X7* lived to receive the Victoria Cross. Among other awards, Magennis was mentioned in despatches.

In February 1945 the depot ship HMS *Bonaventure* sailed from Scotland for the Pacific and the war in the Far East carrying six XE-craft, an improved version of X-craft. Such was the secrecy that they were covered and marked aircraft. On board was Magennis, who had trained as a diver. At Labuan Island, off northern Borneo, orders for Operation Struggle were received – an attack on the Japanese heavy cruisers *Myoko* and *Takao* at Singapore. *XE1* was assigned the *Myoko* and *XE3* the *Takao*.

As in the attack on the German warships, *XE1* and *XE3* were towed a long distance by submarines – *Spark* and *Stygian* – before operational crews took over. In command of *XE3* was Lieutenant Ian Fraser DSC, who had picked his crew, Sub-Lieutenant William Smith, Engine Room Artificer Charles Reed and Leading Seaman Magennis, whom he regarded as a bit difficult. Fraser would later write: 'I knew that in these three I had got together as good a crew as any midget submarine commander could pray for. Together, we were going out to meet trouble.'

In the early hours of 30 July 1945, Fraser and his men took over from *XE3*'s passage crew, and *Stygian* continued to tow the midget submarine, which settled down to a depth of 90 feet. That night, nearing the Strait of Johore, the cable was slipped. *XE3* was on her own. The mission required expert navigation. There was something else on Fraser's mind: 'I knew that on the journey in and out several minefields, British, Dutch and Japanese, were close by, and indeed I had been told that I would have to pass through all of them. I could see no point in getting overwrought at that thought. Instead, I decided to ignore the minefields and plough straight on by the quickest and shortest route, taking the philosophical attitude that any mines would be too deep for our shallow draft vessel to strike.'

At 0305 the next day Fraser sighted a crucial buoy and was surprised that it did not show a light, as intelligence reports had indicated. As *XE3* moved nearer on the surface he suddenly realised it was a fishing boat and ordered a change of course. There was a full moon and they were lucky not to be spotted. At 0425 two ships were seen closing at fairly high speed and *XE3* dived and remained on the bottom for half an hour. Surfacing, Fraser saw the ships were still on the same bearing and dived again.

At 1030, in a calm, oily sea, *XE3* passed through a defence boom near the entrance to the strait at a periscope depth of 10 feet. If the boom had been closed, Magennis would have left *XE3* to cut a way through. The 9,850-ton *Takao* was anchored some 11 miles further on, and at 1250 the cruiser was sighted, heavily camouflaged. There was another scare when Fraser saw through his periscope a cutter 'loaded down to the gunwhale with Japanese sailors' 25 yards away. There was a quick down periscope. Fraser recalled: 'So close had they been that I could make out their faces quite distinctly, and even had time to notice that one of them was trailing his hand in the water.'

XE3 bumped her way along the bottom at depths ranging from 22 feet to 15 feet and ended up striking the cruiser and making enough noise 'to awaken the dead'. Fraser tried to manoeuvre the craft alongside the hull but discovered she was jammed in a hole. It took eight minutes, with the motors churning the waters, to get free. Another run-in was made and this time *XE3* slid into a deeper hole under the keel. 'We were resting on the bottom with the hull of the *Takao* only a foot above our heads,' Fraser noted.

Magennis was ready in his rubber suit and strapped on his breathing apparatus. Fraser patted him on the shoulder as he went to the escape chamber. His job was to place six limpet mines along the hull. Magennis could not open the hatch fully because it touched the hull, but he managed to squeeze out. There was a problem placing the limpets because the hull was covered with barnacles and seaweed. The task took about 30 minutes, but for Fraser 'it seemed like thirty days. I cursed every little sound he made, for every little sound was magnified a thousand times by my nerves.'

It was boiling inside *XE3* because the fan and motor had to be switched off. Those inside drank tin after tin of orange juice. At one point the *Takao* was sitting on top of the boat because the tide had dropped. When Magennis returned, it was time to release the port and starboard charges, each containing two tons of explosives with six-hour timers. The port charge fell away but the starboard charge would not budge. Although exhausted, Magennis volunteered to leave the boat again and try to release it. Armed with 'an elephant-size spanner' he succeeded after struggling for seven minutes. The tension had been too much for Fraser: 'I bit my fingers, swore and cursed at him, swore and cursed at the captain and all the staff on board *Bonaventure* who had planned this operation, at the Admiralty, and finally at myself for ever having been so stupid as to volunteer for this life and, having volunteered, for being so stupid as to work hard enough to get myself this particular operation … I had told Magennis to make no noise, but his hammering and bashing, in what I thought to be really the wrong place, was loud enough to alarm the whole Japanese navy.'

It was time to escape, but a further problem arose. The changing density of the water affected *XE3*'s trim. About a mile from the *Takao*, the boat suddenly broke the surface. Once again, they were not spotted. *XE3* managed to dive 'smartly'. There was one more fright. A high-powered motorboat passed directly above them when they were barely submerged. There was, luckily, no bang. *XE3* negotiated the boom and early on 1 August rendezvoused with *Stygian*. The *Takao* was badly damaged.

XE1 failed to reach her target because of delays in avoiding enemy craft and instead dumped her explosives alongside the *Takao*. The boat had a successful rendezvous with *Spark*.

In a report on Operation Struggle to the Commander-in-Chief, Pacific Fleet, Captain William Fell of the 14th Submarine Flotilla stated:

In the event the attack proved to be one of extreme difficulty, and very considerable hazard, and the courage and determination shown by Lieutenant I. E. Fraser, DSC, RNR, is beyond all praise. Any man not possessed of a relentless determination to achieve his object in full would have been content with his limpets on the target and have dropped his side cargo alongside the target, where its effects would have been very considerably minimised, and such an action would have been fully justified. Lt Fraser, however, fought doggedly on until he had forced his craft under the very centre of the target and there placed his limpets and dropped his charge. There was so little 'headroom' that it was not possible to raise the antennae under the cruiser's keel.

Fell added that the part played by Magennis was 'fully up to the fine standard' set by his commanding officer. On 13 November it was officially announced that Fraser and Magennis had been awarded the Victoria Cross.

Atomic bombs ended the war with Japan shortly after the attack on the *Takao*. Fraser and Magennis were able to take well-earned breaks in Australia before flying back to Britain. During a stopover in Singapore, Fraser took the opportunity to visit the *Takao*. He was delighted to see a large hole in one side of the cruiser, which was resting on the bottom of the harbour. But then came 'the greatest shock I experienced in all the war'. The Japanese had written off the ship the previous year after she was torpedoed by an American submarine and seriously damaged. 'Our plans, our worries, our whole dangerous journey had accomplished nothing,' Fraser admitted. 'Worse, they had been entirely unnecessary.'

In a letter to his brother William, Magennis told of the attack on the *Takao*: 'Under target 1400 1st August. Clear of boom and out 2130. 2200 till 2300 loud explosions and clouds of shit. Joy in our hearts.'

Magennis returned to Belfast on leave, but was given a mixed reception. The ruling Protestants were not happy that Northern Ireland's only recipient of the Victoria Cross during the war was a Catholic. Lord Mayor Sir Crawford McCullagh, who was also Grand Master of the County Grand Orange Lodge of Belafast, allowed a ceremonial welcome but opposed suggestions that Magennis should receive the freedom of the city. A 'shilling fund' was launched, and McCullagh was no doubt surprised to find that contributions totalled £3,066, a large sum in those days, especially as many in the city were still struggling to survive.

Prejudice was not confined to Protestants. A significant number of Catholics saw Magennis as a British hero. When he went to visit his old primary school, St Finian's on the Falls Road, he was snubbed. One former pupil recalled: 'No one stood up. I remember feeling proud that I hadn't honoured king and country. For years afterwards I could still see his kind, smiling face and his elderly mother as we sat stubbornly in our seats.' A teacher told one class: 'He didn't do it for Ireland.'

Fraser was concerned about all the attention he was getting, offering thoughts that Magennis might have been wise to take on board: 'A man is trained for the task that might win him the VC. He is not trained to cope with what follows. He is not told how to avoid going under in a flood of public adulation. Three months after I received my VC I refused all further invitations to functions in my honour. All this flattery was becoming dangerous.'

Of the donations, Magennis said: 'The money rolled into the lord mayor's fund for me. The donations appeared in the local newspapers. It was like looking at the Tote returns every night. Then, on the steps of the city hall, I was handed a cheque for £3,066. Three years later I had spent the lot. I was still in the navy and drawing pay. But I was living it up. In those days money was for spending, for having a good time. I had just married Edna and as we moved around, living in digs, this was a steady drain on the £3,000. We were living above our means.' He was also generous to relatives and friends. One day in 1952 Magennis, then an electrician but off work due to illness, went to a shop – 'I buy anything' – in Smithfield Market, Belfast, and sold his Victoria Cross for £75. He was broke. His decision caused uproar.

'My pride prevented me from going begging to the British Legion,' he said. 'Obviously I had spent the money the city saved for me. It did not seem right to go begging. I decided to sell my VC. The dealer had promised to keep quiet about it. But after a few weeks he announced publicly he would present it to the Belfast Museum. My name was on it and everyone knew it was my VC. What a stink it caused. What a blow-up. The world protested. I got hundreds of letters, mostly condemning me. Some were sympathetic, others rude and scurrilous.'

Such was the adverse publicity that the dealer returned the medal to Magennis and did not ask for the £75. Magennis said he had acted foolishly, adding: 'What a relief it is to have it back. I didn't realise it meant so much to me but now I shall never part with it again – no matter what happens.'

Ex-submariner George Fleming pointed out: 'This was the beginning of a period of re-evaluation for Mick. The people of Belfast did not seem to hold him in high regard; some people even tried to downgrade his act of bravery. He realised that the limelight he had briefly basked in was gone forever. His critics had come out into the open and he now knew where he stood. It was clear that he was not wanted in Protestant Unionist East Belfast and neither was he wanted in Catholic Nationalist West Belfast.'

In February 1955 Magennis moved to Yorkshire, 'where he and his wife were made much more welcome than in Belfast'. He was employed as an electrician in a coal mine at Rossington, near Doncaster. Later the family moved to Bradford. At some point he worked as a TV repairman, but he endured a spell of unemployment and the return of hard times. On 12 February 1986 he died of bronchitis in hospital, aged sixty-six. He had four sons, one of whom was killed as a youngster by a bus in Belfast.

After a long campaign, a memorial to James Magennis VC was unveiled in the grounds of Belfast City Hall in October 1999. Unionists righted a wrong. Bigotry, however, still prevailed. Sinn Fein councillors boycotted the ceremony. One councillor who asked not to be named was quoted as saying: 'Of course it was outrageous. We should have been there to honour James Magennis. But the party ruled otherwise.' Sinn Fein leader Gerry Adams had been to the same primary school as Magennis.

Appendix
Location of Victoria Crosses

William Johnstone (Chapter 1)
Natural History Museum of Los Angeles County. Not on display. Recipient would also have been entitled to the Baltic Medal.

John Byrne (Chapter 2)
Location not known. Other awards: Distinguished Conduct Medal; Crimea Medal with clasps Balaklava, Inkermann [Inkerman], Sebastopol; New Zealand Medal 1860–66; Turkish Crimea Medal.

Edward St John Daniel (Chapter 3)
Lord Ashcroft collection. Other awards: India General Service Medal 1854–95 with clasp Pegu; Crimea Medal with clasps Inkermann [Inkerman], Sebastopol; Indian Mutiny Medal with clasps Lucknow, Relief of Lucknow; Legion d'Honneur; Sardinian Medal for Valour; Order of the Medjidie (5th Class); Turkish Crimea Medal.

James McGuire (Chapter 4)
National Army Museum, London. Other awards: India General Service Medal 1854–95 with clasp Pegu; Indian Mutiny Medal with clasps Delhi, Lucknow.

Michael Murphy (Chapter 5)
Officers' Mess Royal Logistic Corps, Deepcut, Surrey. Other awards: Indian Mutiny Medal.

Valentine Bambrick (Chapter 6)
Location not known. Other awards: Indian Mutiny Medal.

Evelyn Wood (Chapter 7)

National Army Museum, London. Other awards: Knight Grand Cross, Order of the Bath (GCB); Knight Grand Cross, Order of St Michael and St George (GCMG); Crimea Medal with clasps Inkermann [Inkerman], Sebastopol; Indian Mutiny Medal; Ashantee Medal 1873–74 with clasp Coomassie; South Africa Medal 1877–79 with clasp 1877–8–9; Egypt Medal 1882–89 with clasp The Nile 1884–5; Jubilee Medal 1897; Coronation Medal 1902; Coronation Medal 1911; Legion d'Honneur; Grand Cross of the Order of Leopold; Grand Cross of the Medjidie; Order of the Medjidie (5th Class); Turkish Crimea Medal; Khedive's Star 1882–91.

Thomas Lane (Chapter 8)

Royal Hampshire Regiment Museum, Winchester, which has two Victoria Crosses named to Lane. Other awards: Crimea Medal with clasps Alama, Inkermann [Inkerman], Sebastopol; China War Medal 1857–60 with clasps Taku Forts 1860, Pekin 1860; South Africa Medal 1877–79 with clasp 1879 (Natal Horse but unclaimed); Turkish Crimea Medal.

Duncan Boyes (Chapter 9)

Lord Ashcroft collection. No other awards.

Robert Jones (Chapter 10)

Lord Ashcroft collection. South Africa Medal 1877–79 with clasp 1877–8–9.

Redvers Buller (Chapter 11)

The Royal Green Jackets (Rifles) Museum, Winchester, Hampshire. Other awards: Knight Grand Cross, Order of the Bath (GCB); Knight Commander, Order of the Bath (KCB); Companion, Order of the Bath (CB); Knight Grand Cross, Order of St Michael and St George (GCMG); Knight Commander, Order of St Michael and St George (KCMG); China War Medal 1857–60 with clasps Taku Forts 1860, Pekin 1860; Canada General Service Medal 1866–70 with clasps Fenian Raid 1866, Fenian Raid 1870, Red River 1870; Ashantee Medal 1873–74 with clasp Coomassie; South Africa Medal 1877–79 with clasp 1878–9; Egypt Medal 1882–89 with clasps Tel-el-Kebir, El-Teb-Tamaai, The Nile 1884–85, Suakin 1885; Queen's South Africa Medal 1899–1902 with clasps Cape Colony, Tugela Heights, Orange Free State, Relief of Ladysmith, Laing's Nek, Belfast; Jubilee Medal 1897; Order of the Osmanieh (3rd Class); Khedive's Star 1882–91.

Edmund Fowler (Chapter 12)

Cameronians (Scottish Rifles) Collection, Low Parks Museum, Hamilton, Lanarkshire. Other awards: South Africa Medal 1877–79 with clasp 1877–8–9; Egypt Medal 1882–89; Khedive's Star 1882–91.

Henry D'Arcy (Chapter 13)

Location not known. Other awards: South Africa Medal 1877–79 with clasp 1877–8–9.

James Collis (Chapter 14)

Lord Ashcroft collection. Other awards: Afghanistan Medal 1878–80 with clasp Kandahar.

Frederick Corbett (Chapter 15)

The Royal Green Jackets (Rifles) Museum, Winchester, Hampshire. Other awards: Egypt Medal 1882–89 with clasp Tel-el-Kebir; Khedive's Star 1882–91.

George Ravenhill (Chapter 16)

Royal Highland Fusiliers Museum, Glasgow. Other awards: Queen's South Africa Medal 1899–1902 with clasps Cape Colony, Relief of Ladysmith, Transvaal; King's South Africa Medal 1901–02 with clasps South Africa 1901, South Africa 1902; 1914–15 Star; British War Medal; Victory Medal.

Michael O'Leary (Chapter 17)

The Guards Museum, Wellington Barracks, London. Other awards: 1914–15 Star; British War Medal; Victory Medal with MiD; Defence Medal 1939–45; War Medal; Coronation Medal 1937; Coronation Medal 1953; Order of St George (3rd Class).

William Mariner (Chapter 18)

Location not known. Other awards: 1914–15 Star; British War Medal; Victory Medal.

Hugo Throssell (Chapter 19)

Australian War Memorial, Canberra. Other awards: 1914–15 Star; British War Medal; Victory Medal with MiD.

John Sherwood-Kelly (Chapter 20)

Ditsong National Museum of Military History, Johannesburg, South Africa. Other awards: Companion, Order of St Michael and St George (CMG); Distinguished Service Order; British South Africa Company Medal 1890–97 with clasp Matabeleland; Queen's South Africa Medal 1899–1902 with clasps Rhodesia; Relief of Mafeking; Orange Free State; Transvaal; King's South Africa Medal 1901–02 with clasps South Africa 1901, South Africa 1902; Africa General Service Medal 1902–56 with clasp Somaliland 1902–04; 1914–15 Star; British War Medal; Victory Medal.

John Grant *(Chapter 21)*
National Army Museum, Waiouru, New Zealand. Other awards: 1914–15 Star; British War Medal; Victory Medal; Coronation Medal 1937; Coronation Medal 1953.

Martin Doyle *(Chapter 22)*
Lord Ashcroft collection. Other awards: Military Medal; 1914–15 Star; British War Medal; Victory Medal; Coronation Medal 1937.

Gordon Steele *(Chapter 23)*
Trinity House, London. Other awards: 1914–15 Star; British War Medal; Victory Medal; Defence Medal 1939–45; War Medal; Coronation Medal 1937; Coronation Medal 1953; Jubilee Medal 1977.

Clive Hulme *(Chapter 24)*
National Army Museum, Waiouru, New Zealand. Other awards: 1939–45 Star; Africa Star; Defence Medal; War Medal; New Zealand War Service Medal; Coronation Medal 1953; Jubilee Medal 1977.

John Nettleton *(Chapter 25)*
Location not known. Other awards: 1939–45 Star; Air Crew Europe Star with clasp France & Germany; Defence Medal; War Medal with MiD.

John Kenneally *(Chapter 26)*
The Guards Museum, Wellington Barracks, London. Other awards: 1939–45 Star; Africa Star with clasp 8th Army; Italy Star; Defence Medal; War Medal; General Service Medal with clasp Palestine 1945–48; Coronation Medal 1953; Jubilee Medal 1977.

James Magennis *(Chapter 27)*
Lord Ashcroft collection. Other awards: 1939–45 Star; Atlantic Star; Africa Star; Pacific Star; War Medal with MiD; Coronation Medal 1953; Jubilee Medal 1977.

Chapter References

1 The Mystery Sailor: William Johnstone

1. Award to Bythesea and Johnstone. Despatch from Captain Yelverton to Admiral Napier, 31 January 1856. Supplement to *The London Gazette*, 24 February 1857.
   Research on Bythesea's VC, Spink catalogue for 19 April 2007. *The Victoria Cross and the George Cross, The Complete History, Volume 1* edited by Christopher Wright and Glenda Anderson.
2. Bythesea's career. Service record. Information from the National Museum of the Royal Navy.
3. Muster lists for HMS *Arrogant* and HMS *Brunswick*.
4. *Brunswick*'s log, 20 August 1857.
5. Captain's out letter book, *Brunswick* 1856–60.
6. *British Orders, Decorations and Medals in the Robert B Honeyman Jr Collection* compiled by David Workman. Information from the Natural History Museum of Los Angeles County.
7. Napier's career and the Baltic campaign. *Black Charlie, a Life of Admiral Sir Charles Napier KCB 1787–1860* by Priscilla Napier. *The History of the Baltic Campaign of 1854 From Documents and Other Materials Furnished by Vice Admiral Sir C Napier KCB* edited by George Earp.

2 A Police Siege and Suicide: John Byrne

1. Life in Castlecomer. Information from Kilkenny County Library, local studies department. The National Library of Ireland, Collection List No. 52 Prior-Wandesforde Papers.
2. Byrne's military career/campaigns. Information from the Light Infantry (Durham Light Infantry). *The Silver Bugle* spring 1984, spring 1986. *Supreme Courage, Heroic Stories from 150 Years of the Victoria Cross* by General Sir Peter de la Billière, chapter 4. *Faithful, The Story of the Durham Light Infantry* by S. G. P. Ward. *The Victoria Cross and the George Cross, The*

Complete History, *Volume 1* edited by Christopher Wright and Glenda Anderson. *British Battles and Medals* by John Hayward, Diana Birch and Richard Bishop.
3. Byrne's suicide. *The Monmouthshire Merlin and South Wales Advertiser*, 11 and 18 July 1879. *The Cardiff Times & South Wales Weekly News*, 12 and 19 July. The *Cardiff Weekly Mail and South Wales Advertiser*, 19 July.

3 Vanishing Act: Edward St John Daniel
1. Background on Daniel. Article by J Bryant Haigh in *The Bulletin* of The Military Historical Society, November 1971. *The Victoria Cross at Sea* by John Winton. Sotheby's auction catalogue for 21 March 1988, lot 491 Daniel's VC. Research by Michael Daniels. *The Victoria Cross and the George Cross, The Complete History, Volume 1* edited by Christopher Wright and Glenda Anderson.
2. *From Midshipman to Field Marshal* by Evelyn Wood, chapters 4–9 on Crimean campaign. *Evelyn Wood, Pillar of Empire* by Stephen Manning, chapter 2.
3. VC forfeiture. Various War Office minutes in July, August and September 1861, mainly involving Sir George Lewis, General Sir Edward Lugard and Major General Richard Crofton. Letter from Sir George Lewis to Queen Victoria dated 23 August 1861.
4. Daniel's funeral. *The West Coast Times*, 22 May 1868.
5. Background on Daniel's time in New Zealand. *The New Zealand Herald*, 10 December 1971.
6. *The People of the Abyss* by Jack London, chapter 7.
7. *Ships of the Royal Navy* by J. J. Colledge and Ben Warlow.

4 Jailed over a Cow: James McGuire
1. Background. Information from John Cunningham, Fermanagh Authors' Association. *The Victoria Cross and the George Cross, The Complete History, Volume 1* edited by Christopher Wright and Glenda Anderson.
2. Second Burmese War. *British Battles and Medals* by John Hayward, Diana Birch and Richard Bishop. *The History of the Bengal European Regiment* by Lieutenant Colonel P. R. Innes, chapter 17.
3. Indian Mutiny and VC action. *British Battles and Medals* by John Hayward, Diana Birch and Richard Bishop. *The History of the Bengal European Regiment* by Lieutenant Colonel P. R. Innes, chapters 18 and 19. *Behind the Scenes in Many Wars* by Lieutenant General Sir George MacMunn. Information from the National Army Museum, London. *Irish Winners of the Victoria Cross* by Richard Doherty and David Truesdale, chapter 3.
4. McGuire's conviction and forfeiture of VC. Court report in the *Impartial Reporter* newspaper, 31 July 1862. Court witness statements, undated. War Office minutes for the attention of General Sir Edward Lugard, various dates in September, October, November, December 1862. India Office letter to General Lugard from Sir Charles Wood, 16 September 1862. Petition from

James McGuire with support from magistrate dated 18 May 1863. War Office minutes showing General Lugard's approval of restoration of VC, 3 June 1863.

5. McGuire's apparent death and burial. Information from John Cunningham, Fermanagh Authors' Association.

5 Oats, Hay and Prison: Michael Murphy

1. Background. *The Victoria Cross and the George Cross, The Complete History, Volume 1* edited by Christopher Wright and Glenda Anderson. Information from the Royal Logistic Corps. Article in Royal Corps of Transport magazine by Lieutenant Colonel P. L. Morgan, date unknown. Article in *The Journal of The Victoria Cross Society* by Lieutenant Colonel D. J. Owen, October 2008.

2. Indian Mutiny. *British Battles and Medals* by John Hayward, Diana Birch and Richard Bishop. *The Indian Mutiny 1857–58* by Gregory Fremont-Barnes, The final campaigns, January-December 1858. Divisional orders issued by Major General Sir James Outram, 23 December 1857.

3. Murphy's court case. *Hampshire Telegraph* and *The Hampshire Advertiser*, 9 March 1872. Mr Baron Bramwell, *Oxford Dictionary of National Biography*.

6 Despair in Pentonville: Valentine Bambrick

1. Valentine Bambrick, 11th Light Dragoons, and John Bambrick, 11th Light Dragoons, father and uncle of Valentine Bambrick VC. Service records.

2. 11th Light Dragoons and 11th Hussars. Information from the National Army Museum, London.

3. John Bambrick and Charge of the Light Brigade. *Honour the Light Brigade* by William Lummis and Kenneth Wynn, page 146. *A Victorian RSM: From India to the Crimea* by George Smith, based on his diaries. *Left of Six Hundred* by William Pennington. *Hell Riders, The Truth about the Charge of the Light Brigade* by Terry Brighton, chapters 7, 8, 9, 11.

4. The Indian Mutiny. *The Annals of the King's Royal Rifle Corps, Volume III*, by Lieutenant Colonel Lewis Butler, chapters 7, 8, 9, 10. *The Indian Mutiny 1857–58* by Gregory Fremont-Barnes, The final campaigns, January–December 1858. *British Battles and Medals* by John Hayward, Diana Birch and Richard Bishop. Research by William Lummis, undated.

5. Bambrick's court case. *Hampshire Telegraph* and *The Hampshire Advertiser*, 5 December 1863. *The United Service Gazette*, 9 April 1864.

6. Bambrick's suicide. *The United Service Gazette*, 9 and 16 April 1864. Research by William Lummis, undated.

7 For the Love of Money: Evelyn Wood

1. Background on Wood's military career. *The Victoria Cross and the George Cross, The Complete History, Volume 1* edited by Christopher Wright and Glenda Anderson. Army service record (The National Archives WO 27/489). *From Midshipman to Field Marshal* by Evelyn Wood, two volumes. *Evelyn Wood VC, Pillar of Empire* by Stephen Manning. Article in *The Journal of The Victoria Cross Society* by Brian Best, March 2008.

2. Fight over Aunt Ben's will and Katharine Wood's divorce. *The Uncrowned Queen of Ireland, The Life of 'Kitty' O'Shea* by Joyce Marlow, chapters 14, 15 and 16. *Evelyn Wood VC, Pillar of Empire* by Stephen Manning, chapter 10. *The Uncrowned King of Ireland* by Katharine O'Shea, chapter 38. High Court divorce document No 3419.

8 The Deserter: Thomas Lane

1. Attack on Taku forts. *The Chinese Opium Wars* by Jack Beeching, chapter 8. Article on Thomas Lane by Joe West in *The Journal of The Victoria Cross Society*, part 1, March 2004. *The Royal Hampshire Regiment* by Alan Wykes, chapter 4. *British Battles and Medals* by John Hayward, Diana Birch and Richard Bishop.
2. 47th (Lancashire) Foot in Crimean War. Website of the Lancashire Infantry Museum. Article on Lane by Joe West in *The Journal of The Victoria Cross Society*, part 1, March 2004.
3. Lane's biographical details. *The Victoria Cross and the George Cross, The Complete History, Volume 1* edited by Christopher Wright and Glenda Anderson.
4. Lane in New Zealand. Article by Trevor Turner in *The Journal of The Orders & Medals Research Society*, June 2012, quoting the *Otago Witness* of 27 March 1875.
5. Lane in South Africa. Article on Lane by Joe West in *The Journal of The Victoria Cross Society*, parts 1 and 2, March and October 2004. Information from the McGregor Museum, Kimberley. William Lummis files, National Army Museum, London. *The African Review*, April 1889.
6. VC forfeiture. War Office records, various dates in 1882. Kimberley Criminal Court record book for 1881. Article on Lane by Joe West in *The Journal of The Victoria Cross Society*, part 2, October 2004.

9 Suicide at Dunedin: Duncan Boyes

1. Family and naval background. Article by Ian Ruxton in *Cheltonian Society News*, 1998–9 No 19, magazine for former pupils of Cheltenham College. Article by Brian Mitchell in *The Review*, spring 2008, journal of the Naval Historical Collectors & Research Association.
2. Fighting in Japan. Spink catalogue for 21 July 1998, lot 212, sale of Boyes's VC.
3. Presentation of VC. *Hampshire Telegraph*, 23 September 1865.
4. Naval record. The National Archives, ADM 196/36/439, ADM 112/754.
5. Boyes's death. *Otago Daily Times*, 27 January 1869. *North Otago Times*, 23 February 1869. Probate documents filed at the Supreme Court Otago and Southland District, 26 February 1869, 1 March 1869.
6. Daniel Dutton. *Otago Witness*, 29 May 1907.
7. Esme Harman. Letter to 'Cousin Barbara', date unknown.
8. Boyes's grave. *Truth*, 25 May 1955. *Review*, June 1955, journal of the Returned and Services' Association. *Otago Daily Times*, 31 July 2004.
9. Horace Martineau's army career and VC action. *The Victoria Cross and the George Cross, The Complete History, Volume 1* edited by Christopher Wright and Glenda Anderson. *The London Gazette*, 6 July 1900.

10. Summary of evidence against Martineau, 20 September 1915. Letter from Captain M. H. Berry, commanding officer of Sidi Bishr camp, to senior officers, 21 September 1915, with comments by Brigadier C. R. McGregor, also 21 September. Minute to Minister of Defence James Allen from Brigadier A. W. Robin, 15 January 1916. All Archives New Zealand.

10 Condemned by the Church: Robert Jones

1. Isandlwana. *The Washing of the Spears* by Donald Morris, part two. *Journal of the South African Military History Society*, volume 4, January 1979, G. A. Chadwick. *British Battles and Medals* by John Hayward, Diana Birch and Richard Bishop.
2. Rorke's Drift. *The Washing of the Spears* by Donald Morris, part two. *Journal of the South African Military History Society*, volume 4, January 1979, G. A. Chadwick. *British Battles and Medals* by John Hayward, Diana Birch and Richard Bishop. Information from the Regimental Museum of the Royal Welsh. *Gallantry Awards at Rorke's Drift* by James Bancroft.
3. Jones's account of his fighting at Rorke's Drift. *The Strand Magazine*, volume 1, January to June 1891.
4. Background on Jones. Information from the Regimental Museum of the Royal Welsh. *The Victoria Cross and the George Cross, The Complete History, Volume 1* edited by Christopher Wright and Glenda Anderson.
5. Death of Jones, inquest and burial. *Hereford Times*, 10 September 1898. Research by Herefordshire Archive Service, burial register for parish of Peterchurch, 1898.
6. Campaign over Jones's grave. *The Sunday Telegraph*, 6 September 1998. Mirror Online, 25 April 2010. WalesOnline, 20 May 2010.
7. Joseph Trewavas. *The Victoria Cross and the George Cross, The Complete History, Volume 1* edited by Christopher Wright and Glenda Anderson.
8. Charles Lumley. *The Victoria Cross and the George Cross, The Complete History, Volume 1* edited by Christopher Wright and Glenda Anderson. Charles Lumley VC, a tragic final act, article by Brian Best, *The Journal of The Victoria Cross Society*, October 2005, which quotes the *Brecon Journal and County Advertiser* of 23 October 1858. Comments to the author by the Very Reverend Dr Paul Shackerley, March 2015.

11 A Disastrous General: Evelyn Wood

1. Buller's competence. *The Little Field Marshal, A Life of Sir John French* by Richard Holmes, chapter 1.
2. Buller's early life and career. *The Victoria Cross and the George Cross, The Complete History, Volume 1* edited by Christopher Wright and Glenda Anderson. *Buller: A Scapegoat?* by Geoffrey Powell, chapters 1 and 2. Crediton Parish Church website.
3. Hlobane. *Buller: A Scapegoat?* by Geoffrey Powell, chapter 3. *The Washing of the Spears* by Donald Morris, part two. Disquiet over Hlobane's VCs by Ron Lock, article in *Medal News*, April 2008. Charles Hewitt's Zulu war and how Buller won his VC, article by Brian Best, quoting letter written by Hewitt to his sister Annie in January 1920, *The Journal of The Victoria Cross Society*, March 2014.

4. Second Boer War. *Buller: A Scapegoat?* by Geoffrey Powell, chapters 9 and 10, with references to the Royal Commission on War in South Africa. *British Battles and Medals* by John Hayward, Diana Birch and Richard Bishop.

12 *The Sympathetic Queen: Edmund Fowler*

1. Fowler's background and army career. *The Victoria Cross and the George Cross, The Complete History, Volume 1* edited by Christopher Wright and Glenda Anderson. Service record.
2. Battles of Hlobane and Kambula. *Evelyn Wood VC, Pillar of Empire* by Stephen Manning, chapter 7. *The Washing of the Spears* by Donald Morris, part two. Horror at the Devil's Pass by John Young, rorkesdriftvc.com
3. VC. *The London Gazette*, 7 April 1882. Gallantry, patronage and cover-ups – the Zulu War VCs, article by Brian Best, *The Journal of The Victoria Cross Society*, October 2002. *The Victorians at War* by Ian Beckett, chapter 4.
4. Queen's refusal to strip Fowler of VC. Letter from Sir Henry Ponsonby to Lieutenant General Sir George Harman, Aix les Bains, 10 April 1887.
5. Colchester court appearance. *Essex Newsman*, 16 February 1901.
6. Funeral. *The Essex County Telegraph*, 3 April 1926.

13 *A Faked Death?: Henry D'Arcy*

1. D'Arcy's background and career. *The Victoria Cross and the George Cross, The Complete History, Volume 1* edited by Christopher Wright and Glenda Anderson. *What Happened to a VC* by Patricia D'Arcy, part one. *Zulu War Victoria Crosses* by James Bancroft.
2. Hlobane and Kambula. *The Washing of the Spears* by Donald Morris, part two. *New Zealand Herald*, 28 January 1882. *What Happened to a VC* by Patricia D'Arcy, part three.
3. VC action. *The London Gazette*, 9 September and 10 October 1879. *The Washing of the Spears* by Donald Morris, part two. Colonial VCs of the Zulu War, article by Brian Best, *The Journal of The Victoria Cross Society*, March 2004. Gallantry, patronage and cover-ups – the Zulu War VCs, article by Brian Best, *The Journal of The Victoria Cross Society*, October 2002.
4. D'Arcy's disappearance. *The Victoria Cross and the George Cross, The Complete History, Volume 1* edited by Christopher Wright and Glenda Anderson. *What Happened to a VC* by Patricia D'Arcy, part five, quoting *The Journal*, 31 August 1881. Colonial VCs of the Zulu War, article by Brian Best, *The Journal of The Victoria Cross Society*, March 2004. *In the Face of the Enemy, The Complete History of the Victoria Cross and New Zealand* by Glyn Harper and Colin Richardson, chapter 3. *Daily Mail*, 17 September 1992.

14 *The Womaniser: James Collis*

1. Second Afghan War, battle and retreat from Maiwand. *British Battles and Medals* by John Hayward, Diana Birch and Richard Bishop. James Collis VC disgraced hero, article by Brian Best, *The Journal of The Victoria Cross Society*, March 2006. Dix Noonan Webb catalogue, 17 September 2004, listing the campaign medals of Major George Blackwood, Royal Horse

Artillery. My God – Maiwand, David Gore, britishempire website, listing Report on Operations 26–28 July by Brigadier Burrows and Report on Operations of Cavalry Brigade on 27 July by Brigadier Nuttall.

2. Collis's account of Maiwand. *The Strand Magazine*, volume 1, January to June 1891.

3. Background on Collis. *The Victoria Cross and the George Cross, The Complete History, Volume 1* edited by Christopher Wright and Glenda Anderson. *The Times*, 9 May 1998. The hero who was stripped of his VC, article by Lord Ashcroft, *Daily Express*, 24 October 2014.

4. Old Bailey trial. *The Times*, 27 November 1895.

5. Forfeiture of Victoria Cross. War Office letter to Home Office, 22 January 1896. Metropolitan Police (Peckham) letter, 6 April 1896. New Scotland Yard letter to War Office, 26 May 1896. *The Victoria Cross and the George Cross, The Complete History, Volume 1* edited by Christopher Wright and Glenda Anderson.

6. Cambridge workhouse. *Cambridge Chronicle*, 5 July 1912.

7. Lieutenant Colonel Gaskell. Contemporary Biographies – Gentry and Magistrates, covering Lancashire. *Liverpool Post and Mercury, Daily Courier*, Liverpool, various dates in September 1925.

8. Victoria Cross sales. James Collis VC disgraced hero, article by Brian Best, *The Journal of The Victoria Cross Society*, March 2006 (this article refers to the VC being taken illegally from the War Office). The hero who was stripped of his VC, article by Lord Ashcroft, *Daily Express*, 24 October 2014. Information from Nimrod Dix, of auctioneers Dix Noonan Webb. Information from James Morton, of auctioneers Morton & Eden.

15 A Real Bad Hat: Frederick Corbett

1. Background of Embleton and Corbett's army career. *The Victoria Cross and the George Cross, The Complete History, Volume 1* edited by Christopher Wright and Glenda Anderson. Triple cross – the story of a dishonoured Victoria Cross, article by Fred Feather (originally published in *Essex Family Historian*, September 2004), *The Journal of The Victoria Cross Society*, October 2005. Information from the National Army Museum, London.

2. Egypt campaign. *British Battles and Medals* by John Hayward, Diana Birch and Richard Bishop. Information from the King's Royal Rifle Corps Association.

3. VC action. *The Tablet*, 12 August 1882. *The London Gazette*, 16 February 1883. Triple cross – the story of a dishonoured Victoria Cross, article by Fred Feather (originally published in *Essex Family Historian*, September 2004), *The Journal of The Victoria Cross Society*, October 2005. Article in *The Journal of The Orders & Medals Research Society* by P. A. G. Embleton, summer 1991. Article in *The Journal of The Orders & Medals Research Society* by Irvin Mortenson, spring 1990.

4. VC forfeiture. Petition from the War Office to Queen Victoria, 10 December 1884. Note from Osborne House, 18 December 1884.

5. VC copies. Article by E. J. Martin in *The Bulletin* of The Military Historical Society, May 1951. Article in *The Journal of The Orders & Medals Research Society* by P. A. G. Embleton, summer 1991. Triple cross – the story of a

dishonoured Victoria Cross, article by Fred Feather (originally published in *Essex Family Historian*, September 2004), *The Journal of The Victoria Cross Society*, October 2005.

6. Canon Lummis's comments. Letter to Captain A. G. Rumbelow, 17 November 1956.

16 The Hungry Mouths: George Ravenhill

1. Ravenhill's background and army career. *The Victoria Cross and the George Cross, The Complete History, Volume 1* edited by Christopher Wright and Glenda Anderson. Research by Alan Tucker and the Royal British Legion, Chipping Norton. AngloBoerWar.com, Royal Scots Fusiliers.
2. Colenso. *The Boer War* by Thomas Pakenham, chapters 19 and 20. *Buller: A Scapegoat?* by Geoffrey Powell, chapter 10. AngloBoerWar.com, Royal Scots Fusiliers.
3. Workhouse court case. *News of the World*, 21 April 1906.
4. Parliamentary questions. *Hansard*, 30 April and 13 May 1908.
5. Theft court case. *The Birmingham Daily Post*, 25 August 1908.
6. Forfeiture of VC. Royal warrant, 24 August 1908.
7. Sale of VC. *The Times*, 16 December 1908.
8. First World War. Service record. Research by the Royal British Legion, Chipping Norton.
9. Death and funeral. *Birmingham Daily Mail*, 18, 20 and 23 April 1921. *Birmingham Gazette*, 19, 21, 22, 25 and 26 April 1921.

17 A Bootlegging Scandal: Michael O'Leary

1. O'Leary and Irish Guards in First World War. *The Irish Guards in the Great War, The First Battalion* by Rudyard Kipling, 1914 Mons to La Bassee, 1915 La Bassee to Laventie. Michael O'Leary, the first Western Front VC, Cuinchy, France 1 February 1915, article by Brian Best, *The Journal of The Victoria Cross Society*, March 2015.
2. Parents' comments on VC. *Daily Mirror*, 20 February and 23 April 1915.
3. Letter to parents. *Daily Mirror*, 20 February 1915.
4. Description of VC action by Company Quartermaster Sergeant J. G. Lowry. *Marlborough Express* [New Zealand], 16 April 1915.
5. Report of O'Leary's death. *Daily Record*, 31 May 1915 and *Daily Mirror*, 2 June 1915.
6. Investiture. *Daily Record*, 23 June 1915.
7. Strain of recruiting. *Daily Record*, 13 August 1915.
8. Ballaghaderreen. *Nationalism and the Irish Party, Provincial Ireland 1910-1916* by Michael Wheatley, page 245, with reference to *Roscommon Herald*, 27 November 1915.
9. O'Leary's background. *The Victoria Cross and the George Cross, The Complete History, Volume II* edited by Christopher Wright and Glenda Anderson. Michael O'Leary, the first Western Front VC, Cuinchy, France 1 February 1915, article by Brian Best, *The Journal of The Victoria Cross Society*, March 2015.

10. Police appointments. *The Globe*, Toronto, 8 March and 7 September 1921, 16 June 1923.
11. Smuggling charge. *The Toronto Daily Star*, 7 February and 26 May 1925. *The Globe*, Toronto, 10 and 23 February 1925, 6 April 1925, 5, 9 and 26 May 1925.
12. Crystal Beach arrest. *The Globe*, Toronto, 10 September 1925. *Fort Erie Times*, 11 and 25 September and 4 December 1925.
13. Ordeal of fighting bootleggers. *The Toronto Daily Star*, 9 October 1926.
14. Departure from Canada. *The Toronto Daily Star*, 2 and 25 October and 18 December 1926. *The Globe*, Toronto. 14 and 15 October 1926.
15. Hotel commissionaire. *The Toronto Daily Star*, 12 June 1936.
16. Hero sons. Information from the Royal Air Force Museum, London. *The London Gazette*, 25 April and 29 September 1944. *The Distinguished Flying Cross and How It Was Won 1918–1995* by Nick and Carol Carter.

18 The Burglar: William Mariner

1. VC action. Report written by Lieutenant James Price, military intelligence, 6 February 1918. Spink catalogue offering Mariner's VC for sale, 23 November 2006. Account written by Jack [John] Laister in 1991, reported in the *Daily Mail*, 13 November 2006. [Laister was 94 in 1991 and his memory may have been hazy].
2. Eyre's account. *Somme Harvest* by Giles Eyre, chapter 3.
3. Award of VC and reaction. *The London Gazette*, 23 June 1915. *Manchester Evening News*, 24 June and 9 August 1915. *Daily Record*, 13 August 1915.
4. Mariner's background. Information from the King's Royal Rifle Corps Association. Spink catalogue offering Mariner's VC for sale, 23 November 2006. *The Victoria Cross and the George Cross, The Complete History, Volume II* edited by Christopher Wright and Glenda Anderson.
5. Mariner's criminal record and Scotland Yard tribute. *Manchester Evening News*, 16 and 24 February 1914. VC who was once a convict, article in *The Journal of The Victoria Cross Society*, October 2003. *Daily Sketch*, 21 August 1916. *Daily Mail*, 4 April 1921.

19 A Speech Too Far: Hugo Throssell

1. Northam speech. *My Father's Son* by Ric Throssell, chapter 7. *Gallipoli Victoria Cross Hero* by John Hamilton, chapter 15. *The Australian*, 25 August 2012. *The Gallipolian*, journal of the Gallipoli Association, winter 2001–02 (Derek Hunt).
2. Communism and military intelligence. *My Father's Son* by Ric Throssell, chapter 7. This book quotes various documents in a large file compiled by the Australian Security Intelligence Organisation (ASIO).
3. Throssell's background. *Australian Dictionary of Biography* (Suzanne Welborn). *My Father's Son* by Ric Throssell, chapters 2 and 3. *Gallipoli Victoria Cross Hero* by John Hamilton, chapters 1–3. *The Victoria Cross and*

the George Cross, The Complete History, Volume II edited by Christopher Wright and Glenda Anderson.

4. Gallipoli and VC action. *My Father's Son* by Ric Throssell, chapters 4 and 5. *Gallipoli Victoria Cross Hero* by John Hamilton, chapters 7-11. *The London Gazette*, 15 October 1915. Information from the Australian War Memorial.

5. Throssell's business ventures. *My Father's Son* by Ric Throssell, chapters 9-12. *Gallipoli Victoria Cross Hero* by John Hamilton, chapters 16 and 17.

6. Suicide. *My Father's Son* by Ric Throssell, chapter 13, quoting *The West Australian*, 20 November 1933. *Gallipoli Victoria Cross Hero* by John Hamilton, chapter 18. The *Western Argus*, 21 November 1933.

7. VC sale controversy. *The Australian, The Age*, both 28 September 1984.

20 *Churchill's Outspoken Critic: John Sherwood-Kelly*

1. Family background. *Undefeated* by Philip Bujak, chapter 1. A burned out case, article by Brian Best, *The Journal of The Victoria Cross Society*, October 2008. *The Victoria Cross and the George Cross, The Complete History, Volume II* edited by Christopher Wright and Glenda Anderson.

2. Early campaigns. *Undefeated* by Philip Bujak, chapter 2. *British Battles and Medals* by John Hayward, Diana Birch and Richard Bishop.

3. Gallipoli. *Undefeated* by Philip Bujak, chapter 4. A burned out case, article by Brian Best, *The Journal of The Victoria Cross Society*, October 2008.

4. VC action. Intelligence report by Captain James Lloyd, 17 January 1918. *The London Gazette*, 8 January 1918. *The Royal Inniskilling Fusiliers in the Great War* by Frank Fox, chapter 9.

5. Controversy in South Africa. Letter from Brigadier Martyn to War Office, 7 March 1919.

6. *City of Karachi* complaint. Letter from South African high commissioner to War Office, 30 November 1918. War Office minutes, 6 December 1918. Statement by Sherwood-Kelly, 30 December 1918. Report by Major General Thompson to War Office, 12 February 1919. War Office minutes, 3 March 1919. Army Council letter giving decision on complaint, 22 March 1919.

7. North Russia campaign (all dates 1919). Letters from Sherwood-Kelly to a Mrs Cameron in Somerset and a Mr Janson in London, both 26 July. Report by Major General Ironside, 17 August. War Office minutes, 3 and 6 September. Statements by Lieutenant G. E. Hill, 17 September, and Captain A. W. Warwick, 19 September, on Sherwood-Kelly's criticism of senior officers. Report by General Lord Rawlinson, 18 September. Report by Brigadier Grogan, 22 September. *Daily Express*, 6 and 13 September. A burned out case, article by Brian Best, *The Journal of The Victoria Cross Society*, October 2008.

8. Court martial. War Office minutes 6, 22 and 24 September 1919. List of charges, sentence and confirmation, October and November 1919.

9. Attempt to join Foreign Legion. Letter from military attaché at French embassy to General Burnett-Stuart, 28 August 1925. Reply, 5 September.

10. Later life. *The Times* obituary, 19 August 1931. *The Victoria Cross and the George Cross, The Complete History, Volume II* edited by Christopher Wright and Glenda Anderson.

21 *Her Ladyship Is Not Amused: John Grant*

1. Mountbatten reception. *In the Face of the Enemy* by Glyn Harper and Colin Richardson, chapter 8. Corinne Grant, Australian website Daily Life, 9 March 2012. Fairfax NZ News, 2 July 2008. *New Zealand Herald*, 12 April 2006.
2. Grant's background and army career. *The Victoria Cross and the George Cross, The Complete History, Volume II* edited by Christopher Wright and Glenda Anderson.
3. First World War campaigns. Victoria University of Wellington Library: *The Wellington Regiment (NZEF) 1914–1919* by W. H. Cunningham, C. A. L. Treadwell and J. S. Hanna, and *The New Zealand Division 1916-1919* by Colonel H. Stewart.
4. Victoria Cross. *The London Gazette*, 27 November 1918.
5. Grant's return to New Zealand. *New Zealand Herald*, 27 October 1919. *In the Face of the Enemy* by Glyn Harper and Colin Richardson, chapter 8, quoting personal file and letter from Colonel Duigan to general headquarters, 10 May 1935.

22 *The IRA Terrorist: Martin Doyle*

1. Doyle's background and British Army career. *The Victoria Cross and the George Cross, The Complete History, Volume II* edited by Christopher Wright and Glenda Anderson. Article in *Ireland's Own* magazine, Unsung Irish hero of three wars, date unknown. *The Irish Times*, 10 November 2015. *The Irish Sword*, journal of the Military History Society of Ireland, volume XVI.
2. Royal Dublin Fusiliers in First World War. Information from the Irish Great War Society.
3. Royal Munster Fusiliers in First World War. *History of the Royal Munster Fusiliers 1861 to 1922* by Captain S McCance, chapters 4–6.
4. VC action. *The London Gazette*, 28 January 1919. *Irish Winners of the Victoria Cross* by Richard Doherty and David Truesdale, chapter 6.
5. Conflict in Ireland 1913–23. *The Anglo-Irish War* and *The Irish Civil War 1922–23*, both by Peter Cottrell.
6. Doyle in the IRA. Information from Irish author Padraig Og O Ruairc. From hero to terrorist, article by Ron Gittings, *Medal News*, March 2007.
7. IRA in Clare. Information from Irish author Padraig Og O Ruairc. *Blood on the Banner* by Padraig Og O Ruairc, chapters 6–9. Information from the Bureau of Military History, Dublin, which provided witness statements by the following men of the IRA's Mid-Clare Brigade who took part in the war of independence: Joseph Barrett, Seamus Connelly, Patrick Devitt, John Jones, Patrick Kerin, Edward Lynch, Seamus McMahon, Sean McNamara,

Anthony Malone, Patrick Mulcahy, John Neylon, Andrew O'Donohue, Sean O'Keeffe, Peter O'Loughlin, Thomas Shalloo.
8. Doyle in National Army. Military Archives, Dublin.

23 The Lusitania Avenged: Gordon Steele

1. Steele's background and naval career. *The Victoria Cross and the George Cross, The Complete History, Volume II* edited by Christopher Wright and Glenda Anderson. Service record. *The Victoria Cross at Sea* by John Winton.
2. *Baralong* as Q-ship. *Gallant Gentlemen* by E. Keble Chatterton, chapter 7. *Slaughter at Sea* by Alan Coles, chapter 3. Imperial War Museum interview with *Baralong* gunner George Hempenstall, 1986.
3. *Baralong*'s attack on *U-27*. Herbert's original report, 20 August 1915, and later statement by him, undated. Admiralty minute sheet, 22 August. Admiralty letter to Vice Admiral Commanding, Queenstown, 27 August. *Gallant Gentlemen* by E. Keble Chatterton, chapter 8. *Slaughter at Sea* by Alan Coles, chapter 4.
4. US newspaper reports alleging atrocity. *The New York Times*, 11 September. *New York World*, 7 October. *The Boston Traveler*, 8 October. *Chicago American*, 15 October. All 1915.
5. Admiralty response to allegations. Various statements and notes involving Naval Secretary, October-December. Despatch from British embassy, Washington, 19 September, but forwarded by Foreign Office to Admiralty on 19 October. Report on sinking of SS *Ruel*, 22 August. All 1915.
6. *The Times* report on Reichstag debate, 19 January 1916.
7. VC action. *The London Gazette*, 11 November 1919. Steele's private written account, undated, Imperial War Museum. *The Victoria Cross at Sea* by John Winton.
8. Steele's comments on *Baralong* attack. *Gallant Gentlemen* by E. Keble Chatterton, chapter 8. *Slaughter at Sea* by Alan Coles, chapter 15.

24 A War Criminal?: Clive Hulme

1. Hulme's background and army career. *The Dictionary of New Zealand Biography. The Victoria Cross and the George Cross, The Complete History, Volume III* edited by Christopher Wright and Glenda Anderson. Obituary *New Zealand Herald*, 4 September 1982. Obituary *Te Puke Times*, 21 September 1982.
2. Campaign in Greece. *23 Battalion, The Official History of New Zealand in the Second World War* by Angus Ross, chapters 3 and 4.
3. Campaign in Crete. *23 Battalion, The Official History of New Zealand in the Second World War* by Angus Ross, chapter 5. *Crete, The Battle and the Resistance* by Antony Beevor, chapters 10, 14 and 16.
4. Hulme's comments on fighting at Maleme. Letter from him, dated 16 May 1942, to a relative of Lloyd Hume, who had been killed in action.
5. War crime allegation. *In the Face of the Enemy* by Glyn Harper and Colin Richardson, chapter 11 (at the time of publication Harper was head of the Massey University Centre for Military Studies and Richardson had taught

military history and strategy at the Australian Army Command and Staff College). *The Daily Telegraph*, 10 April 2006. *Bay of Plenty Times*, 10 and 25 April 2006.

25 'He Raped Me': John Nettleton

1. Nettleton's background. *The Victoria Cross and the George Cross, The Complete History, Volume III* edited by Christopher Wright and Glenda Anderson. Article by Brian Best, *The Journal of The Victoria Cross Society*, March 2011.
2. Augsburg raid. *The Augsburg Raid* by Jack Currie, chapters 2–5. Article by Brian Best, *The Journal of The Victoria Cross Society*, March 2011. *The Times*, 18 and 20 April 1942, *The Daily Telegraph*, 18 and 20 April, *Daily Mail*, 20 and 21 April. Briefing note for RAF press conference, 27 April.
3. Selborne's criticism. Letter to Churchill, 27 April 1942. Memo to Churchill, 2 May.
4. Award of Victoria Cross. Recommendation for Nettleton and Sherwood, 19 April 1942. *The London Gazette*, 28 April.
5. Sheila Mercier's rape claim. *Annie's Song* by Sheila Mercier, chapter 3. *Daily Mail*, 6 September 1994, *The Mail on Sunday*, 11 September 1994.

26 The Phoney Irishman: John Kenneally

1. Kenneally's early life. *The Honour and the Shame* by John Kenneally, chapters 1–3. John Kenneally the Brummie Irishman, article by John Kenneally (son), *The Journal of The Victoria Cross Society*, March 2008. *The Victoria Cross and the George Cross, The Complete History, Volume III* edited by Christopher Wright and Glenda Anderson.
2. Irish Guards. *The Honour and the Shame* by John Kenneally, chapter 4.
3. VC action. *The London Gazette*, 17 August 1943. *The Honour and the Shame* by John Kenneally, chapters 5 and 6. Obituaries, *The Times* and *The Daily Telegraph*, 28 September 2000.
4. Later life. John Kenneally the Brummie Irishman, article by John Kenneally (son), *The Journal of The Victoria Cross Society*, March 2008. Obituaries, *The Times* and *The Daily Telegraph*, 28 September 2000.
5. False identity and Neville Blond. *Sunday Express*, 17 September 1967 and 2 February 1992.

27 The Wild Submariner: James Magennis

1. Detention. *Magennis VC* by George Fleming, chapter 8. Submarine Service record card.
2. Early life. *Magennis VC* by George Fleming, chapter 1. *Belfast Telegraph*, 5 February 1997. *Causeway* magazine, winter 1995.
3. Naval career. *The Victoria Cross and the George Cross, The Complete History, Volume III* edited by Christopher Wright and Glenda Anderson. *Magennis VC* by George Fleming, chapters 2–5. Submarine Service record card.

4. VC action. *Frogman VC* by Ian Fraser, chapters 15-19. Captain William Fell's report on Operation Struggle to Commander-in-Chief, Pacific Fleet, 18 August 1945. Article on attack written for the *US Undersea Warfare Newsletter* after request from British Joint Services Mission, Washington, to Director of Torpedo, A/S & Mine Warfare, Admiralty, 22 May 1950. *The Victoria Cross at Sea* by John Winton, section on Fraser and Magennis. *The London Gazette*, 13 November 1945. Magennis letter to brother William, written on board submarine *Voracious*, 19 September 1945.

5. Shilling fund. *Belfast Telegraph*, 22, 24, 26 and 27 November 1945.

6. Sale of VC and criticism. *Belfast Telegraph*, 16 and 18 September 1952. *Sunday Express*, 21 September 1952. *Daily Mail*, Irish edition, 7 April 1960.

7. Move to England. *Magennis VC* by George Fleming, chapter 8. *The Mail on Sunday*, 24 October 1999.

8. Belfast memorial. *The Times*, 9 October 1999.

Bibliography

Arthur, Max, *Symbol of Courage, The Men Behind the Medal* (Pan Books, 2005)

Ashcroft, Michael, *Victoria Cross Heroes* (Headline, 2006)

Ashcroft, Michael, *Special Forces Heroes* (Headline, 2008)

Bancroft, James, *Gallantry Awards at Rorke's Drift* (Bancroft Publishing, 2014)

Bancroft, James, *Zulu War Victoria Crosses* (Bancroft Publishing, 2014)

Beckett, Ian, *The Victorians at War* (Hambledon Continuum, 2003)

Beeching, Jack, *The Chinese Opium Wars* (Hutchinson, 1975)

Beevor, Antony, *Crete, The Battle and the Resistance* (John Murray, 1991)

Bew, Paul, *Enigma, A New Life of Charles Stewart Parnell* (Gill & Macmillan, 2011)

Billière, de la, Peter, *Supreme Courage, Heroic Stories from 150 Years of the Victoria Cross* (Little, Brown, 2004)

Bowyer, Chaz, *For Valour, The Air VCs* (Grub Street, 1992)

Brighton, Terry, *Hell Riders, The Truth about the Charge of the Light Brigade* (Viking, 2004)

Bujak, Philip, *Undefeated, The Extraordinary Life and Death of Lt Col Jack Sherwood Kelly VC, CMG, DSO* (Forster Consulting, 2008)

Butler, Lewis, *The Annals of the King's Royal Rifle Corps Volume III* (John Murray, 1926)

Brazier, Kevin, *The Complete Victoria Cross* (Pen & Sword, 2010)

Brown, Malcolm, *The Imperial War Museum Book of the Somme* (Sidgwick & Jackson, 1996)

Carter, Nick and Carol, *The Distinguished Flying Cross and How It Was Won* (Savannah Publications, 1998)

Chatterton, E. Keble, *Gallant Gentlemen* (Hurst & Blackett, 1931)

Coles, Alan, *Slaughter at Sea, The Truth Behind a Naval War Crime* (Robert Hale, 1986)

Colledge J. J., Warlow, Ben, *Ships of the Royal Navy* (Chatham Publishing, 2006)

Cottrell, Peter, *The Anglo-Irish War, The Troubles of 1913-1922* (Osprey, 2006)

Cottrell, Peter, *The Irish Civil War 1922–23* (Osprey, 2008)

Cunningham, W. H., Treadwell, C. A. L., Hanna, J. S., *The Wellington Regiment (NZEF) 1914-1919* (Ferguson & Osborn, 1928)

Currie, Jack, *The Augsburg Raid* (Goodall Publications, 1987)

D'Arcy, Patricia, *What Happened to a VC* (Dundalgan Press, undated)

Doherty, Richard, and Truesdale, David, *Irish Winners of the Victoria Cross* (Four Courts Press, 2000)

English, Richard, *Armed Struggle, The History of the IRA* (Pan Books, 2012)

Eyre, Giles, *Somme Harvest, Memories of a PBI in the Summer of 1916* (London Stamp Exchange reprint, 1991)

Fox, Frank, *The Royal Inniskilling Fusiliers in the Great War* (Constable, 1928)

Fraser, Ian, *Frogman VC* (Angus & Robertson, 1957)

Fleming, George, *Magennis VC* (History Ireland, 1998)

Fremont-Barnes, Gregory, *The Indian Mutiny 1857–58* (Osprey, 2007)

Hamilton, John, *Gallipoli Victoria Cross Hero, The Price of Valour: The Triumph and Tragedy of Hugo Throssell VC* (Frontline Books, 2015)

Hamilton, Robert, *Victoria Cross Heroes of World War One* (Atlantic, 2015)

Harper, Glyn, and Richardson, Colin, *In the Face of the Enemy, The Complete History of the Victoria Cross and New Zealand* (HarperCollins, 2007)

Hayward, John, Birch, Diana, Bishop, Richard, *British Battles and Medals* (Spink, 2006)

Holmes, Richard, *The Little Field Marshal, A Life of Sir John French* (Cassell, 2005, first published by Jonathan Cape in 1981)

Hywel-Jones, Ian (project co-ordinator), Wright, Christopher, Anderson, Glenda (editors), *The Victoria Cross and the George Cross, The Complete History*, three volumes (Methuen and The Victoria Cross and George Cross Association, 2013)

Innes, P. R., *The History of the Bengal European Regiment* (Simpkin, Marshall & Co, 1885)

Kenneally, John, *The Honour and the Shame, Bravery Has No Rules* (Headline, 2008, first published by Kenwood in 1991)

Kipling, Rudyard, *The Irish Guards in the Great War, The First Battalion* (Spellmount, 1997)

Laffin, John, *British VCs of World War 2, A Study in Heroism* (Sutton, 1997)

Laffin, John, *The Agony of Gallipoli* (Sutton, 2005)

London, Jack, *The People of the Abyss* (Journeyman Press, 1977, first published in Britain in 1903)

Lummis, William, and Wynn, Kenneth, *Honour the Light Brigade* (Hayward, 1973)

McCance, S., *History of the Royal Munster Fusiliers 1881 to 1922* (Naval & Military Press reprint, undated)

MacMunn, George, *Behind the Scenes in Many Wars* (John Murray, 1930)

Manning, Stephen, *Evelyn Wood VC, Pillar of Empire* (Pen & Sword, 2007)

Marlow, Joyce, *The Uncrowned Queen of Ireland, The Life of 'Kitty' O'Shea* (Weidenfeld & Nicolson, 1975)

Mercier, Sheila, *Annie's Song, My Life & Emmerdale* (Titan Books, 1994)

Moloney, Ed, *A Secret History of the IRA* (Penguin, 2003)

Bibliography

Morris, Donald, *The Washing of the Spears, The Rise and Fall of the Zulu Nation* (Jonathan Cape, 1965)

Mulholland, John, and Jordan, Alan, *Victoria Cross Bibliography* (Spink, 1999)

Murphy, James, *Liverpool VCs* (Pen & Sword, 2008)

Napier, Charles, *The History of the Baltic Campaign of 1884, From Documents and Other Materials Furnished by Vice Admiral Sir C Napier KCB* (Naval & Military Press reprint, undated)

Napier, Priscilla, *Black Charlie, A Life of Admiral Sir Charles Napier KCB 1787-1860* (Michael Russell, 1995)

O'Shea, Katherine, *The Uncrowned King of Ireland* (Nonsuch, 2005, first published in 1914)

Pakenham, Thomas, *The Boer War* (Weidenfeld & Nicolson, 1979)

Parry, D. H., *Britain's Roll of Glory* (Cassell, 1899)

Pennington, William, *Left of Six Hundred* (privately printed London, 1887)

Powell, Geoffrey, *Buller: A Scapegoat? A life of General Sir Redvers Buller* VC (Leo Cooper, 1994)

Ross, Angus, *23 Battalion, The Official History of New Zealand in the Second World War* (Historical Publications Branch, 1959)

Ruairc, Padraig Og O, *Blood on the Banner, The Republican Struggle in Clare* (Mercier Press, 2009)

Smith, George, *A Victorian RSM, From India to the Crimea* (Costello, 1987)

Steele, Gordon, *To Me God Is Real* (Arthur Stockwell, 1973)

Stewart, H., *The New Zealand Division 1916-1919, A Popular History based on Official Records* (Whitcombe and Tombs, 1921)

Thomas, David, *Crete 1941, The Battle at Sea* (Cassell, 2003)

Throssell, Ric, *My Father's Son* (William Heinemann Australia, 1989)

Ward, S. G. P., *Faithful, The Story of the Durham Light Infantry* (Naval & Military Press reprint, 2004)

Wheatley, Michael, *Nationalism and the Irish Party, Provincial Ireland, 1910-1916* (Oxford University Press, 2005)

Winton, John, *The Victoria Cross at Sea* (Michael Joseph, 1978)

Wood, Evelyn, *From Midshipman to Field Marshal* (Methuen, 1906)

Workman, David, *British Orders, Decorations and Medals in the Robert B Honeyman Jr Collection* (Los Angeles County Museum of Natural History, 1979)

Wykes, Alan, *The Royal Hampshire Regiment* (Hamish Hamilton, 1968)

Acknowledgements

Many people have helped with the research for this book, and I would especially like to thank the following: Bob Barltrop, Orders & Medals Research Society; Julie Barnes, Dunedin Library; Peter Beirne, Clare County Library; Brian Best, *The Journal of The Victoria Cross Society*; Dr Robert Blyth, National Maritime Museum; Damien Brett, Kilkenny County Library; the British Library; John Cunningham, Fermanagh Authors' Association; Nimrod Dix, Dix Noonan Webb; Stephen Farish, Regimental Museum of The Royal Welsh; Sean Fleming, Fort Erie Library; Sally-Ann Greensmith, Cambridgeshire Archives; Hampshire Record Office; Herefordshire Archive Service; the research and photograph archive departments at the Imperial War Museum, London; Peter John, Naval Historical Collectors & Research Association; Emma Knowles, Otago Settlers Museum; George Malcolmson, Royal Navy Submarine Museum; James Morton, Morton & Eden; The National Archives, London; the National Army Museum, New Zealand; the National Library of New Zealand; Keeba Roy, *The Mail on Sunday*; Padraig Og O Ruairc; the Royal Air Force Museum, London; the Very Reverend Dr Paul Shackerley, Dean of Brecon; Sunet Swanepoel, McGregor Museum, Kimberley; the Templer Study Centre, National Army Museum; Martin Tregoning, Association of Old Worcesters; Beth Werling, Natural History Museum of Los Angeles County; Lieutenant Colonel Bob Wyatt, The Military Historical Society; Anna Zanardo, Toronto Reference Library.

I have greatly appreciated Duncan McAra's help and guidance. My thanks also to Amberley's Shaun Barrington and Alex Bennett.

Brian Izzard

Index

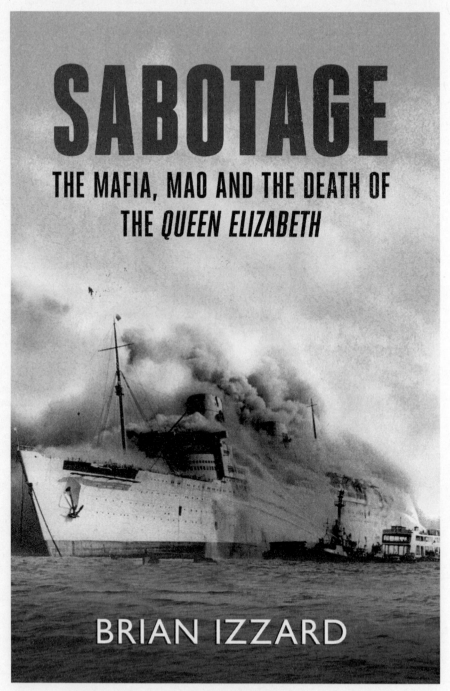